Sharon G. Mijares, PhD
Gurucharan Singh Khalsa, PhD
Editors

The Psychospiritual
Clinician's Handbook
Alternative Methods
for Understanding
and Treating Mental Disorders

Pre-publication
REVIEW . . .

"**P**sychotherapy is undergoing a quiet revolution by integrating spiritual perspectives with modern diagnostic know-how. This handbook provides a wide range of clinical cases, innovative techniques, and illuminating discussions on how to treat the whole person. It is essential reading for therapists, teachers, and students interested in integrative approaches."

Daniel Deslauriers, PhD
Director, East-West Psychology Program,
California Institute of Integral Studies

The Psychospiritual Clinician's Handbook

Alternative Methods
for Understanding
and Treating Mental Disorders

TITLES OF RELATED INTEREST

The Psychospiritual Clinician's Handbook
Alternative Methods for Understanding and Treating Mental Disorders

Sharon G. Mijares, PhD
Gurucharan Singh Khalsa, PhD
Editors

The Haworth Reference Press™
An imprint of The Haworth Press, Inc.
New York • London • Oxford

For more information on this book or to order, visit
http://www.haworthpress.com/store/product.asp?sku=5369

or call 1-800-HAWORTH (800-429-6784) in the United States and Canada
or (607) 722-5857 outside the United States and Canada

or contact orders@HaworthPress.com

Published by

The Haworth Reference Press™, an imprint of The Haworth Press, Inc., 10 Alice Street, Binghamton, NY 13904-1580.

Book cover design illustrations and those on chapter title pages created by Gabo Carabes, copyright 2005, <http://www.melkocha.com>.

Cover design by Jennifer M. Gaska.

Kundalini Research Institute

Library of Congress Cataloging-in-Publication Data

The psychospiritual clinician's handbook : alternative methods for understanding and treating mental disorders / Sharon G. Mijares, Gurucharan Singh Khalsa, editors.
    p. cm.
    Includes bibliographical references and index.
    ISBN-13: 978-0-7890-2323-0 (hc. : alk. paper)
    ISBN-10: 0-7890-2323-7 (hc. : alk. paper)
    ISBN-13: 978-0-7890-2324-7 (pbk. : alk. paper)
    ISBN-10: 0-7890-2324-5 (pbk. : alk. paper)
    1. Psychotherapy—Religious aspects. 2. Mental Illness—Alternative treatment. 3. Mentally ill—Religious life. 4. Psychiatry and religion. 5. Spiritual life.
[DNLM: 1. Psychotherapy—methods. 2. Complementary Therapies—methods. 3. Religion and Psychology. 4. Spiritual Therapies—methods. WM 400 P97417 2005] I. Mijares, Sharon G. (Sharon Grace), 1942-. II. Khalsa, Gurucharan Singh.

RC489.S676P79 2005
616.89'14—dc22

                                        2004024739

CONTENTS

ABOUT THE EDITORS

Sharon G. Mijares, PhD, is a Self-Relations Psychotherapist and a graduate of the Union Institute and University. She is a member of the Sufi Ruhaniat International, the International Association of Sufism's Psychology and Sufism Forum, and the American Psychological Association's Division on the Psychology of Religion, and has a black belt (Shodan) in Aikido. She is a core adjunct faculty member of Chapman University's Counseling Psychology program and National University's Psychology Department and has served on several doctoral committees as adjunct faculty of the Union Institute and University. Sharon is the editor of *Modern Psychology and Ancient Wisdom: Psychological Healing Practices from the World's Religious Traditions* (Haworth, 2003). She has authored several articles and recently contributed a chapter, "At every moment a new species arises in the chest," for Stephen Gilligan and Dvorah Simon's edited book *Walking in Two Worlds: The Relational Self in Theory, Practice, and Community* (2004). She can be contacted at (760) 436-3518 or through her Web site <www.psychospiritual.org> or by e-mailing <sharonmijares@aol.com>.

Gurucharan Singh Khalsa, PhD, LPCC, is a well-known teacher of Kundalini yoga, therapist, writer, and researcher. He is a leader in the use of positive lifestyle and psychospiritual approaches for mental, emotional, and spiritual health. He has been a student of Yogi Bhajan, PhD, "the master of Kundalini yoga and founder of Humanology," since 1969. Gurucharan is the director of training for the Kundalini Research Institute, where he develops international standards and materials for yoga teachers. He taught yoga and wellness at MIT for over 15 years and currently co-directs the yoga and integrative health program at University of Guadalajara, Mexico. His experience, first in mathematics and the sciences and then in psychology and yoga, bridges the conversation between science and spirit, and West and East. His most recent books, co-authored with Yogi Bhajan, were *Breathwalk* (2000) and *The Mind* (1998). He travels widely training teachers and therapists and resides in New Mexico. Gurucharan can be contacted by e-mail at <YogaMaster@aol.com>. His Web sites are <www.gurucharankhalsa.com> and <www.breathwalk.com>.

CONTRIBUTORS

Kyrai Antares recently completed her bachelor of arts in eating disorders counseling at Union Institute and University and is beginning her graduate studies in depth psychology at Vermont College. Kyrai's struggle with and triumph over anorexia and bulimia inspired her first book, *Finding a Break in the Clouds: A Gentle Guide and Companion for Breaking Free from an Eating Disorder* (Trafford Publishing, 2001). She offers lectures, workshops, and personal coaching for women, their families and friends, and for all who seek a deeper understanding of disordered eating. She can be contacted at <www.findingabreakinthe clouds.com>.

Celia A. Drake, PhD, is a licensed psychologist in private practice in Phoenix, Arizona. She graduated from the California School of Professional Psychology and practices clinical and forensic psychology. A student of Kundalini Yoga, she meditates regularly. E-mail may be sent to <cdmy@att.net>.

Henry Grayson, PhD, is the founder and chairman of the board of the National Institute for the Psychotherapies in New York City and director of its Center for Spirituality and Psychotherapy. Co-author of several books, he is most recently the author of *Mindful Loving: 10 Practices for Creating Deeper Connections* (Gotham/Penguin, 2003) and the six-tape Sounds True audio series, *The New Physics of Love* (Sounds True, 2000). He is also the president of the Association for Spirituality and Psychotherapy. Dr. Grayson has integrated spirituality and the new physics into psychotherapy for over twenty years. He lectures widely across the United States and abroad and practices in New York City and in Westport, Connecticut. He can be reached at <Hengray@aol.com> or <www.mindfulloving.com>.

Elizabeth (Liz) Z. Gulliford, MPhil, was first enthused by the interface between theology and psychology at the University of Oxford, from which she graduated in 1998 with a BA in Theology. She subsequently obtained a MPhil in Theology at the University of Cambridge, specializing in psychology and theology, Eager to be able to fire on both theological and psychological cylinders, Liz studied for a BPS accredited psychology BSc while working as a research assistant for the Psychology and Religion Research Programme at the University of Cambridge, from which she graduated last year. Her special research interest has been forgiveness, the subject of the book she has recently co-edited with Fraser Watts and the topic of a number of lectures she has delivered both at conferences and to the general public. She also enjoys working on a variety of other fields of interest with the project and is about to embark on an interdisciplinary study on gratitude. Her publications include *Forgiveness in Context: Theology and Psychology in Creative Dialogue* edited by F. Watts and L. Gulliford (T&T Clark, 2004), and Forgiveness and Faith: Psychology and Theology in Dialogue, *Ministry Today* 31, 6-15.

Arife Ellen Hammerle, PhD, JD, is the clinical director of the Community Healing Centers, an integrative psychotherapy group practice. She has published many articles on psychology and Sufism as well as her first book, titled *The Sacred Journey: Unfolding Self Essence* (IAS, 2000). She is an active member of the International Association of Sufism, Sufism Psychology Forum, Institute for Sufi Studies, and is president of the board of the Marin Interfaith Council. She is the coordinator for the United Nations Department of Public Information for the International Association of Sufism Non-Governmental Organization. Dr. Hammerle teaches psychology and Sufi courses at the Institute for Sufi Studies and Santa Rosa Junior College. She is a senior student of the Uwaiysi Tariqat of Sufism.

Anita Johnston, PhD, is the director of the Anorexia and Bulimia Center of Hawaii, which she cofounded in 1982, and the clinical director and founder of the 'Ai Pono Intensive Outpatient Eating Disorders Programs in Honolulu and Maui. She is the author of *Eating in the Light of the Moon: How Women Can Transform Their Relationship with Food Through Myths, Metaphors, and Storytelling* (Gruze Books, 2000), which has been published in five languages. Dr. Johnston has a private practice specializing in women's issues and eating disorders in Kailua, Hawaii, and conducts workshops and professional trainings throughout the country.

Dwight H. Judy, PhD, is associate professor of spiritual formation at Garrett-Evangelical Theological Seminary in Evanston, Illinois, where he directs doctor of ministry and spiritual formation programs. He is an ordained United Methodist minister, licensed as a psychologist in California, and a member of the American Association of Pastoral Counselors. He makes his home in Syracuse, Indiana, with his wife and two teenaged sons, where he also serves as director of spiritual formation for the Oakwood Christian Spiritual Life Center. His teaching focus is preparing persons for specialized ministries in spiritual formation. Previously, he was on the faculty of the Institute of Transpersonal Psychology in Palo Alto, California. He is a past president of the Association for Transpersonal Psychology. His books include *Quest for the Mystical Christ: Awakening the Heart of Faith* (OSL Publications, 2003); *Christian Meditation and Inner Healing* (OSL Publications, 2000); *Embracing God: Praying with Teresa of Avila* (Abingdon, 1996); and *Healing the Male Soul: Christianity and the Mythic Journey* (Crossroad, 1992). He has contributed chapters to *Textbook of Transpersonal Psychiatry and Psychology* (Basic Books, 1996); and *Modern Psychology and Ancient Wisdom: Psychological Healing Practices from the World's Religious Traditions* (The Haworth Press, Inc., 2003).

Bruce Kerievsky was a student of Thomas Hora, the developer of metapsychiatry spiritual teaching, for three decades. He is president of his own computer consulting firm, the author of numerous articles for spiritually oriented newsletters and of several essays for journals of psychotherapy and of computers, the webmaster for three psychospiritual Web sites, the treasurer of the PAGL (Peace, Assurance, Gratitude, and Love) Foundation, an advisor to the board of Association for Spirituality and Psychotherapy (ASP), an editor of the ASP newsletter, and a teacher of metapsychiatry. He has compiled a book of Dr. Hora's aphorisms, with his commentary, titled *Only Understanding Heals: Spiritual Solutions to Problems in Living* (unpublished manuscript). He can be reached at <kbruce@optonline.net> or <www.meaningandtruth. com>.

Dharma Singh Khalsa, MD, has served as the president and medical director of the Alzheimer's Prevention Foundation International (APFI) since its inception in 1993. He is the only physician to testify before the United States Congress about an integrative brain longevity platform. Born in Ohio and raised in Florida, Dr. Khalsa graduated from Creighton University School of Medicine and received his training in anesthesiology at the University of California–San Francisco, where he was chief resident. Dharma is also a graduate of the UCLA Medical Acupuncture for Physicians program and participated in Harvard Medical School's Mind/Body Medical Institute's basic and advanced curriculum. He is board certified in anesthesiology, pain management, and antiaging medicine. He is the author of four critically acclaimed books, with other works in progress including The Better Memory Kit (Hay House, September 2004). He can be reached through the following Web sites: <www.drdharma.com>, <info@alzheimersprevention.org>, or <www.AlzheimersPrevention. org>.

Manjit Kaur Khalsa, PhD, is a psychologist and workshop leader with more than twenty years of experience using psychospiritual approaches to help people overcome their personal limitations in order to achieve their dreams (The Radient Woman Press,1995). She is coauthor of the book *Radiance and Victory: A Woman's Way to Prosperity* (The Radient Woman Press, 1995). She is also the executive director of the 3HO Foundation of Massachusetts and the director of the Baba Siri Chand Yoga Center. Her offices are located in Wellesley and Millis, Massachusetts, and you can contact her through her Web site at <DoctorKhalsa.com>.

Peggy J. Kleinplatz, PhD, is a clinical psychologist, certified sex therapist, and sex educator. Since 1983, she has been teaching human sexuality at the School of Psychology, University of Ottawa, where she was awarded the Prix d'Excellence in 2000. She also teaches sex therapy at the affiliated Saint Paul University's Institute of Pastoral Studies. She deals with sexual issues in individual, couples, and group therapy and offers workshops on sexuality and spirituality. Her work focuses on eroticism and transformation. She is the editor of *New Directions in Sex Therapy: Innovations and Alternatives* (Brunner-Routledge, 2001), a book intended to combat the increasing medicalization of human sexuality. She can be contacted at <kleinpla @uottawa.ca>.

Stanley Krippner, PhD, is an internationally renowned researcher in the fields of dreams, shamanism, and human sexuality. At Brooklyn's Maimonides Medical Center, he conducted research on the dreams of pregnant women. In 1972, he began teaching full-time at San Francisco's Saybrook Graduate School, designing the course in human sexuality, among others. In 1973, he was elected president of the Association for Humanistic Psychology and has also served as president in two divisions of the American Psychological Association. He is a Fellow in the Society for the Study of Human Sexuality, and has written, edited, co-written, or co-edited over 1,000 articles and book reviews, as well as fifteen books, including *Personal Mythology* (Jeremy Tarcher, 1988); *Varieties of Anomalous Experience* (APA, 2000); *The Psychological Impact of War Trauma on Civilians* (Praeger, 2003); and *Broken Images, Broken Selves* (Brunner/Mazel, 1997). He has taught a certificate program in human sexuality at the Institute de Medicina y Tecnologia Avanzada de la Conducta in Ciudad Juarez, Mexico, and delivered a paper at the World Congress of Sexology in Havana, Cuba, in 2003. He can be contacted at <www.stanleykrippner.com>.

Deborah J. Lewis, PhD, is a graduate of the California School of Professional Psychology. She is a professor of psychology at Argosy University in Phoenix, Arizona. She also is in private practice, specializing in forensic and neuropsychology. She has been studying alternative healing techniques since 1988. She may be contacted via e-mail at <DLewis@Argosyu.edu>.

David Lukoff, PhD, is a professor of psychology at Saybrook Graduate School and a licensed psychologist in California. He is co-author of the new DSM-IV diagnostic category "Religious or Spiritual Problem" and author of fifty publications on religious and spiritual issues. He lectures internationally on spirituality in mental health and mental disorders, and is copresident of the Association for Transpersonal Psychology. He trained in psychology and anthropology at the University of Chicago, Harvard University, and Loyola University Chicago, and has been a member of the faculties of Harvard, UCLA, Oxnard College, California Institute of Integral Studies, and the Institute of Transpersonal Psychology. He can be contacted at <dlukoff@comcast.net> or <www.spiritualcompetency.com>.

John E. Mack, MD, professor of psychiatry at Harvard Medical School and founder of the Center for Psychology and Social Change, explores how extraordinary experiences can affect personal, societal, and global transformation. He authored many books detailing how one's perceptions shape relationships with others and with the world, including the Pulitzer Prize–winning biography of T. E. Lawrence, *A Prince of Disorder* (Little, Brown & Co., 1976), and most recently, *Passport to the Cosmos: Human Transformation and Alien Encounters* (Crown, 1999). Dr. Mack died in 2004 while on a speaking engagement in London.

Jeffrey Rediger, MD, MDiv, is medical director at McLean Hospital Southeast and an instructor in the department of psychiatry at Harvard Medical School. He has a master of divinity degree from Princeton Theological Seminary and publishes in the fields of medicine, psychiatry, and spirituality. He is cohost of the television program *In a True Light* and is medical director of the Institute for Psychological and Spiritual Development in Cambridge, Massachusetts.

Colin A. Ross, MD, is an internationally renowned clinician, researcher, author, and lecturer in the field of traumatic stress and trauma-related disorders. He is the founder and president of the Colin A. Ross Institute for Psychological Trauma. Dr. Ross provides treatment for patients with trauma-related disorders and symptoms. He is the executive medical director of three programs located at Timberlawn Mental Health System in Dallas, Texas; Forest View Hospital in Grand Rapids, Michigan; and Del Amo Hospital in Torrance, California. Dr. Ross has authored over 100 professional papers and books. He has reviewed for numerous professional journals, and is a member of the American Psychiatric Association and the International Society for the Study of Traumatic Stress. Visit his Web site at <www.rossinst.com>.

Jeffrey M. Schwartz, MD, a leading neuroscientist and research professor of psychiatry at UCLA School of Medicine, is a seminal thinker and researcher in the field of self-directed neuroplasticity. He is the author of over 100 scientific publications in the fields of neuroscience and psychiatry. Dr. Schwartz has also authored three popular books with HarperCollins, *Brain Lock: Free Yourself From Obsessive-Compulsive Behavior* (1997), *The Mind and the Brain: Neuroplasticity and the Power of Mental Force* (2002), and *Dear Patrick: Life is Tough—Here's Some Good Advice* (2003). His major research interest over the past two decades has been brain imaging/functional neuroanatomy and cognitive-behavioral therapy, with a focus on the pathological mechanisms and psychological treatment of obsessive-compulsive disorder. He has also been a devoted practitioner of mindfulness meditation in the Pali Buddhist tradition for over twenty-five years.

Jessica Stier, BA, is an actress and a writer living in Los Angeles. In the spring of 2000 she began working as a writer for the Westwood Institute for Anxiety Disorders, Inc. As a result of her fascination with the cognitive therapy and mindfulness-based treatments she began her training to become a clinical assistant in the program. For the past two years she assisted in the intensive treatment program for obsessive-compulsive disorder where she helped patients to use mindful awareness in combination with the four steps developed by Jeffrey M. Schwartz. Contact her at <jessicacastier@msn.com>.

Margo Thienemann, MD, is a psychiatrist on the faculty in the Division of Child and Adolescent Psychiatry and Child Development at Stanford University. She directs the Anxiety Disorders clinic there, treating children and their families with cognitive-behavioral and pharmacological interventions, incorporating mindfulness techniques. Current research includes child and family group interventions for pediatric anxiety disorders and work investigating biological correlates of symptom change. Contact her at <mthiene@stanford. edu>.

Selene Vega, MA, LMFT, is a workshop leader, ritual facilitator, and psychotherapist (MFC #32604) with an MA in clinical psychology (from John F. Kennedy University) and a BA in ritual and the arts in cross-cultural perspective (from the University of California, Santa Cruz). Since 1972 she has guided individuals and groups into the realms of psyche and spirit, bringing movement and trancework to the fields of addictions, eating disorders, psychospiritual crisis and ecopsychology. Selene co-authored *The Sevenfold Journey: Reclaiming Mind, Body, & Spirit through the Chakras* with Anodea Judith (The Crossing Press, 1993). She is former editor of the *Spiritual Emergence Network Newsletter* and past president of Santa Cruz, CA CAMFT (California Association of Marriage and Family Therapists). Visit her Web site at <www.spiritmoving.com>.

Foreword

I first came across a comment on the need for linking psyche and spirit in a book written in the fifteenth century by Marsilio Ficino. It is not a new idea, then, but one desperately needed in our time. There can be no doubt that we are now in cultural liminality: We find ourselves in a transition between modernity, with its de rigueur quantitative studies, its laboratories, and its evidence-based approach to healing, and an unknown but clearly different sensibility generically labeled "postmodern." Today's interest in bridging the psychological and the spiritual is part of that shift in paradigm.

In many areas of contemporary life—medicine, psychotherapy, and religion, for example—people are demanding attention to the spiritual dimension. We often express their hunger with the question, "Is this all there is to life?" We have had a century and more of technological, materialistic development, and now we are discovering that a human being is more than a body. Once we work hard enough to afford the house, the car, and the electronics, we step back and think, "I still don't feel good. I'm not fulfilled. Could there be something more?"

These questions may occur in an apparently happy life, but they also find expression in painful and disorienting symptoms: depression, marital dissatisfaction, loneliness, addictions, and serious phobias, to name a few. One of the habits of modernity was to separate such symptoms from meaning. They were treated as diseases, autonomous developments that came from nowhere and represented our failure to make medicines and treatments fast enough. The word *disease* often has in it the implication that a certain problem has no relation to lifestyle or personal history. We believe that smoking can cause cancer, but we do not think much about a connection between a society devoted to the work ethic and widespread depression.

Modernity also tended to see the spiritual life as a matter of belief and morals. One hopes that, stewing in our current spiritual liminality, we might finally deepen our idea of religion and spirituality, moving beyond a list of beliefs, which often amount to a simplified ideology, and discovering a translucent morality, a deep sense of community, and an awareness of fate and personal transcendence. Religion as we have known it in the West is largely attuned to childhood and has many infantile aspects. Dietrich Bonhoeffer, speaking for his own Christianity, declared that religion was coming of age, when even the notion of God would need to be seriously reimagined.

This point leads me to offer a caution as we go about inventing a psychospiritual approach to healing. Let us not do it within the context of the fading era. Let us move on from modernity completely, enjoying its achievements but acknowledging a shift to a new way of imagining life and culture. Let us psychoanalyze, in the best sense, for example, our habit of quantifying human experience. Is there any subtle defensiveness in such a practice? Let us be careful in our use of language. Could we be more poetic and imagistic, labeling less and looking for subtle, individual, and complex insight?

I also expect the new era to heal the split between secularity and spirituality. Let us not worry about exploring spiritual and even religious issues in the context of our work, which is usually taken to be secular. Of course, we do not want to get caught in theocracies of any kind or any flirtation with proselytizing, but we can notice the spiritual implications in what are often taken to be secular ideas and literature. The spirituality people crave may not be satisfied with religion or spiritual practices as we know them. In a new era, transcendence may be directly immersed in individual and cultural experience.

Art in the modern period tended to approach the spiritual obliquely and even negatively, through heavy criticism and satire. However, art is always close to the spiritual, and I expect art therapy to become a more important part of psychospiritual work in the near future. It, too, must abandon its attachment to modernity, which is often a defensive way of justifying itself. Art, like psychotherapy, stands at the edge of the numinous and senses a certain inadequacy in the face of its challenge. It may try to be like its respected cousins, the physical sciences and the various technologies, instead of admitting to its spiritual role. In psychotherapy, art could be an important connection between the psychological and the spiritual.

In a similar vein, in the new era we might become more aware of the individual's own spiritual evolution, which may or may not be expressed in conventional religious or spiritual ways. The effort to get out of a bad marriage may be a form of transcendence. Remaining in a marriage with emotional generosity and caring for children at the cost of personal desires may also be a form of spiritual practice, not justified by any formal spiritual language or forms.

In language with which I am more familiar, I would hope that the spirit remains in touch with the soul. I would like to see us shift from the "mind/body" paradigm, a dualistic way of thinking, to a "body/soul/spirit" image, the one that was used in the Renaissance revival of culture. By soul, I mean the depth of experience found in ordinary life and relationships. Modernity, for example, speaks highly of the family, but its values weaken the family and favor corporate and elite satisfactions. In a new era, we could understand how body, soul, and spirit are all part of the family and require our serious attention.

A psychospiritual outlook must focus not only on whole persons but also on a whole world. The new era now dawning will not separate the individual's health from the health of the planet. It will not divide intellectual, emotional, and moral health from the health of the human body and of the planet. We now know how tightly all of this life is connected. The move toward spirit is only a first step toward a full reimagination of culture. Ultimately, along with some of my colleagues, I would expect a return to the etymological roots of the word *psychotherapy,* which could be translated "soul care," in which the soul is not just human but also a dimension of the communities in which we live and of the world as a whole. The purpose of soul care would be to enrich life and not just prevent or treat problems.

A vast new world is waiting for us, as we try to cut the cord that keeps us tied to modern style. We are now feeling the ties loosening and we are glimpsing our future. It is a dangerous time but also a period of promise. More than anything, it calls for imagination and deep intelligence. This book is an important step in that direction. It allows a community of voices to speak, and it follows a strong intuition that spirituality matters. It is the beginning of a necessary linking of worlds that were formerly separated, a marriage of everyday life and spirituality.

Thomas Moore, PhD
Author, Care for the Soul; Soul Mates; Meditations

Acknowledgments

We are pleased to have the opportunity to express our gratitude for the many influences which have contributed to this collection. Our lives have been deeply blessed by our spiritual teachers. In particular, Sharon is grateful for both her Sufi guide, Saadi Neil Douglas-Klotz, and her psychotherapy mentor, Stephen Gilligan. Their influences have contributed much to her development and influence the contributions to this book. Likewise, Gurucharan Singh Khalsa is grateful for the years of teachings from Yogi Bhajan, his spiritual teacher, who never failed to inspire, challenge, awaken, and bless. His vision of human potential and the reality of spirit infuses and informs all that Gurucharan does.

We want to acknowledge all the authors who contributed to this book. Each one was excited about and dedicated to this project. John Mack who completed his chapter just before his death, was a luminary in many spheres of life. In addition to his wordcraft and intellectual acuity for which he received a Pulitzer prize, he was a leader in developing models of mental health delivery to serve communities and opened the way for many new ideas. Above all, he was compassionate and never failed to see the unique heart of each person he worked with. Gurucharan and John shared profound conversations for over twenty years as they worked together to explore the scope of human potential and the structure of the mind. We are very pleased to have his contribution in this volume frame the importance of the worldviews we hold and clinical approaches we use. We are also most appreciative for Thomas Moore's Foreword and contribution to the conversation of the psychospiritual practitioner. Certainly the "care of the soul" is a powerful theme for all of the contributors. Also, we want to thank Gabo Carrabes/Harimandir Singh for the offering of such exquisite artwork, both on the book cover and the first page of every chapter.

The Haworth Press staff have been most helpful and professional throughout each stage of this book. Amy Rentner, Peg Marr, and

Dawn Krisko guided us through the production. Copyeditors Linda Mulcahy and Anissa Harper are to be commended for an incredible final editing of our book. Also, Jennifer Gaska is appreciated for her work with Gabo Carrabes/Harimandir Singh's cover design.

Finally, we want to express our appreciation to the many psychotherapists who recognize the value and application of a psychospiritual orientation.

Introduction

Sharon G. Mijares
Gurucharan Singh Khalsa

The field of psychology is rapidly undergoing a quiet revolution. It is revolution born of evolution. It arises from the increasing need to locate the human being in the center of the therapeutic process. As human beings we have a unique, sophisticated sensitivity in our consciousness and spirit that can direct the mind and heal the body. It is underused and underdeveloped, and yet it holds the keys to a therapeutic process that is at once effective, adaptable, and transformational. The field of clinicians that use a psychospiritual approach to better the lives of their clients is expanding.

People are seeking alternative approaches in medical care and mental health care. When nearly half of patients who visit traditional doctors also subscribe to some form of alternative treatment, our institutional efforts clearly are not satisfying some key client needs. People want to prevent problems not just alleviate symptoms after they appear. They also need help sorting out the confusion, stress, and conflicts of our fast-paced, globally connected lives in order to be happy. They ask for guidance in making and enacting positive lifestyle choices that integrate the energy of the body with the goals of the mind. Perhaps most important, they want to deal with what is uniquely human in each of us so they can live a life imbued with meaning, connecting to their deepest resources of spirit and consciousness.

The demand to align our therapeutic agenda with this instinct for personal dignity, integrity, and strength has come to the door of the clinic. The revolution begins with clinicians addressing those needs as they reexamine their therapeutic worldviews and attitudes to focus on the right problems to solve. It moves ahead with an array of techniques that are enriching the healing interactions with clients as they integrate the best of science with the practices of many wisdom traditions. Those practices cultivate profound experiences within the person that are the resources for the transformational work that evokes the caliber, character, and resilience in each of us. This collection of essays is a window on the revolution and a practical introduction to some of the worldviews and most effective practices used by psychospiritually oriented therapists.

Keyes and Haidt (2003) identify the three historical missions of psychology before World War II:

> The first was to cure mental illness. The second was to make everyone's lives happier and more productive and fulfilling, with the burgeoning of industrial psychology as the paradigm example. The third was to identify and nurture high talent and genius. (p. xiv)

As a profession, we took on that charge with great energy after the war and focused on what seemed most pressing—identifying and curing mental illness and developing a viable profession of providers of mental health care. To our credit, we have identified many syndromes and can claim some victories on eliminating symptoms for several of the major mental illnesses. However, we have also failed. In our pursuit of illness, we have largely forgotten how to help people fulfill themselves; lead happy productive lives; develop their innate areas of genius; and awaken the conversation with their consciousness and soul in a uniquely human way.

We chose a fork on the road to solutions that left the whole person behind. The result is that our approach to therapy and psychology in general does not speak to the majority of problems that we now face individually and collectively. We have many sophisticated and amazing instruments that can peer into the body and patterns of the brain, but we have lost the disciplined subjectivity needed to actually see human beings and grasp in their uniqueness all that can be perceived but not measured, categorized, and put into simple laws.

The 1998 American Psychological Association convention assessed therapists' efforts at prevention of illness. An important conclusion for many therapists was that operating too narrowly on a disease model has limited our success and our relevance:

What we have learned over 50 years is that the disease model does not move us closer to the prevention of those serious problems. Indeed, the major strides in prevention have resulted from a perspective focused on building competency, not on correcting weakness. Human strengths act as buffers against mental illness. (Keyes and Haidt, 2003, p. xv)

Now voices are rising to call for positive psychologies, for psychospiritual approaches that build the person's capacities for resilience.

The worldview each therapist brings to the healing process is equally a factor for our relevance and effectiveness. The worldview adopted by psychology was strongly biased to make progress in the same manner that the hard sciences of physics and chemistry had. We have indeed made progress, but the narrowing of the approaches was unnecessary. Putting a human into the container of general laws and molecular mechanisms is like squeezing an ocean into a thimble— much will be lost and it will be painful. Leshan (2002) offered a critique of worldviews and their impact on our approach in this way:

Psychology has so thoroughly sold its birthright, has so completely abandoned any contact with human existence, that it is widely believed in our society that it would be useless to look to it for help in a time of overwhelming peril. . . . The root cause of this situation is that psychology was using an inappropriate set of assumptions.

He elaborated:

It was accepted that the new science of mind and behavior would find the same sort of mechanisms and mechanical interactions that the nineteenth century had found as it perfected the steam engine. . . . No meaningful or important aspects of human life fit that mechanical model. . . . Men and women of great dedication and sincerity made this choice in the deep belief that it would lead to a rich and productive path. . . . Only slowly have we begun to realize they were inapplicable to a science of human consciousness and behavior. (pp. 157-159)

Psychospirtually oriented practitioners often bring a worldview that is centered in a spiritual, humanistic, or experiential perspective. They accept the beneficial accomplishments and useful questions raised in the mechanistic approaches but find what is truly important to be absent. They bring a fresh view of what to attend to and what can be done with and by the client. In each chapter we asked the practitioner to share worldviews as well as technique.

For many psychospiritual clinicians, one more fundamental principle fuels the change in approach—the reality and use of consciousness and the spirit. In the mechanical version of the person, consciousness is a simple epiphenomenon of the brain and tissue. It is what the brain does. In many other perspectives, consciousness or spirit is taken as a primary—as basic as time, space, and energy. When consciousness is applied and spirit is invoked, the problems we face are transformed. They are framed in a different light. To encounter the problem fully and embrace its meaning in our life is as important as eliminating it as a symptom. Symptoms are understood as communications between the body, mind, and spirit, not just as illness. The power is not just in a cure but in the healing capacity of the mind and the encounter of the disturbance.

James Hillman is a strong iconoclastic voice who challenges worldviews and asks the questions we do not want to ask. He says a primary problem in therapies is the belief that you must first perceive or have an insight before willfully acting. Sometimes conation, willful action, opens perception. Commitment is the first act of a healthy human being. Therapy can remove us from the world and the need to act as a way in which we know ourselves and create real change. Many wisdom traditions emphasize service, commitment, and taking consistent actions to build character. Testing ourselves in the face of challenge is a kind of therapy as well. The mechanical view of the person made us look at the person from the past forward, but this buries the dynamic dialogue between the timeless dimensions of spirit and the timely moment we live in. Hillman and Ventura (1992) put it this way:

> Suppose you take it the other way and read a person's life backward . . . Suppose we look at the kids who are odd or stuttering or afraid, and instead of seeing these as developmental problems we see them as having some great thing inside them, some des-

tiny that they're not yet able to handle. . . . You read your childhood as a miniature example of your life, as a cameo. (pp. 18-19)

We could have a destiny inherent to our souls that reveals itself in
the pattern of circumstances and challenges in our lives. Within that
we can choose and embrace what we encounter even as we act and
create change. The result of our effort is fulfillment, not simply the
absence of symptoms. The result of therapy is our conscious presence
as human beings, not the absence of past traumas. "We've had a hundred years of analysis, and people are getting more and more sensitive, and the world is getting worse and worse. Maybe it's time to look
at that" (Hillman and Ventura, 1992, p. 3).

Psychospiritual approaches also face the challenge of recognizing
that many forms of extraordinary experience, of nonnormative feelings and behaviors, can be golden doorways to a deep level of change.
In many traditional wisdom cultures,

> the challenge of what we would call psychotherapy consisted of
> bringing a person back to a normal life without stamping out the
> impulse toward transformation in the process of treatment. To
> do this, a practitioner would have to recognize the difference be-
> tween thwarted normal psychological functioning and the un-
> satisfied yearning "that comes from nowhere (as one Sufi
> teacher has described it), for the evolution of consciousness."
> (Needleman, 1982, p. 78)

The practitioners in this collection have started to do just that.
Psychospiritually oriented psychotherapy offers a positive, integrative approach that enables clients' lives to open in new and ever-deep-
ening ways. The authors in this anthology realize that the psychotherapist's belief system and personal influence can be a crucial point in
the client's healing. If the psychotherapist has a limited worldview or
therapeutic paradigm, he or she may focus primarily or wholly on diagnoses and their symptoms. If the psychotherapist includes the client's deeper beliefs, especially values associated with faith and spiritual practices, research has indicated that healing is accelerated
(Richards, 2000). Integrative healing is incomplete without an in-
depth application of the spiritual influences affecting clients' inner
and outer lives (Mijares, 2003).

The human experience is an evolutionary process. We learn and develop through stress, difficulties, problems with significant relationships, and myriad other life situations. Disappointments and frustrations can be opportunities for growth or they can shut us down.

The therapeutic paradigm our profession has pursued since World War II has focused primarily on pathological conditions. It isolates symptoms from the rest of the client's life experience. Psychotherapists trained in this overly reductionist paradigm become limited in their approach to understanding and treating mental disorders. Alternative models and treatments are disallowed as health maintenance organizations (HMOs) and managed care companies constrain their practitioners to follow a rigidly categorized diagnostic and treatment paradigm. Clients are viewed as passive objects. The clinician views the client in terms of his or her diagnosis. The clients then identify with the diagnoses given to them by the "experts," and many opportunities for growth remain unexplored.

Recently health care groups have increasingly responded to the market pressure to include lifestyle approaches such as yoga and meditation. Many doctors and clinicians have issued manifestos demanding a complete revamping of our health care system. Even in these rumblings of change, the person is not the focus. Symptoms continue to divert approaches that engage the unique wholeness and spirit of a person. The construct of the hard sciences of an objective removal of the self inhibits exploration and use of disciplined subjectivity and perception beyond categorization. Health plans add yoga as an allowable tool, but only if we strip it first of the spirit, of personal encounter, of challenge, and of ecstatic or extraordinary states that are a signature of wellness. We need to add courage, creativity, and sensitivity to high standards for professional practice as we explore the many uses of psychospiritual approaches. The authors in this collection have done just that in many areas of application. Their examples provide a vision for the future.

RISING DEMAND FOR AND RESEARCH IN INTEGRATIVE PSYCHOSPIRITUAL THERAPY

Increasing numbers of practitioners are integrating spiritual perspectives along with meditation, prayer, breathing practices, intoning (mantric sound), and creative imagery to enhance psychotherapeutic healing. According to the American Psychological Association's Division 36 (Richards, 2000), clients were willing to pay approximately $27 billion out of their own pockets for alternative therapies. Many clients are making choices for holistic healing paradigms; they want more than what is offered by traditional models of psychotherapy. As clinicians we need to be flexible enough in our worldviews and techniques that we can go beyond the immediate presenting symptoms and known syndromes to open the field of awareness of the client and the therapeutic encounter. By this we invite transformation and allow new solutions for change to emerge. We empower the client, the therapist, and the unused potentials for self-healing that reside in consciousness and the spirit.

A 2003 edition of the American Psychological Association's *Monitor* (DeAngelis, 2003) reports that the National Center for Complementary and Alternative Medicine (NCCAM) hired psychologist Margaret A. Chesney as their deputy director. Researchers at NCCAM are studying the effects of meditation and alternative healing practices with a plan for disseminating their findings to the health care professionals and the public. These new research areas are expanding the field of psychological understanding in that the majority of psychiatric research had previously focused on pathology. The following provides some history on the development of the diagnostic model.

In 1917 the American Medico-Psychological Association, which became the American Psychiatric Association in 1921, began gathering data to formulate a classification of "severe psychiatric and neurological disorders." The DSM-IV notes in its history of development that this intended to help formulate a system of proper diagnosis and treatment of those who had originally been lumped into one category: "idiocy/insanity." Certainly, this was an improvement in order to better diagnose and treat many suffering persons, for it promised a more humanistic treatment for those in need.

In 1952 the move toward a symptom-based description was taken to go beyond all the theoretical conflicts that often obscured the real patterns in the client. A Freudian, a behaviorist, a Jungian analyst, and a Gestalt-oriented therapist would use language and concepts so disparate that it allowed no coherent tracking and research.

From a few dozen original symptom patterns it has now grown to over 400. Clinicians know that it is not adequate. Major revision is scheduled for 2010. What that will look like is not known yet. Many people recognize the complete absence of the factors and lifestyles that create or protect good mental/emotional health. They want to add in new scales to draw attention to the positive resources of the client. Others want to integrate all the genetic information coming from the genome projects and create an extended causal chain description that goes from gene to cognition to environment (Helmuth, 2003). This is a healthy discussion. We encourage all psychospiritual practitioners to join that discussion and open new perspectives.

Spirituality as a primary concern and tool to promote psychological health has spurred a number of special volumes by journals. They take note of rising levels of research and new evidence for spirituality itself as a valid treatment variable. In a special issue of the *American Psychologist* (Miller and Thoresen, 2003) a review of research concludes, "the evidence is clearly suggestive and, though not definitive or conclusive, is sufficient to warrant further methodologically sound investigation that will clarify health risk or protective effects of spiritual/religious factor" (p. 24).

HISTORICAL MOVEMENTS TOWARD A MODEL OF PSYCHOSPIRITUALITY

Sigmund Freud's (1856-1939) theories had a profound divisive influence on the development of Western psychology. Freud was not a religious man, but he did study some of the Kabbalistic teachings of the Jewish mystics. This is actually the background for core elements of psychoanalytic thought. The Kabbala (to receive) teaches followers meditative processes related to the unfolding journey of the Self. These teachings are found in the Zohar (the Book of Radiance). The Zohar contains teachings known as the Three Stands of the Soul related to various aspects of human consciousness (Kramer, 2003). For example, the *Nefesh* refers to one's actions, whereas *Ruach* is related to emotions. *Neshamah* is the term for higher Self. Freud reinterpreted these strands as id *(Nefesh),* ego *(Ruach),* and superego *(Neshamah).* The superego was related to introjected parental, societal, and religious morals. His interpretation of the *Neshamah* did not include spiritual experience and realization. Freud's dedication to the new sciences of neurology and physiology stopped him from even trying to penetrate and comprehend the deeper spiritual realities (perhaps a victim of modernity?) found in Jewish and other mystical teachings. This closed the door to the relationship of spirituality and positive psychological development, as evidenced in the following quote:

> Religion is an attempt to master the sensory world in which we are situated by means of the wishful world which we have developed within us as a result of biological and psychological necessities. But religion cannot achieve this. Its doctrines bear the imprint of the times in which they arose, the ignorant times of the childhood of humanity. . . . If we attempt to assign the place of religion in the evolution of mankind, it appears not as a permanent acquisition but as a counterpart to the neurosis which individual civilized men have to go through in their passage from childhood to maturity. (Küng, 1979, p. 51)

This perspective does not account for the vast history of exceptionally mature and influential persons acknowledging spiritual and religious experience as an integral force in their lives, for example, Mohandas Gandhi, Mother Teresa, Carl Jung, William James, and Rollo May, along with numerous other teachers, leaders, authors, artists, and great musicians found in every century of human history.

The separation between Freud and Carl Jung was primarily in relationship to their disagreements in the area of the transcendent function and spirituality. Jung studied all of the world's religious writings, including the alchemists' allegorical references to spiritual transcendence and the development of one's full human potential. Jung based his theory of individuation on this process leading to wholeness. His theories were not accepted in mainstream academia because of his mystical leanings.

William James (1842-1910) took a very different route from Freud in that he, like Jung, included spiritual experience. Unlike Freud, he differentiated the discipline of psychology from the study of neurology and philosophy (Fadiman and Frager, 1994) by choosing to define psychology as "the description and explanation of states of consciousness" (James, 1892, p. 1). His book *The Varieties of Religious Experiences* (1997), first published in 1902, explored the religion of healthy mindedness, conditions related to a sickness of soul, the unification of the divided self, religious conversion, saintliness, and mysticism. James was the third president of the American Psychology Association. He believed that all humans had the capacity for improving their lives and emphasized the training of will. James also correlated emotions to the body and in so doing emphasized a multilevel approach to understanding consciousness. James stood for an integrative approach in that he included mind, body, and spirit in his research and writings, but Freudian philosophy and behaviorism were to dominate the field of psychiatry and psychological theory for the rest of the century.

Abraham Maslow (1908-1970) is credited with founding both humanistic and transpersonal psychologies. In particular, he criticized both psychoanalysis and radical behaviorism; psychoanalysis focused on pathological states rather than psychological health, and behaviorism failed to acknowledge the larger potential and values within the human being. Maslow promoted research into spiritual and religious development.

Italian psychiatrist Roberto Assagioli (1888-1974) was another contributor to psychospiritual healing paradigms. Assagioli began his career as a psychoanalyst. He embraced the initial wave of psychoanalytic thought but soon realized it failed to include the broader fields and potentialities within human development. Like Freud, Assagioli studied the mystical writings of Jewish Kabbalistic teachers. Whereas Freud had reinterpreted these mystical writings in secular terms, Assagioli accentuated the spiritual teachings and incorporated them into a process of psychospiritual development. Assagioli studied the writings of Gershom Scholem (a modern Jewish mystic), developed a friendship with Martin Buber (a renowned Jewish theologian and philosopher), and was the Italian translator for the Sufi teacher Hazrat Inayat Khan.

Assagioli is particularly significant in the field of psychospirituality. He recognized the problems "that can occur as the result of a spiritual awakening in an ill-prepared or undeveloped personality" (Scotton, Chinen, and Battista, 1996, p. 59). For example, many persons seek out spiritual teachers and practices to escape their psychological pain and developmental issues. Assagioli recognized that this could create an "inflation of the personal I that can occur when a person is unable to integrate and assimilate the flow of light and spirit into the personality" (p. 59). He developed a program called psychosynthesis that encouraged recognition of subpersonalities and psychological needs as an integral part of psychospiritual development. In this work, a strong psychic foundation is developed that enables a deeper integration of spiritual energies accompanying psychospiritual awakening.

More recently, the transpersonal theories of Ken Wilber have had a large impact on the developing integration of psychology and spirituality. Wilber examines the various theories of psychological thought as related to different phases of development (Wilber, 2000, 2001). This suggests "that consciousness displays a spectrum of levels and states with corresponding unconscious structures. He contends that different schools of psychology address different levels of this spectrum" (Walsh and Vaughan, 1996, p. 63). Wilber's writings have had a broad influence by showing a developmental spectrum that includes the spiritual and its many levels. He brought together many teachings from wisdom schools and matched them to contemporary observations about pathology and healthy development. He has also been one of the strongest voices to warn of the perils of confounding the spiritual and emotional in psychospiritual therapies:

> If you confuse experiential feelings with that emptiness, then you will confuse emotionalism and sentimentalism with spirit, and this is often the first step on a regressive slide into the unending world of your own subjective fascination. You don't transcend the self, you simply feel the self intensely. (Wilber, 2003, p. 3)

His brilliant integration of many realms and ways of knowing has culminated in the formation of the Integral Institute, which actively develops his ideas and seeks practical applications including therapies. His efforts have generated rich dialogues and equally serious critics. Stanislav Grof (2003) represents many therapists when he notes,

> His knowledge of the literature is truly encyclopedic, his analytical mind systematic and incisive, and the clarity of his logic re-

markable. . . . Since speculations concerning consciousness, the human psyche, and spiritual experiences represent the corner stone of Ken's conceptual framework, it is essential to test their theoretical adequacy and practical relevance against clinical data. Ken himself does not have any clinical experience, and the primary sources of his data have been his extensive reading and the experiences from his personal spiritual practice. For this reason, evaluating his ideas in the light of actual experiences and observations from transpersonal therapy and from modern consciousness research seems particularly important and necessary. (p. 1)

This move toward the integration of ways of knowing will be a powerful influence in the development of therapeutic approaches as well.

Most recently we see the growing influence and integration of the perspectives from Buddhist psychology and the practice of meditation. Several authors in this book elaborate those. Yoga practices that integrate a refined meditative skill with physical exercise, nutrition, and lifestyle have joined mainstream culture. Yogi Bhajan's Humanology has introduced a pragmatic codification of the applied psychology of Kundalini yoga and meditation. It has a growing impact on the approaches to the mind and exemplifies the equal use of the body, mind, and spirit for treatment. Several examples of this are included in this collection.

In Western psychology many pioneers have kept love, authentic presence, and spirituality central to the healing process. Notably the late Carl Rogers (1902-1987) brought this reality of compassion into the field of psychotherapy when he emphasized "unconditional positive regard" for one's patients. In this editor's (SGM) opinion, all disorders of thought, feeling, and relationship can be seen as a lack of love—the lack of love for oneself and thereby a true lack of love for others. This lack of love creates disharmony and manifests itself in body, mind, and spirit. Therefore, in order for psychotherapists to truly heal, they must open their hearts to authentic love and caring.

AUTHORS IN THIS COLLECTION

We have invited a number of leaders in the psychospiritual approaches to contribute to this book. We picked a select number of categories that cover major recognizable syndromes without trying to be exhaustive. We also picked areas where psychospiritual approaches have made a real contribution and demonstrate the differences in worldview. Our hope is that this will inspire more practitioners to explore these approaches. The chapters are also an opportunity to reflect on our current treatments and ask how we can effectively include the dimensions of consciousness, spirit, and lifestyle as part of a complete healing program. Theories and treatments have been presented for many of the most common mental disorders. Although spirituality is frequently included in substance abuse treatment programs, spirituality is rarely, if ever, included in treating these other disorders.

Each author offers the reader a combination of worldview and applied practice. The emphasis is on applications and approaches that can broaden our understanding of the client and the client's strengths. Many of the chapters introduce readers who are unfamiliar with these approaches to the basics of alternative treatment. Besides a clear clinical awareness of the need to reduce presenting symptoms, the approaches in this volume put the client and the innate healing processes and potential of the client at the center of an integrative approach. Communication, insight, integration, lifestyle intervention, and spiritual clarity are all part of a treatment that respects the known and unknown parts of the client's body, mind, and psyche.

We start with John Mack (1929-2004), a leading psychiatrist and Pulitzer Prize winner, who has explored extraordinary experiences and their implications for therapeutic approaches and for our worldview. He gives us the big picture and underscores the need for the therapist to pay attention to the context and process of the client. Dwight Judy explores how life changes and adjustment disorders invite us to adopt new life structures. Chapter 3, "Breathing into Fear," explains the power of using breathing and awareness as a primary intervention for anxiety disorders. Selene Vega illustrates its application along with the perspective of Stephen Gilligan's self-relations psychotherapy. In Chapter 4, Sharon Mijares guides the reader on the use of traumatic experiences and PTSD to transform the scope and depth of a person's identity. Anita Johnston and Kyrai Antares demonstrate the craft of narrative therapy used with the sensibilities of a psychospiritual approach to eating disorders.

Gurucharan Singh Khalsa introduces the use of Yogi Bhajan's Humanology using yoga and meditation for ADHD and attentional disorders. Colin Ross, a leader in dissociative identity disorders, opens a thorough discussion of the often overlooked spiritual conflicts and contexts that arise with multiple personalities. Manjit Kaur Khalsa looks at personality disorders, focusing on borderline and narcissistic syndromes and further exploring the Humanological perspective and the work of Linehan whose dialectical behavioral therapy draws from Zen and cognitive-behavioral therapies. The area of conduct disorders and antisocial personalities is filled with complex personal and societal value issues. Celia Drake and Deborah Lewis bring clarity to all of those challenges with a moral reasoning model that supports a pragmatic psychospiritual approach.

The important area of bipolar personality disorders is given new perspectives by Jeff Rediger, drawing on deep Western philosophical roots and extensive psychiatric and psychospiritual experience. Psychotic disorders have always fueled much controversy about treatment and the conflating spiritual openings with madness. David Lukoff brings a critical eye to spiritual emergencies and psychotic episodes with guidelines for a psychospiritual clinician. Depression as a spiritual ailment is presented from a Sufi perspective by Arife Ellen Hammerle.

A very important question for the psychospiritual treatment approach is how profoundly awareness itself can create neurological and emotional change. Jeffrey M. Schwartz, Elizabeth Gulliford, Jessica Stier, and Margo Thienemann combine their wide range of talents to examine the potential and mechanisms of neuroplasticity as they artfully explain the use of mindfulness for obsessive-compulsive disorders. They also address the broader topic of integrating biological and psychospiritual approaches. Peggy Kleinplatz and Stanley Krippner discuss the artificial divide between human sexuality and religion. They provide a model for integrating spirituality in the clinical treatment of sexual disorders. Dharma Singh Khalsa keeps with the biological focus when he lays out practical methods to prevent and treat Alzheimer's disease. He gives stress a central focus and presents treatments that range from nutrition to meditation. The final chapter by Henry Grayson and Bruce Kerievsky, surveys some of the organizations and therapeutic communities that support psycho-spiritual treatment options.

The chapters are independent and can be browsed according to the interest of the reader. The blend of perspectives and practical applications provide insight and new information. Clinicians who want to explore this area will find each chapter very accessible. Psycho-spiritual practitioners can use these chapters as windows into the expanding field of alternative treatment that strives for effectiveness, integrity, and creativity in the use of the spirit of each person.

REFERENCES

DeAngelis, T. (2003). Psychologist to help direct the Nation's Alternative Health Practice. *APA Monitor,* 34(1), 72.

Fadiman, J. and Frager, R. (1994). *Personality and Personal Growth,* Third Edition. New York: HarperCollins College Publishers.

Grof, S. (2003). Ken Wilber's Spectrum Psychology by Stanislav Grof, MD <http://primal-page.com/grofken.htm>, p. 1.

Helmuth, L. (2003). In Sickness or in Health? *Science,* 302, 808-810.

Hillman, J. and Ventura, M. (1992). *We've Had a Hundred Years of Psychotherapy—And the World's Getting Worse.* San Francisco: Harper San Francisco.

James, W. (1892). *Psychology: The Briefer Course.* New York: Holt, Rinehart and Winston. Reprint, New York: Harper and Row, 1961.

James, W. (1997). *The Varieties of Religious Experiences.* New York: Simon and Schuster, Inc.

Keyes, C.L. and Haidt, J. (2003). *Flourishing: Positive Psychology and the Life Well-Lived.* Washington, DC: American Psychological Association.

Kramer, S.Z. (2003). Jewish Spiritual Pathways for Growth and Healing. In Sharon G. Mijares (Ed.), *Modern Psychology and Ancient Wisdom: Psychological Healing Practices from the World's Religious Traditions* (pp. 97-122). Binghamton, NY: The Haworth Press, Inc.

Küng, H. (1979). *Freud and the Problem of God.* New Haven, CT: Yale University Press.

Leshan, L. (2002).*The Dilemma of Psychology: A Psychologist Looks at His Troubled Profession.* New York: Allworth Press.

Mijares, S.G. (Ed.) (2003). *Modern Psychology and Ancient Wisdom: Psychological Healing Practices from the World's Religious Traditions.* Binghamton, NY: The Haworth Press, Inc.

Miller, W.R. and Thoresen, C.E. (2003). Spirituality, Religion and Health: An Emerging Research Field. *American Psychologist,* 58(1), 24-35.

Needleman, J. (1982). *Consciousness and Tradition.* New York: Crossroad/Herder and Herder Publishers.

Richards, P.S. (2000). Spiritual Influences in Healing and Psychotherapy. *Psychology of Religion Newsletter,* Winter (pp. 1-12). Washington, DC: American Psychological Association Division 36.

Scotton, B.W., Chinen, A.B., and Battista, J.R. (1996). *Textbook of Transpersonal Psychiatry and Psychology.* New York: Basic Books.

Walsh, R. and Vaughan, F. (1996). The Worldview of Ken Wilber. In Scotton, B.W., Chinen, A.B., and Battista, J.R. (Eds.), *Textbook of Transpersonal Psychiatry and Psychology* (pp. 62-74). New York: Basic Books.

Wilber, K. (2000). *Integral Psychology Consciousness, Spirit, Psychology, Therapy.* Boston: Shambhala Press.

Wilber, K. (2001). *The Eye of Spirit: An Integral Vision for a World Gone Slightly Mad,* Revised Edition. Boston: Shambhala Press.

Wilber, K. (2003). Online interview transcript. Ken Wilber Online. <http://wilber.shambhala.com/html/interviews/Shambhala_interview.cfm/>, p. 4.

Chapter 1

Approaching Extraordinary Experiences in the Mental Health Field

John E. Mack

EXTRAORDINARY EXPERIENCES

In 1990 I began to see clients who were having what have usually been called alien abduction experiences. After working with more than fifty such individuals I came to realize that my psychiatric training had not provided me with a way to approach such clients, let alone to understand what they were undergoing. For here were people who, from a clinical standpoint, were describing events that seemed to have actually occurred in their lives but were, from the standpoint of our society's consensus reality, simply not possible. The incredulity, and even outrage, that greeted my taking these reports seriously has led me to consider the whole question of how, as mental health professionals, we are to work with people whose experiences are extraordinary from the standpoint of our culture's dominant worldview.

Psychiatrists and other mental health professionals will inevitably encounter patients/clients who present with what might be called extraordinary or "anomalous" experiences.[1] When confronted with events or phenomena with which they are unfamiliar, human beings inevitably relate their experiences to what they already know or believe that they know, and psychiatrists and psychologists are no exception (Coady, 1992). This tendency can, however, result in serious misunderstandings and potential harm when the category to which the person is assigned is inappropriate. Clinicians must be able to approach individuals who present with unfamiliar or extraordinary experiences from a perspective that is unbiased and open-minded. In this chapter I will attempt to provide the elements of such a perspective and consider its implications for diagnosis, patient care, and research.

Consider, for example, the not infrequent instances in which a patient reports that he or she has been visited during the night by a recently deceased relative (I have a number of such cases in mind). For many, if not most, clinicians, especially those raised and trained in Western societies, such "spirits" are not thought to exist in any real— i.e., actual, literal, or material—sense. The only alternative usually available in our culture, then, would be to consider them to be the product of the inner world or imagination of the individual. Assuming this to be the case, the therapist will then turn his or her attention to the possible motivation behind, or diagnostic implications of, such an experience—whether, for example, it reflects unresolved grief, expresses a kind of wish fulfillment, or is simply a form of hallucination. The point here is not that this approach on the part of the clinician is altogether mistaken; the timing, for example, of the spirit's appearance may indeed be related to desires or longings of the bereaved person. Rather, we must recognize that such assumptions are reflective of a worldview that may preclude a more useful approach to such an experience. Later in this chapter I will describe what might be a more constructive way of thinking about and treating such experiences.

It is beyond the intention of this chapter to provide a complete list of the anomalous or extraordinary experiences that a mental health practitioner may encounter. Some of the more common ones would include, in addition to spirit visitations, so-called kundalini awakenings (unexplained bodily energies or vibrations that reach disturbing intensity and seem to be associated with spiritual development) and various mystical or ecstatic experiences; near-death experiences (NDEs); episodes of clairvoyance, precognition, telepathic communication, and other "psychic" experiences, particularly when they are unwelcome or unexpected; UFO encounters (especially alien contact or "abduction" experiences); hauntings; psychokinetic phenomena; apparently inexplicable manifestations of light perceived in the patient's environment; and ecstatic religious experiences, including perceiving apparitions of the Virgin Mary (or other manifestations of a Divine Mother archetype).

Czech-born psychiatrist Stanislav Grof, working with his wife Christina, realized that such experiences may have a consciousness-expanding or "spiritual" significance while also being intensely troubling to the individual, especially if not recognized for what they are. The Grofs originated the term *spiritual emergency* (later *spiritual emergence*) to describe them (Grof and Grof, 1990), and founded the Spiritual Emergency Network (SEN) to provide a "hotline" to which people who are undergoing such experiences can turn.

WORLDVIEWS

A particular experience is considered extraordinary or anomalous in relation to a set of assumptions that are usually, for the most part, unconscious, which define for an individual or society what is or can be possible or real. A worldview is rather like the air we breathe or the way water might seem to a fish.[2] It is so much an intrinsic part of the organism's environment as to be taken for granted, or not even perceived, unless called to its attention by some inescapable truth with which the presumption is in conflict. When this occurs, for human beings, the individual is forced to make a choice: either the old worldview must be stretched, sometimes to bizarre lengths, or it must be modified or abandoned to make room for information that does not fit within its limits.

Philosopher Neal Grossman gives a striking example of such "stretching" that occurred when he discussed with a member of his department examples of near-death experiences in which patients were able to provide accurate information about what had been happening inside and outside the operating room after coming out of a coma during which they were, in effect, brain dead: "They just subconsciously heard the conversation in the operating room," or "that's just a coincidence or a lucky guess," the man suggested. When pressed further by Grossman, his colleague said, "Even if I were to have a near death experience, myself, I would conclude I was hallucinating rather than believe that my mind can exist independently of my brain" (Grossman, 2002, p. 8).

A worldview is, in essence, a psychological organizing system, a mental structure comprising a set of assumptions about "the way things are" or "must be." It could be thought of as functioning like the "operating system" of the cosmos, telling us what exists and guiding us in our relationship to that reality. In the material or external realm, a worldview is not so much the physical laws themselves but the conviction that those laws are the fixed parameters for defining the physical universe. In the mental or inner world, a worldview defines the boundaries of the humanly possible with regard to capability, perception, and the relation of the mental to the physical world. Until quite recently, for example, it was assumed that action and perception at a distance were not possible, but in recent decades it has been discovered that prayer can affect healing of individuals who do not know they are being prayed for, and under proper conditions people can be trained to identify targets far removed from them in time and space ("remote viewing") (Dossey, 1989, 1992, 1997, 2001; Sicher et al., 1998; Targ, 2000, 2002; Targ and Katra, 1998).

For a given individual a worldview functions as if it were the very foundation of the psyche, the concrete upon which it is based and the glue that holds it together. It seems to orient us in time and space, and even in our relationships to others. For this reason a threat to the integrity of a worldview may be met at the very least with strong resistance, and sometimes with anger and even violent behavior (see the case example of Michael in this chapter). In the political realm worldviews manifest as ideologies, rigid assumptions about how large groups must function to bring about a desired result for a particular society; they have provided the justification for most of the terrible wars throughout human history.

The worldview that until quite recently dominated Western society has been variously called Newtonian/Cartesianism, scientific materialism (labeled "scientism" in its extreme form), or anthropocentric humanism (Zimmerman, 1991). According to this view, the physical or material world is the dominant or "objective" reality and conforms to established laws or mechanisms. Psychological experience obviously exists but is secondary or "subjective," and therefore assumed to be less amenable to scientific study. A "scientific" approach to understanding human experience has generally consisted of efforts to discover the "mechanisms" of the mind's functioning, or to reduce the activities of the psyche to the workings of the brain. Furthermore, in this framework the inner and outer realms are treated as quite separate, and apparent connections are regarded as "coincidences."

The matter of worldviews clearly has great significance in the mental health field. The worldview of the therapist will determine how he or she regards the experiences that the patient reports. Most of us, especially psychiatrists and doctorate-level psychologists, have been schooled in the traditions of scientific materialism and believe, for the most part, that mental phenomena have, ultimately, a material or biological explanation. Phenomena that clearly defy established physical laws are regarded with suspicion. The effectiveness of medication in certain psychiatric disorders is taken as evidence for the biological basis of the condition. Less consideration tends to be given, instead, to the possibility that a given distress or apparent psychopathology is an expression of the troubled state of the person as a whole, and that *any* effective intervention—pharmacological, psychological, or spiritual—will inevitably impact the individual in all of these dimensions. Differences of worldview tend to come to the forefront when a significant cultural or religious divide separates the clinician from the patient or client.

Case Example: Michael—A Clash of Worldviews

Michael's case, though extreme in several respects, illustrates dramatically how a lack of understanding based on a clash of worldviews can cause serious harm.

Michael is a pioneering physicist, now in his forties, who underwent an extraordinary spiritual awakening when he was eighteen, which so frightened his father that he forced Michael on two occasions in a six-month period into a psychiatric ward. I will describe only the first of these hospitalizations here. The second followed pretty much the pattern of the first but was less coercive, partly because by this time Michael had learned how to behave in a way that enabled him to "go along with the program."

As a teenager Michael developed somewhat precocious interests in yoga, meditation, and quantum physics, and read a number of works that sought to integrate developments in physics with Eastern philosophy and the transformation of consciousness. Shortly before he was to begin college at a California university, Michael began to have spontaneous mystical experiences of a profound nature. Over a period of several months he had a number of periods in which he had ecstatic sensations of intense currents of energy and heat flowing through his body, accompanied by feelings of bliss. On several occasions the universe and his own ego seemed to dissolve or melt into "tidal waves" of light, and he would experience the "perfection of the divine order." Reality became timeless or eternal, and nothing was separate. There would be "formless ecstatic radiance that had absolutely no features to it, and there was this unbelievable feeling of being Home." The "wonderful abundance" that seemed to characterize the cosmos contrasted painfully with the destructive behavior Michael saw in human society. As he radiated love to those around him, birds seemed to come to Michael, as if he were a modern day St. Francis.

Michael was able to do his college work during the fall of his freshman year, but when he came home for Christmas vacation he was shocked by the "iron-fisted crushing response" that he received, especially from his father, when he talked about his transformational experiences. His father was an eminent biologist who was convinced that Michael was undergoing some form of psychosis. He even had a theory that the cause of all this was a "mutant gene" of schizophrenia, which Michael's disorder would help him identify. As Michael tried to explain that nothing was wrong with him, his father seemed to grow more distant and alarmed and took a lot of notes. On Christmas Eve he virtually dragged Michael into a car, explaining that he wanted him to meet with "this guy who had a similar view of the brain." Michael did not resist too much, as he felt certain that he was quite rational and could reason effectively with anyone he might see.

But his father drove him to a local university psychiatric institute where the doors soon closed behind him. Despite Michael's protestations, his father and members of the hospital staff forced him into a closed ward. A bizarre breakdown of communication occurred, as each thing he said seemed to be misinterpreted. The open-hearted sharing of "a way of being that was more joyous" was treated as part of his madness, and self-descriptions Michael had intended to be metaphoric were taken literally. For example, at one point he said that "the being you call Michael is dead." Later he found that "claims he is dead" was written in the chart.

Michael was told that he had undergone a "break from reality," and Thorazine, a powerful antipsychotic agent used in the 1970s, was recommended. He resisted this, for he had read about the drug and felt certain it would not be good for him. When the nursing staff tried to force him to take the pills, Michael would spit them out, on one occasion spraying the orderlies with orange juice. This struggle went on for several hours, until Michael was placed in a straitjacket and tied to a bed. Finally, exhausted, Michael went to sleep. During the night five orderlies awoke him, shining a flashlight in his eyes. They held each of his legs while another injected into his thigh a dangerously toxic dose of Thorazine. (Michael's wife, a physician, was able years later to review the hospital records and confirm much of the story.) After a period of great mental chaos and confusion, lasting several days, Michael became quite docile.

After several occasions in which his outrage got the better of him, Michael was able, with his mother's help, to develop a strategy that enabled him to leave the hospital. At no time could Michael identify a single person as his doctor or therapist. On the day that Michael was released "to the custody of my parents" a psychiatrist told him that he had had a severe psychotic break and might need to take psychiatric medications for the rest of his life. When he got home Michael was understandably very depressed by the hospital experience. His father, in collaboration with whomever on the psychiatric faculty he had consulted, urged him to take lithium to alleviate his depression. Michael was certain that he did not need this medication and would dispose of the pills. He allowed his parents to believe he was taking the drug, and as he came out of the depression his father said to him, "Thank God for the lithium."

The crisis surrounding Michael's hospitalizations, and the barbaric treatment he received, led to his mother's own spiritual development and his parents' eventual divorce. The mystical awakening Michael experienced in his late teens contained the seeds of his later achievements as a scholar in the forefront of the integration of science and consciousness and the recognition in science of the centrality of human experience as a source of knowledge about the universe and our place in it. Influenced by his son and other leading physicists and scientists of consciousness, Michael's father is gradually softening his rigidly materialistic worldview. After years of estrangement between Michael and his father following the traumatic hospitalizations, they are becoming reconciled and even collaborating on a project that can help to relieve the planet's energy crisis.

Much can be said about Michael's case, not the least of which concerns the barbaric nature of his psychiatric treatment. However, to a large extent the brutality and aggression expressed in Michael's care is secondary to a radical clash of worldviews. Looking back a quarter of a century, we might better think of Michael's late teenage crisis as a dramatic spiritual awakening rather than a form of psychosis. Unfortunately, his father and the psychiatric faculty and staff were completely committed to a worldview that had little place for spirituality at all, and certainly not for the sort of dramatic mystical transformation that Michael was undergoing.

Michael's father, limited by his radically materialistic point of view, could see what was happening to his son only as a frightening form of nervous system breakdown and reacted accordingly. Similarly, for the faculty and staff, such radical openings of the heart and spirit had no place in the psychobiological framework that prevailed then (and to some degree still does) in academic departments of psychiatry. As so often happens in such situations, a terrible catch-22 developed. The poetic and metaphoric language of the heart that Michael used to describe his experience was heard altogether literally, taken as further evidence of his psychosis. Similarly, his inevitable outrage at the cruelty of his treatment was seen as a further expression of madness. The clash of worldviews was radical, hurtful, and, at that time, sadly irreconcilable.

SPIRITUALITY AND RELIGION

Many mental health professionals, especially those with a Freudian background, have been trained according to a secular outlook, which regards religion as, at best, a psychological "crutch" or, worse, a kind of collective obsession or outright delusion. Historical and contemporary abuses on the part of organized religion are sometimes invoked to bolster such viewpoints. Spirituality is frequently equated with religion, regarded as a kind of nebulous high-mindedness, a vain seeking of unrealistic goals.

The clinician's personal relationship to spiritual questions is of critical importance in any consideration of how extraordinary human experience is to be regarded. Many of the experiences we consider to be anomalous, such as NDEs, kundalini awakenings, or religious epiphanies, involve a direct encounter with what has been variously called the Divine, Source, Home, God, or the Ultimate Creative Principle. Other experiences, such as precognition, clairvoyance, telepathy, and various other psychic phenomena, if not spiritual in the sense of a numinous presence, demonstrate the possible existence of a nonmaterial realm that can, potentially, be objectively demonstrated.

I recall a conversation I once had with an incoming chair of our department in Cambridge. As is customary at such times, I reviewed with her my various interests and the projects in which I was engaged. She seemed quite accepting of most of what I had to say, even my explorations of encounters with aliens, but added, "It's only your interest in spirituality that concerns me." She then proceeded to tell me of her unhappy experiences growing up with a grandfather who was a rigid, and evidently rather cruel, orthodox rabbi. For this psychiatrist there was no separation between religion and the whole realm of human spirituality.

Until quite recently it was commonplace to regard mystical experiences themselves as a kind of infantilism or even as a type of delusion (Grof, 1985). The consequences of this extreme expression of materialism have sometimes been horrifying. Because of the pioneering work of the Grofs, David Lukoff, Bob Turner, Arthur Deikman, Nancy Kehoe, Ken Wilber, Eugene Taylor, and many others, what Taylor calls a "psychology of the transcendent" is emerging in the mental health field (Mack, 1999). The American Psychiatric Association's *Diagnostic and Statistical Manual of Mental Disorders* (DSM) now comes close to recognizing the existence of the spiritual realm, by acknowledging that people undergo psychospiritual experiences—experiences involving "questioning of spiritual values that may not necessarily be related to an organized church or religious organization" (American Psychiatric Association, 2000, p. 685).*

WHAT IS CALLED FOR?

Before offering specific recommendations for training mental health professionals in appropriate ways of responding to patients or clients who present because of their (or family members') distress relating to extraordinary experiences, we must return to the matter of worldviews. Ideally, clinicians, in addition to becoming familiar with the great variety of anomalous experiences that clients may report, should themselves undergo explorations of their own into what is usually called "nonordinary" or "altered states" of consciousness. Such journeys, if not resulting in precisely the same sort of exceptional experiences that the clients may present, will enable the clinician to enter psychological realms or states of being in which what has heretofore been regarded as extraordinary may seem less strange, or even possible.

---

*Reprinted with permission from the *Diagnostic and Statistical Manual of Mental Disorders*, Fourth Edition, Text Revision, Copyright 2000, American Psychiatric Association.

Much as mental health professionals have been urged, if not required, to seek personal therapy or psychoanalysis to better understand their patients' psychology, it is not inappropriate to expect that
we undergo some form of practice that will reveal the limitations of
the dominant worldview or will open our awareness to the variety of
experiences for which standard biological or psychodynamic expla-
nations are clearly inadequate. Such a practice might consist of one or
another form of meditation, certain forms of hypnotherapy, modalities such as Grof Holotropic Breathwork (www.holotropic.com),
shamanic journeying (Eliade, 1964; Harner, 1991; Walsh, 1990),
Breathwalking (Bhajan and Singh Khalsa, 2000), and controlled out-
of-body experiences (Buhlman, 2001; Monroe, 1971). What these
journeys share in common is an opening of the experiencer to the realization that the psyche is "transpersonal"; it is not simply contigu-
ous with the body but can seem to extend "beyond the brain" and become capable of perceiving elements of a vastly expanded material
and nonmaterial reality.

Whether or not a mental health professional has chosen to under-
take the personal explorations that might reveal the limitations of his
or her given worldview, mental health clinicians should be taught to
appreciate the great range of human experiences that have heretofore
been improperly regarded as pathological. At the very least, for example, didactic training needs to include a taxonomy of the varieties
of spiritually related experiences that not only do not reflect psychopathology but also may signify a striving for expanded awareness,
transcendent consciousness, or connection with the Divine. Even if
the clinician regards such notions as "unproven," or even nonsensical,
teachers and supervisors must insist that the trainee be aware that his
or her beliefs are not necessarily "the truth." Beliefs should be
suspended at least to the extent that they not be imposed upon the
client.

A few years ago a professional woman in her forties came to see
me because of strange "electrical dreams" associated with bright
lights and the appearance on several occasions of strange humanoid
beings in her room at night. She had recently dismissed another psychiatrist to whom she had been recommended for hypnotherapy to help
understand the source of these unusual experiences. When in the
course of her hypnotic sessions she would recall with powerful emo-

tions her encounters with the strange beings, associated apparently with UFOs, she told me that the doctor had discouraged communications of this sort and would say that he did not "believe" in UFOs. In her letter she thanked him for his services, but also wrote that it was improper for him to allow his treatment approach to be governed by whatever he may or may not have believed.

After fourteen years of studying UFO-related encounters I still have no certain knowledge of their origin. Clearly, however, in case after case my clients, such as the woman just described, have benefitted greatly from my taking such experiences seriously and being open to the possibility that they are altogether "real" in whatever way we are to understand that much maligned word.

DIAGNOSIS

Mental health professionals need to develop adequate skills for assessing extraordinary experiences, but details of what is reported do not, by themselves, tell us how best to consider such communications. Clearly, from what has been said previously, the fact that what a patient or client reports seems strange, or even impossible, according to the experience of the clinician, does not in itself warrant a diagnosis of psychopathology. Furthermore, the clinician must be aware that much of the patient's distress can derive from the fact that he or she, like ourselves, may have been raised in a cultural context in which such things are simply not possible—past-life memories, UFO encounters, and near-death experiences are common examples. I have introduced the term *ontological shock* to distinguish the troubled feelings that result from this discordance of worldviews (on the part of both the clinician and the therapist) from those that are brought about by the troubling aspects of the experiences themselves.

Of course, extraordinary experiences can be associated with various forms of psychopathology (over and above the trauma or stress occasioned by the experience itself). UFO encounters, past-life experiences, and psychic abilities, for example, do not provide immunity from common psychiatric disorders such as addiction, depression, or psychotic states. The clinical picture may be further complicated, however, by the fact that unintegrated elements of the experiences may be the source of considerable emotional distress. This, of course, can be greatly aggravated when relatives and friends are threatened by, or simply do not accept, what the patient is reporting.

The standard mental status examination can be of considerable value in assessing reports of extraordinary experience. The *way* that UFO experiencers, for example, reported what they said had happened to them convinced me that I was not dealing with an ordinary psychiatric problem. The clients' emotions were often of great intensity and appropriate to what they said had happened to them; they spoke like individuals who have participated in a disturbing event. In addition, the fact that they were appropriately doubting and self-critical, appreciating how I or anyone in our society might regard such reports, further persuaded me that these individuals were telling the truth and that something strange had, evidently, happened to them. They did not, like deluded persons, try to convince me of anything.

In addition to the mental status, the context of the person's whole life must be taken into consideration. How is he or she *functioning* in relation to primary life tasks, for example, relations with others, school, work, care of children? Does the clinician know of other such cases—Martian apparitions or NDEs, for example—in which psychopathology does not seem to have been a factor? What do relatives, co-workers, and friends say about the person? Is he or she prone, for example, to self-dramatization, exaggeration of imagination, or outright lying?

Cultural and religious considerations are also important. Is the phenomenon in question—reincarnation, for example—familiar in other cultures? This is obviously important in the case of clients who are themselves from other cultures, but these considerations also apply in those instances in which members of our own society are undergoing experiences which, though not necessarily normally accepted as possible according to the dominant worldview, may be an expression of some form of emotional or spiritual transformation or growth. Some extraordinary experiences, such as Martian apparitions and other encounters with Divine entities, may have a religious significance that needs to be understood before a psychiatric diagnosis is applied.

WITNESSING

I have come to the conclusion that the familiar mental status examination is essentially inadequate for the assessment of most extraordinary experiences. This form of examination tends to objectify the individual, separating the examiner from the patient or client in such a way that something fundamental is lost. The mental status may be useful for evaluating forms of psychopathology, but in the case of extraordinary experiences we are more concerned with the meaning of the phenomena, their transformative power, and the implications they hold for the mental health field and our society's dominant worldview.

In an effort to correct this deficiency I have applied the notion of the witness or witnessing (I am grateful for writings and conversations with Lisa Oakman for the development of this idea). A witness is a person in whose presence one feels a certain truthfulness. This is not based on a cognitive assessment of the reality or likelihood of what is being reported. Rather, it is a feeling of resonance, an intersubjective connection with the person that involves our whole being, sometimes accompanied by the sense that one is hearing something especially meaningful, sacred, or even transcendent. In Oakman's words (2002), when a witness of this sort speaks,

> all recognize they have been in other realms. Sincerity and truth and power of spirit are just as measurable as inches and pounds, but not in the same way. The measuring rod is the sense of pattern ringing true that one feels in the presence of such a person.

THERAPEUTIC APPROACHES

In working with people who come to our attention as a result of distress relating to extraordinary experiences, the task is quite different from what we are accustomed to confronting in approaching psychiatric patients. In these instances we can think of the emotional or psychological problem as secondary, in other words, occurring as a response to an unusual event or experience rather than deriving from elements in the individual biology, personality, or psyche per se. The principal task is not to treat a disorder or bring about a therapeutic result. Rather, we might think of the clinician's role as that of a facilitator, helping the person come to terms with or integrate the experience or experiences.

This has several aspects.

First, the therapist or facilitator must take a sufficiently thorough history to find out the nature and pattern of the experiences, how often they have occurred, and where they fit or do not fit into the person's life.

Second, the facilitator needs to try to help the person come to terms with what has occurred. In order to do this he or she needs to have done the necessary "homework." This consists of becoming familiar with the experience(s) under consideration, while examining biases or preconceptions regarding the matter that may interfere with the clinician's capacity to approach his or her client's report with an open mind.

Third, in certain instances, for example, in the case of alien contact, the facilitator must help the patient "hold" or "bear" and move through the often intense forces or energies that remain in the person's psyche. Unless this is done the person may stay "stuck" in a state of traumatization or remain in some way a victim of what has occurred.

Fourth, the facilitator needs to work with family members, teachers, and others in the client's community to help them understand the nature of the problem and thereby reduce the individual's sense of isolation.

Fifth, it may be useful to suggest therapeutic or spiritual practices that can enable the person to grow or develop in such a way that the experiences can come to seem less extraordinary, and the experiencers, therefore, can be enabled more readily to accept themselves as members of the human community.

Finally, it is often useful to introduce the experiencer to others who have had similar experiences. In the case of the NDE and UFO phenomena, established communities offer support, understanding, and education to individual experiencers and the society as a whole.

FURTHER IMPLICATIONS

Although this book is addressed primarily to mental health clinicians, many of the extraordinary experiences referred to in this chapter carry implications that extend beyond the mental health field. As we shift in regard to such phenomena, for example, as religious visions, near-death experiences, and UFO encounters, from pathologizing or outright denial to a greater acceptance of their nonpsychiatric actuality, our view of ourselves and our place in the cosmos will also change. For example, rather than experiencing ourselves as alone and disconnected in a cosmos devoid of life beyond the Earth, we might come to realize that consciousness can exist "beyond the brain," intelligent entities pervade the universe (whether or not they are embodied), and when our bodies die our consciousness may persist in some form. Notions of soul, spirit, and meaning, long discredited in Western cultures, may once again become part of the experience of being human.

NOTES

1. Rhea A. White, founder of the Exceptional Human Experience Network, has identified 230 types of "exceptional experiences," which she has placed in nine broad classes: death-related, desolation/nadir, dissociative, encounter, exceptional human performance/feats, healing, mystical, peak, and psychical experiences. The emphasis in this chapter is on those frequently encountered in clinical practice (White, 2000).

2. In this context I generally prefer the term *worldview* to *paradigm,* with which it is sometimes used interchangeably, because the latter has come to be associated rather specifically with scientific systems.

REFERENCES

American Psychiatric Association (2000). *Diagnostic and Statistical Manual of Mental Disorders* (Fourth Edition, Text Revision). Washington, DC: American Psychiatric Association.

Bhajan, Yogi and Singh Khalsa, G. (2000). *Breathwalk: Breathing Your Way to a Revitalized Body, Mind, and Spirit.* New York: Broadway Books.

Buhlman, W. (2001). *The Secret of the Soul: Using Out-of-Body Experiences to Understand Our True Nature.* San Francisco: Harper San Francisco.

Coady, C.A.J. (1992). *Testimony: A Philosophical Study.* Oxford: Clarendon Press.

Dossey, L.O. (1989). *Recovering the Soul: A Scientific and Spiritual Approach.* New York: Bantam.

Dossey, L.O. (1992). *Healing Beyond the Body: Medicine and the Infinite Reach of the Mind.* New York: Random House.

Dossey, L.O. (1997). But is it energy? Reflections on Consciousness, Healing, and the New Paradigm. *Subtle Energies,* 3(3), 69-82.

Dossey, L.O. (2001). The Forces of Healing: Reflections on Energy, Consciousness, and the Beef Stroganoff Principle. *Alternative Therapies in Health and Medicine,* 3(5), 8-14.

Eliade, M. (1964). *Shamanism: Archaic Techniques of Ecstasy.* Princeton, NJ: Princeton University Press.

Grof, C. and Grof, S. (1990). *The Stormy Search for the Self.* Los Angeles: J.P. Tarcher.

Grof, S. (1985). *Beyond the Brain: Birth, Death, and Transcendence in Psychotherapy.* Albany: State University of New York Press.

Grossman, N. (2002). On Materialism As Science Dogma. [Published as "Who's Afraid of Life After Death?"] *Journal of Near Death Studies,* 21(1), 5-24.

Harner, M.J. (1991). *The Way of the Shaman: A Guide to Power and Healing* (Third Edition). San Francisco: Harper San Francisco.

Mack, J. (1999). A Wily Reality. *PEER Perspectives,* 3(1), 12-13.

Monroe, R.A. (1971). *Journeys out of the Body.* New York: Doubleday.

Oakman, L. (2002). Witness. Unpublished essay.

Sicher, F., Targ, E., Moore, D., and Smith, H.S. (1998). A Randomized Double-Blind Study of the Effect of Distant Healing in a Population with Advanced AIDS. *Western Journal of Medicine,* 169, 356-363.

Targ, E. (2000). Research in Prayer and Distant Healing: Evidence and Implications. Presented at the 2000 International Conference on Science and Consciousness, April 29-May 3, The Message Company, Santa Fe, New Mexico.

Targ, E. (2002). Research Methodology for Studies of Prayer and Distant Healing. *Complementary Therapies in Nursing and Midwifery,* 8(1), 29-41.

Targ, R. and Katra, J. (1998). *Miracles of Mind: Exploring Nonlocal Consciousness and Spiritual Healing.*

Walsh, R.N. (1990). *The Spirit of Shamanism.* New York: Tarcher/Putnam.

White, R. (2000). List of Potential EHEs (Third Edition). The Exceptional Human Experience Network. <www.ehe.org>.

Zimmerman, M.E. (1991). Deep Ecology, Ecoactivism, and Human Evolution. *ReVision,* 13(3), 122-128.

Chapter 2

Seasons of Change: Adjustment Disorder As Summons to New Life Structure

Dwight H. Judy

INTRODUCTION

Adjustment disorder is defined in the DSM-IV (American Psychiatric Association, 1994) as a time of challenge in adjusting to a life stressor. In this chapter, we explore underlying themes of life change. In many cases, the presenting crisis of the client represents a major life transition process that has not yet been understood or integrated. An underlying theme of our discussion will be the rhythmic nature of our lives. Our human drive toward meaning manifests in life goals. Conflicts may arise between such major issues as our commitment to family and our commitment to our work life. Sometimes, before we realize it, we have achieved a major life goal and are unconsciously asking, "What's next?" A crisis in one or more areas of life will bring the client to counseling. How can we effectively assist in the exploration of deeper life transition issues? In this chapter, we explore a variety of ways of examining the theme of major life transition from models of transpersonal psychological development and from the cycles of transition in the mythic journey of the hero or heroine. Can adjustment disorder become a summons to new life adventure?

DSM-IV DIAGNOSIS

Several variations in diagnostic categories for adjustment disorder are present in the DSM-IV. In all cases a time of challenge has manifest in relationship to a life stressor. The onset should be within three months of an identifiable life stressor. If considered acute, the disturbance lasts for six months or less after the identifiable stressor has terminated. If considered chronic, symptoms persist for more than six months, because the stressor is chronic or because the consequences have enduring effects. Bereavement is not included in the DSM-IV as such a life stressor. The diagnostic categories include Adjustment Disorder with Depression (309.0), with Anxiety (309.24), with Mixed Anxiety and Depressed Mood (309.28), with Disturbance of Conduct (309.3), with Mixed Disturbance of Emotions and Conduct (309.4), and Unspecified (309.9). Such diagnosis may be listed as Axis I or primary diagnosis (American Psychiatric Association, 1994).

The challenge that might evoke the symptoms of adjustment disorder could be a variety of life events, such as divorce or change in marital relationship, change within work or family relationships, divorce of parents, a physical move, and disruption of social circumstances. The stressor might be a sense of vocational crisis, going to college, or adjustment to retirement. It could be the diagnosis of major physical or psychological illness within oneself or a loved one. As adolescents, young adults, midlife adults, or elder adults, we frequently face challenges within the process of making life changes. A relationship with a counselor, psychotherapist, or spiritual director is often indicated for such a period of life transition. The adjustment disorder diagnosis is utilized when symptoms seem beyond the normal range of emotional or behavioral challenges during major life transition.

Adjustment disorder in its acute manifestation may be utilized as a transitional diagnosis. It should not be used for more than six months. At that time, the symptoms will have dissipated or a different diagnosis should be named, as the life stressor or its residual effects have become chronic in nature. For example, rather than continuing the Axis I diagnosis of adjustment disorder with depression, if the depressive symptoms persist, the appropriate Axis I diagnosis would become one of the depressive disorders. Adjustment disorder as a chronic diagnosis may be utilized longer than six months if the life stressor or its effects continue and become chronic themselves. This is a welcome change from DSM-III-R to DSM-IV. Previously, the chronic nature of stressors was not recognized in the diagnostic category (American Psychiatric Association, 1987).

When generally well-functioning individuals find their way into our consulting rooms, we may utilize the adjustment disorder diagnosis while becoming familiar with the client and the presenting issues, to explore recent life changes and emotional tendencies. If after this time of becoming familiar, the acute emotional stress abates but issues of life challenge persist, appropriate diagnoses for Axis I may include V61.1 Partner Relational Problem; V62.81 Relational Problem Not Otherwise Specified; V62.82 Bereavement; V62.3 Academic Problem; V62.2 Occupational Problem; 313.82 Identity Problem; or V62.89 Religious or Spiritual Problem; V62.3 Acculturation Problem; or V62.89 Phase of Life Problem. In therapeutic interaction, a history of sexual or physical abuse might be discovered, in which case the treatment code would be changed to code 995.5 if the abused person is a child or 995.82 if the abused person is an adult.

As is readily apparent from reading a list of such wide variety of possible outcomes, the adjustment disorder diagnosis allows significant time for evaluation of major life stressors, which might indicate the need for further treatment.

In this chapter, I give some perspectives on life transitions that may be at work beneath the presenting symptoms. My focus is toward the general theme that adjustment disorder may be indicative of the broader themes of identity, phase of life, or occupational problems. I also address a perspective on spiritual issues.

PHYSICAL AND RELATIONAL CONCERNS

Whenever emotionally challenging symptoms are present, I always ask when the client has last had a thorough physical examination. Frequently, I have seen emotional changes related to hormonal shifts. Sometimes hormonal replacement therapy has made a significant difference in relationship to symptoms of either anxiety or depression. We owe it to our clients to have a good referral list of physicians, psychiatrists, and/or psychologists who are knowledgeable in the increasing variety of psychoactive medications. Such medication may be indicated to address presenting symptoms of anxiety or depression. Treatment for underlying symptoms sometimes cannot progress without first attending to these issues. Changes of thyroid functioning also seem more frequent than ordinarily diagnosed. This first step, it seems to me, is always indicated.

A good diagnostician may find other underlying health issues that may have been activated by the life stressor. The life stressor itself may be a symptom of other underlying health issues as well.

Simple measures such as attention to balanced diet, sleep, and modest exercise also fall in the realm of the initial care we need to provide. Is structure needed for the individual to provide this basic level of self-care? If so, how do we assist with such self-monitoring, so that normalcy of functioning can begin to be restored? These simple measures are frequently very important.

Are living circumstances adequate? Are there persons within the household or acquaintances, support groups, or a faith community with whom the client regularly relates? Is there a good network of community or is this a support that needs to be built?

We must attend to the most basic physical and relational nurturance of the client as we begin to probe more deeply into underlying struggles and challenges.

Is a belief system or sense of philosophy of life in place? Often the life stressor that leads to adjustment disorder will catapult such a belief system into question. If so, then are we adequately prepared to accompany the client into that arena or do we also need to invite exploration with a spiritual director, pastoral counselor, or pastor concurrent with our particular mode of counseling? Not infrequently the inadequacy of the client's belief system is brought into awareness through such crisis. Can we assist the individual to identify core beliefs about life and then journey through the necessary questioning process in the face of this particular life challenge? Can we assist the client to find a community of support for formulating such a philosophy of life or an adequate religious perspective? Are these matters best referred to others for exploration?

INVITATION TO TRANSLATION
OR TRANSFORMATION

In his groundbreaking book on adult development, *The Atman Project* (1980), Ken Wilber noted the major ways our human consciousness can shift and expand throughout our adult life. Previous discussions of Western developmental psychology focused almost exclusively on the process of development from infancy into young adulthood. It was assumed that once the capacities of adulthood were gained the human psyche was formed. However, drawing on models of adult development as described in Eastern spiritual traditions, Wilber made a very strong case for the continuing development of the human being throughout adulthood. Our consciousness changes throughout the life transitions we encounter in adulthood, allowing for a greater capacity for the intuitive, psychic dimensions and for inner experience facilitated by prayer, meditation, and dreamwork. A similar case could be made for the awakening of unconscious material through depth psychotherapy. Prior to the exploration of early childhood material through analysis or dreamwork, our conscious awareness is at a surface level of self-understanding. Through the plumbing of memory or the expansion of awareness through mystical understanding, our field of consciousness deepens or broadens. That "I" of self-consciousness expands.

Carl Jung spoke of the "ego" as simply the "I." It is that portion of our psyche of which we are aware. Clearly, that sense of "I" shifts and changes through the experiences of life (Jung, 1968). Sometimes we are very deeply engrossed in the examination of our motivations. At other times, we are reacting much more simplistically to life process and decision. I would suggest that we move through our lives with a kind of "island" of self-consciousness (the "I" of whom we are generally aware) in a vast sea of potential consciousness (our personal life history, collective human experience, and cosmic awareness). We have come to a generally comfortable arrangement with this self-consciousness, which may serve us well for several years or even decades. However, when major life change arrives upon us, this changed life circumstance often catapults us into that larger sea of uncharted (i.e., undiscovered, unknown, unconscious) selfhood.

Michael Washburn (1995) has identified this sea of potentiality as the "dynamic ground." He contrasts this dynamic ground of consciousness with the ego, or that portion of consciousness of which we are aware and from which we live our daily lives. At times of major change, we are usually cast into this undifferentiated dynamic ground. The result of engaging this process, if successful, is that we claim new parts of our deep selfhood, access different motivations and creative drives within ourselves, and begin to integrate those in our daily life. Ego has changed by relating to the dynamic ground in a new way. This process itself can be anxiety provoking, because our accustomed way of relating to reality, which we thought was stable (our ego), has had its foundations shaken.

Ken Wilber (1980) described the challenge of such times with the following categories—does this period of life require "translation" or "transformation?" His analogy to illustrate the difference is this: Life is like living in a multistoried apartment building. When we get the urge to make changes within life, translation is moving our furniture to another apartment on the same floor; transformation is moving to another floor within the building—engaging in a different view of life. Transformation requires deep self-examination, because it is working at deep structures of the psyche. Translation does not require deep self-examination. Translation would be related to counseling interventions aimed at problem solving within the existing psychological self-understanding of the client, while transformation is the process of reorientation of the psyche. To be overly simplistic, translation is the work of short-term counseling, clinical social work, and of pastoral care; transformation is the work of psychoanalysis. Pastoral counseling, spiritual direction, long-term counseling, psychotherapy, and the medication interventions of psychiatry may work in either or both domains. The first task in approaching a person in the midst of adjustment disorder is to begin to probe this issue.

Is this a time for translation or for transformation? Is the work to be done within the counseling office to be oriented to assisting a person to make life adjustments within her or his existing psychological self-awareness or is it a time for transformation of psychological awareness? These are matters of fairly great significance. During the throes of loss of a marital relationship, a client may be open to exploring a more primitive sense of loss, or such an individual may need to be held with care, keeping the focus simply on reestablishing a new life structure without doing deep psychological work. Both processes are equally legitimate ways of dealing with adjustment issues. To put it another way, are the presenting symptoms to be relieved by adjustments within current life circumstances or are they the sign of a deeper emergence of selfhood that is seeking to evolve?

Changing Life Structure

A few years ago, I was invited to offer an event on men's spirituality. I pulled from my bookshelf a book I had not read in many years, Daniel Levinson's (1978) *The Seasons of a Man's Life.* This work utilized a very small sample of men and took men only to their mid-forties. I was amazed at its wisdom in charting predictable life stages and concerns for men. Gail Sheehy collaborated on this book and expanded on this research in her best-selling book *Passages* (1976). I now frequently recommend Sheehy's *New Passages* (1996) for women and men in the midst of major life transitions. It offers very helpful information on medical and psychological milestones for both women and men, into their seventies and beyond.

Daniel Levinson (1978) utilized a category that I have found to be extraordinarily helpful in counseling people in the midst of life transitions. He used the term *life structure* to describe the framework within which every person lives. We each have a life structure that has many components. It is literally our home or apartment. It is our neighborhood. It is our employment. Our life structure includes those relationships most important to us—our singleness, marriage, or life partner arrangements, our children and their life stages of development, our relationship to our parents, whether living or deceased. Our life structure includes our economic circumstances and the way our work relates to our income and our economic desires. It is our avocations as well as vocations. I would expand the notion of life structure also to include issues of faith structure, our sense of relationship with nature, religious structures, and the divine. Levinson's research suggests that usually two elements, such as family and work, are most prominent within an individual's concerns at a given time.

To get a sense of the concept of life structure and how it changes over time, simply think back on your life ten to fifteen years ago. It is helpful to name a particular year and note your age. Where did you live, with whom, what was your work like, what were your economic circumstances, what were your family circumstances, what were your career aspirations, did you have children, what was your relationship like with your parents, what was your relationship to spiritual beliefs and practices? Now, think of the same issues in present life circumstances. Obviously, much has changed. Occasionally, a person's external life structure has changed little, yet, even then, others who are significant in one's life will have changed, such as children or parents. Life structure is dynamic.

Levinson utilized this basic premise to approach the normal changes we experience within life. I suggest this is an extremely helpful model to utilize in analyzing the adjustment issues that clients present. The following possibilities exist within our life structure at a given time:

1. advancement within a stable life structure,
2. decline or failure within the life structure,
3. breaking out—trying for a new life structure,
4. advancement which itself produces a change within life structure, and
5. unstable life structure (Levinson, 1978).

Each of these dimensions has its own potentialities and challenges. The issues present in number two, decline or failure within a stable life structure, are those that are most likely to bring an individual into our counseling rooms. Here, a divorce has erupted, a spouse or child or parent has died, a job has been lost, or perhaps a health crisis has emerged. The life structure that was thought to be stable has proven unstable. Life circumstances have brought about unexpected changes. Within these circumstances, the question of whether translation or transformation is the therapeutic task is most important to ascertain. Is this a time for support to reorganize one's life, within the existing psychological framework of the client, or is this change of life structure to be taken as a summons to major self-examination?

We can get some help on this very important issue from notions of human suffering as described in classical Buddhism. An ancient text, the Abhidhamma, describes three kinds of human suffering, (1) ordinary suffering, (2) the suffering created by an unstable sense of self, and (3) the suffering created by a stable sense of self (Engler, 1984). Ordinary suffering is the conflict between desire or impulse and control or inhibitions. To put ordinary suffering in classical Freudian language, it is the conflict between id and superego. We live with this conflict all the time, many times per day. It is the conflict between desire, self-examination, and decision for action. I see a kind of candy I have never tried before. I want it. Then I think about my caloric intake for that day. Hmm, maybe this is not the best day to try it. That is ordinary human suffering.

Sometimes our work in counseling and spiritual direction is simply to assist people to understand these basic conflicts and to bring them to light, so that rather than being vaguely unhappy, we can actually take charge of our more or less unconscious "ordinary suffering" and make more conscious decisions. This issue is very relevant as we help to unpack such complex issues as the quality of a marital relationship, a career path, or the ways we interact in support of our children or other family members. To what degree does our devotion to our children's well-being, for instance, help us decide to commit to a work situation that is not so satisfactory, in other words to choose to "suffer" some on behalf of a greater good? Conversely, to what degree is our "suffering" not a noble cause but an indication of lack of self-worth, or an indication that we need to face directly some very difficult decisions? As we unpack this issue, we can often gain insight into the therapeutic task.

The other two issues are at the heart of the question of whether counseling for adjustment disorder is a time for translation or transformation. Has life structure been so disrupted that the client is thrust into an unstable sense of self? In those circumstances, our task might be to assist in reestablishing stability of work within the same career or in finding a new support system within the same community. To what degree is such a disruption the summons to actually reorient one's life in a major way?

The crisis may fall into that third category—suffering created by a stable sense of self. The stability itself has become stifling to the interior urge for creativity, yet fear holds us back from leaping into a new life structure. Is this perhaps the time to take that leap and go back to graduate school for a career change? Is it time to "unstable" the marriage relationship? Is this a time of life in which a major change must be undertaken with respect to one's religious orientation? If so, what structures of support can assist in this kind of deep transformative work? What are the ideas behind the symptoms of depression or anxiety? What future being imagined at a deep, almost unconscious level brings on these symptoms? Is it fear of further loss and dislocation? That might be an indicator to work strongly on issues of translation, keeping as much of the current life structure in place as possible. Is the imagined future unconsciously leading toward fear of loss of selfhood because of a stifling sense of present limitations? If so, perhaps the work of transformation will lead to envisioning of a new life structure.

Life As Multiple Stories

Clearly, the deep work of transformation does not usually take place within the six-month time frame of the adjustment disorder, in its acute manifestation. However, we have perhaps identified the work of a deep identity problem or phase of life problem (for example) as a more appropriate diagnosis and are continuing the work of transformation within the client. If the life stressor is chronic, such as living with a spouse whose mental health is unstable, adjustment disorder may serve as the appropriate diagnosis for some time.

One of the most effective ways of addressing the major life changes that we all will endure throughout our lives is to think of our life as a series of interlocking stories. We are living a story with relationship to our career or vocational calling. It may have many chapters. Sometimes, it appears, either by our choice or the choice of others, that our career story is cut short. Our job is eliminated, or such personality conflicts exist within our organization that we believe we must leave. Perhaps we reach a dead end in our hopes for advancement and must either adjust our career aspirations downward or make a major change.

One of life's most basic challenges for us as adults is dealing with unexpected change. A sense of stability has been achieved, often through great effort on our part. Then, circumstances shift. The story changes. A new chapter begins, and we did not get to finish the previous chapter in the way we had anticipated. Our story of work has many shifts and changes.

We live many other stories as well. There is our life-partner relationship. Will there be a life partner? Will there be divorce or remarriage? How will we adjust to each other through the many seasons and changes of life? If we have a partner, and that person makes radical change within her or his own life values, actions, or vocation, how must we change to accommodate those changes in our partner? How does the story of our life partner mirror and conflict with the story of our personal vocational aspirations?

Then there is the story of our relationship to parents, children, and other family members. My wife and I entered marriage with an expectation of someday having children but also knowing of a potential problem of infertility. We were in fairly good partnership in the early years of our marriage, while the notion of children was somewhat far off. We even released our names from an adoption agency when our names got too close to the top of the list. Our career aspirations took precedent and we were in harmony. A period of major challenge came as both career aspirations and our differing views on parenthood became focused. It was a very troubled time for us. Only as each one of us gave way to the other on some issues we had thought were essential were we able to continue in our story together. Amazing for us, the story of children became very prominent again, as Ruth dealt with the implications of infertility both emotionally and physically. We adopted two infant boys when we were turning forty-one years of age.

Then, the disruption between the stories of parenting and vocation became very challenging for each of us. For me, it was fairly excruciating trying to build my career in my midforties and attend properly to parenting. The two stories were in great tension.

Other kinds of stories can be dramatically disruptive to our hopes. Disease can surprise us, or we may not be able to adjust to a disappointment in a relationship. We make a move we think is in our best interest only to find ourselves filled with anxiety or depression. Perhaps a person has worked toward a career change for many years and then, once in the new career, is disappointed. Adjustments must be made to reorient or perhaps specialize within this new career option. Others tell us that our behaviors have changed and we are acting in ways that are becoming destructive to ourselves or others. Our reactions to political decisions completely outside our personal level of influence can cause within us deep resentment, anger, or even depression.

One area that is particularly fruitful to explore when symptoms of adjustment disorder erupt is whether a crisis in one area of life has dramatically impinged on the hopes for another area of life. Has a fundamental conflict come into focus between career aspirations of one partner and the other partner's hopes for the environment to raise children, for example? Can adjustment challenge be partially illuminated by seeing the variety of conflicts emerging between life commitments? Are career aspirations in conflict with commitments to care for aging parents? Are career aspirations in conflict with our partner's aspirations? Are religious values of one partner in conflict with the other partner's lifestyle? Have our personal spiritual aspirations come into conflict with our habituated lifestyle?

CALL TO ADVENTURE

Joseph Campbell (1968) gave us a language for these kinds of major life stories. In *The Hero with a Thousand Faces,* Campbell examined mythologies, fairy tales, and sacred stories from around the world. He discovered that these stories, which humanity has used to help give meaning to life, have a universal pattern. Such stories often begin with a breakthrough into "normal" life, which Campbell named the Call to Adventure. An example is the story of Parsifal. Parsifal is sixteen years old when we meet him in the story. His mother has carefully guarded him from all knowledge of the world of knights, because when he was very young, both Parsifal's father and brother had gone off on knightly conquests and never returned. However, when he is sixteen, five knights come riding into their village in shining armor. As soon as Parsifal sees them, he gives himself to that life. He rides off with them.

That is a classic Call to Adventure. Often, in the midst of life going on "as usual" something happens that changes our life story dramatically. That change can be of either a positive nature, such as it was for Parsifal, or a very negative nature as it would have been for his mother. His mother, in this case, might well have been a classic candidate for a diagnosis of adjustment disorder! We can only vaguely imagine the range of emotions she would have dealt with and the old grief for her husband and elder son that might have been stirred up. The few more years she had expected in Parsifal's company were lost to her. Her life story was radically interrupted by Parsifal's answer to a new life story in his Call to Adventure.

A question that is always helpful to ask in times of life transition is: What is my present Call to Adventure? Can I name the character of the story in which I now find myself? Has it surprised me to the degree that it is very difficult to sort this out? What are the expectations of this story? How do I square this story with my previous expectations of an earlier version of the story I thought I was writing in my life? Is there conflict between the essential Call to Adventure in the story of my career, my life-partner relationship, the needs of children in their life stages, or of care for parents in their declining years? Have I been summoned into parenting my grandchildren?

Can even a major life crisis such as a severe health challenge be seen as a Call to Adventure? Can it be turned from only a victimized stance to a sense of empowerment to take charge of aspects of my life I may have been neglecting? Can the symptoms of adjustment disorder be seen as a summons to creatively rethink some of my basic life patterns, commitments, and ways of acting and being?

Threshold Crossing

In the pattern of the hero/heroine's journey, there comes a moment in which one has clearly left one's old life behind. Campbell calls this the *threshold crossing.* William Bridges (1980) calls this passage *the neutral zone* in his book *Transitions: Making Sense of Life's Changes.* At the threshold or neutral zone, one is frequently bewildered. This experience may well be used to illuminate some of the symptoms of adjustment disorder. One begins to be aware that an old way of life has ended but is not yet clear about where life is now leading. Even if one seems to be on a life journey that is in a very positive direction, such as returning to school in midlife for career advancement, enough changes have been made that one can be somewhat overwhelmed at the rapidity of transition. Is there a sense of faith in life to continue on? Is there a sense of religious faith? Is there a sense of self-esteem to carry one through the challenges? Or have the challenges come with such rapidity that one is left reeling in anxiety?

This experience is sometimes called *liminality*. The limen is the board on the floor of the threshold of a door. To be in liminality is to literally be in the doorway, neither in the room just left or the room into which one is headed. One is "in between."

The in-between state can evoke deep memories of previous emotionally challenging transitions. The emotion may precede the understanding. We may find ourselves needing to plumb repressed memories, to recover lost aspects of ourselves, which are needed for this new phase of our life. Hence, the adjustment disorder may well be the challenge to "transformation" rather than "transition."

Bridges suggested that the neutral zone experience requires two or three years to navigate well. Recent advances in brain research have discovered physiological correlates to this time frame. About three years are needed for short-term memory experiences to be fully integrated into our long-term memory. Hence, in doing deep transformative work of any kind, self-identity would be in flux for approximately three years, while the brain structures are being reoriented. The relationship between brain function and our internal life stories is discussed extensively in *Remembering the Future; Imagining the Past: Story, Ritual, and the Human Brain* (Hogue, 2003).

Midlife change may come more than once. Conflicts among our stories occur in varieties of ways. Simply to help name the major nature of the transition sometimes relieves anxiety.

Adjustment Disorder to Adventure Call

I have been privileged in my counseling and spiritual direction work to see many midlife adults entering a time of major life transition and passing through to renewed life purpose. In the interests of confidentiality, I will not present individual case studies. Examples have already been cited in the illustrations I have used to name some of the areas of conflict. Here, I will add some of the other some themes and symptoms that have marked such transitions.

- Anxiety in the midst of deep conflict within work environment
- Challenges to life work based on gender discrimination

- Crisis of faith due to a series of deaths and other losses
- Advancement into position not congruent with personality
- Struggles of commitment to partner in shared life work
- Health crisis challenging deep vocational self-identity
- Challenge of partner's sense of career with time to give to children's development
- Challenge of vocational aspiration with limitations in advancement
- Loss of job due to merging of organizations
- Developing new career based on inner motivations
- Work challenges based on conflicts of values with others in the organization
- Naming current vocational mission after retirement

All of these have presented deep ethical, existential, and relational challenges. Often basic structures of faith and personal self-understanding needed to be maneuvered. Frequently, issues of early childhood physical or sexual abuse were uncovered in the midst of adult transitions. Relationship issues were renegotiated. However, sustaining the process has been the underlying question, What is the current Call to Adventure? When we have discovered ourselves in such times of transition, a year or more may be needed to actually name the new life, the new Call to Adventure, which is now summoning us. Frequently, then, challenges to other commitments to family, self, and place, will need to be thought through and negotiated in light of the new Call.

As a minister and spiritual director, I often ask that question in a theological way. What is God asking of you now in your life? What are the gifts you are being asked by God to bring forth now? How is God sustaining you for this challenging life transition? As secular counselors, we can still ask those questions in deep and penetrating ways. What is the deepest source of life meaning for you? What is the creative gift that you need to give to life now? With what deep attitudes of compassion do you wish to engage your partner, your children, your parents, and your world?

Underlying the demands of the Call to Adventure is a sense of life as an ongoing process of creative self-renewal. If people do not have such a sense of life as a creative adventure, they are extremely challenged when life sends hardships upon them. With that faith in life, our transitions can still be extremely challenging. We often need the counselor's ear to help us speak these new longings into reality.

Tests and Helpers

The hero/heroine's journey always has tests and helpers in this new adventure. A particularly helpful frame of reference to keep in mind is that point. Who (actual persons) or what (attitudes, persistent personality challenges, external stumbling blocks) are my current tests? Naming these is helpful. Otherwise, it is extraordinarily easy to slip into thoughts of victimization. To concretely, specifically name them allows us to see which ones we can actually do anything about and which ones we need to accept as permanent, if unpleasant, realities.

Who (persons) or what (attitudes, practices of self-nurture, prayer, community support, new ideas) are our helpers? Once we realize that we have entered a new phase of our life story in this particular challenge, we need to realize that we can actually reach out to a new community of support. Sometimes for this new venture a new physical or spiritual discipline is needed that can be a helper. Sometimes the task is to look around and name some people whose friendship we might cultivate. One of the greatest gifts of Joseph Campbell's work on the hero/heroine's journey is that in the mythologies, fairy tales, and religious stories, there are always helpers! Often, the help comes from surprising sources. This idea of intentionally seeking helpers is extremely significant. It can be very helpful in the midst of deep life transitions to be reassured that helpers can be found and that they may well come from very unexpected sources. We may need to consciously name them in order to claim their help.

Often once these steps have been taken, we have begun to find the resources needed to relieve our anxiety, depression, or destructive behaviors enough to resume the adventures of life in a positive way. We may have remembered previous experiences of transition within our life in which we were successful and we draw strength from them. We may have had to revisit previous transitions that we did not make successfully and claim the gifts and unresolved challenges from those experiences.

FINDING TREASURE AND SHARING THE ELIXIR

The hero/heroine's journey involves finding the particular treasure of this unique stage of life journey. It may be something quite ephemeral, such as developing a deeper level of compassion. It may be very material, such as coming to a point of financial stability. It may be the achievement of a certain creative act in which we were so deeply engaged that we did not even realize it was the goal until we saw it in reality.

It can be very helpful to attempt to tentatively identify the treasure that we are seeking—again in the multiple domains of our life stories. What is the nature of our career service now? How would we know if we were successful? What are our hopes for our life with our partner? What dreams do we have for our children at this stage of their lives?

Finally, Campbell challenges us to see the broader social context of our own life journey. Is there an elixir to share with others that we have gained from our own struggles? *Elixir* is an old-fashioned word; it means a life-enhancing tonic. Can your life story and struggles be used for the benefit of others? That is our ultimate sense of meaning.

Elixir giving can be very simple gestures of support and kindness to others. It can be the gift of a lifetime of achievement in our chosen field. The issue is that we see our own life story within the great life story of a society seeking greater health.

ADJUSTMENT DISORDER IN THE FACE OF WORLD DISORDER

I think over the next few decades we are likely to see increasingly difficult issues of adjustment disorder in response to global challenges. No doubt, many persons sought some kind of treatment in the wake of the tragedies of September 11, 2001. We seem to have entered an era of increasing global fear and uncertainty, just when we had thought the world was going to find some stability with the end of the tensions of the Cold War.

I would not be surprised me to begin to see a kind of floating anxiety or dysthymic reaction to global crisis. A crisis within our communities close to home or the death of a community member on distant shores in the armed services might well evoke a crisis of adjustment disorder in any of its manifestations. Certainly, economic uncertainties abound, with many people facing career-related challenges.

Questions of life meaning may take on deep significance. When our social order itself is "unstable," when our institutions, including our religious institutions, are "unstable," when there is very little job security, then we are each thrust into a challenging Call to Adventure. Such a Call requires a unique combination of ego strength and flexibility. We must be strong within our own sense of self and yet adapt to constantly changing circumstances.

Guides who have journeyed their own depths are much needed to enable others to negotiate the challenging rapids of change.

REFERENCES

American Psychiatric Association (1987). *Quick reference to the diagnostic criteria from DSM-III-R*. Washington, DC: American Psychiatric Association.

American Psychiatric Association (1994). *Quick reference to the diagnostic criteria from DSM-IV*. Washington, DC: American Psychiatric Association.

Bridges, W. (1980). *Transitions: Making sense of life's changes,* Second edition. New York: Perseus Publishing.

Campbell, J. (1968). *The hero with a thousand faces,* Second edition. Princeton, NJ: Princeton University Press.

Engler, J. (1984). Therapeutic aims in psychotherapy and meditation: Developmental stages in the representation of self. *Journal of Transpersonal Psychology,* 16(1):25-61.

Hogue, D.A. (2003). *Remembering the future; imagining the past: Story, ritual, and the human brain.* Cleveland, OH: Pilgrim Press.

Jung, C. (1968). *Aion: Researches into the phenomenology of the self,* Volume 9, Part II, *The collected works of C. G. Jung,* Second edition, trans. R. F. C. Hull. Bollingen Series 20. Princeton, NJ: Princeton University Press.

Levinson, D.J. (1978). *The seasons of a man's life.* New York: Ballantine Books.

Sheehy, G. (1976). *Passages: Predictable crises of adult life.* New York: E.P. Dutton.

Sheehy, G. (1996). *New passages: Mapping your life across time.* New York: Ballantine Books.

Washburn, M. (1995). *The ego and the dynamic ground: A transpersonal theory of human development,* Second edition. Albany: State University of New York Press.

Wilber, K. (1980). *The atman project: A transpersonal view of human development.* Wheaton, IL: The Theosophical Publishing House.

Chapter 3

Breathing into Fear: Psychospiritual Approaches for Treating Anxiety

Selene Vega

This chapter discusses approaches to the treatment of anxiety from a psychospiritual perspective. It includes a review of the traditional cognitive-behavioral and pharmacological techniques for treating anxiety, with attention to the latest trends in treatment, including acceptance-based and mindfulness approaches. The author places anxiety disorders in the larger context of global events and trends that have impacted the general feeling of safety in the Western world and contributed to the rise of anxiety in general. A client example illustrates the use of Stephen Gilligan's self-relations psychotherapy, spiritually oriented cognitive therapy, transpersonal bibliotherapy, hypnosis, and breath awareness.

INTRODUCTION

We live in an age of anxiety. Certainly this is not the first time in history when a large proportion of the population lives under the shadow of fear. In the United States, the sense of safety and detachment from terrorist acts and wars in other parts of the world was shattered on September 11, 2001, when four commercial airplanes were hijacked and turned into weapons that killed thousands. The United States is currently involved in a war in Iraq where the death toll on both sides rises daily, and in too many places on the earth people live with constant awareness of the violence that may touch them at any time.

Given the current state of the world and the media's ability to bring it to our attention, many people are feeling an increased level of anxiety. Primary physicians have seen a rise in cases of anxiety over the past eighteen years (Harman et al., 2002), reminding us that anxiety is not just a response to the most recent events but to the larger context of our world psyche that is exhibiting great distress. Many people around the world fear for their lives each day, and their fears are not ungrounded. In addition to the dangers in our immediate environment, anywhere we live or travel we are aware that we could be attacked by terrorists at any time. Our fears are fueled by the emotionally evocative language and visual imagery used by the daily media, but the dangers are indeed real.

Humans have always needed to be wary of their environment in order to survive amid the many threats to individual existence. Our nervous systems are wired to react to survival threats to support our readiness to deal with them effectively. Anxiety is part of a biological warning system activated by real or imagined dangers. In a potentially dangerous situation, the automatic vigilance that helps us notice and respond quickly to a threat is an adaptive response. In contemporary times, the dangers may be more psychological. Fear of failing at a task, for example, can generate moderate anxiety that can improve performance, motivate action, and stimulate creativity. However, when anxiety becomes a chronic state or the level increases from moderate to severe, it can be incapacitating. When thoughts of all the catastrophes that might occur in the future fill the mind, the performance of even simple tasks is hampered, action becomes impossible, and creativity is frozen.

Our individual attention to survival needs is somewhat attenuated by working collectively. As part of a tribe, a village, a community, and even a gang, individuals do not need to take sole responsibility for their safety. "Safety in numbers" implies that each individual needs to pay attention to only part of the situation and trust that others will take care of the rest. At the same time, membership in a group carries awareness of the need for survival of the group as a whole. Each individual must be vigilant about the safety of others in the group as well as his or her own safety.

With global communication and the connectedness it creates, awareness of the world beyond our individual shelter has expanded; fear for survival has broadened to include not just all of humankind, but nonhuman inhabitants of this planet as well. The scope of effects from human actions is now global and threatens the sustainability of life as we know it on Earth. Our fears are not just for individual survival or the survival of our small immediate tribe. We have reason to fear for the survival of all the inhabitants of our planet. This fear is an undercurrent in the world around us. As Macy and Brown (1998) put it,

> [The] future seems ever more fragile. With wars igniting around the globe, the forests falling, the hungry and homeless on our streets, the poisons in our food, water, air, and breast milk, and the extinction of whole species and cultures, it grows harder to take hope in our common journey. We are tempted to shut down, narrowing our sights to our own and our family's short-term survival. (p. 6)

In the "shutting down" process Macy and Brown refer to, what often remains is the general worry and anxiety that characterize generalized anxiety disorder (GAD). When threats feel so large and beyond our control, worry can take a smaller and more personalized form, as if that would give us more control. This allows us to avoid confronting fears as large and external as fear for the planet's future, and as individual and internal as fear of one's sense of worthlessness.

When people seek therapy due to anxiety and worry, they may or may not be aware of the larger cultural forces and external factors contributing to their discomfort. In addition, therapists may not be trained or willing to recognize those forces and factors and include them in their understanding and treatment. Traditional training in psychotherapy generally teaches therapists to interpret concerns about the environment as metaphorical and encourages them to look for intrapsychic attributions for the feelings (Hillman and Ventura, 1993).

Both therapists and clients may attribute fear and anxiety to situations that seem personally specific, focusing on problems in the immediate life situation that feel overwhelming. Acknowledging the many possible sources for anxiety, both internal and external, past and present, can widen the perspective. Therapists can help clients sort out fears that may be unfounded ("I'm afraid that my child will be kidnaped/that I'll be ridiculed and rejected/killed in a plane crash," etc.) and those that may be quite realistic ("I'm afraid my job may be downsized out of existence in the worsening economy/that I won't be able to support my family/that something terrible may happen to me or my loved ones/that our environment will be destroyed by the greed of corporations," etc.), but worrying about them will not help the client change or deal with the situation.

When we burrow under these fears, the personal and planetary, the threat of terrorism, the reality of wars and death, we come face to face with what existentialists believe is the root of anxiety, deep within the individual, "in a fear of nonexistence, nonbeing, or nothingness" (Barlow, 2002, p. 8). Rollo May (1979) reminds us that

> [Anxiety is] the apprehension cued off by a threat to some value that the individual holds essential to his existence as a personality. The threat may be to physical life (a threat of death), or to psychological existence (the loss of freedom, meaninglessness). Or the threat may be to some other value which one identifies with one's existence (patriotism, the love of another person, "success," etc.). (p. 180)

Stanislav Grof (1985) goes even further, pointing out sources for symptoms that go beyond the personal history or present circumstances of the client:

> Experiential therapies bring overwhelming evidence that childhood traumas do not represent the primary pathogenic causes, but create conditions for the manifestation of energies and contents from deeper levels of the psyche. The typical symptoms of emotional disorders have a complex multilevel and multidimensional dynamic structure. The biographical layers represent only one component of this complex network; important roots

of the problems involved can almost always be found on the perinatal and transpersonal levels. (p. 153)

Grof (2000) asserts that we need to clear out these old programs by allowing them to emerge into consciousness, a process that can plunge the client into "a sense of all-pervading anxiety and impending catastrophe of enormous proportions" (p. 52). This may happen in the course of therapy, or it may be triggered by a personal or spiritual process the client is engaged in.

With consciousness of these deeper issues underlying anxiety, we are confronted with our task as therapists: to assist our clients in their struggle with learning how to live and find joy and pleasure in life, while maintaining consciousness of pain and suffering in the world as well as in our own individual existence. From there, our clients have a foundation for making conscious choices concerning actions they may take to mitigate real dangers.

TRADITIONAL DIAGNOSIS AND PSYCHOTHERAPEUTIC TREATMENT

The anxiety disorder section of the DSM-IV-TR includes several diagnostic categories: panic attacks, agoraphobia, specific phobias, social phobia, and generalized anxiety disorder (American Psychiatric Association, 2000). (Post-traumatic stress disorder and obsessive-compulsive disorder are also considered to be manifestations of anxiety, but given their specific characteristics, they are addressed in separate chapters in this book.) When we include all of these, the prevalence of anxiety disorders is quite high. A 1994 National Comorbidity Survey (NCS) (Kessler et al., 1994) found a total of 17.2 percent for anxiety disorders over the prior twelve months; 24.9 percent reported a lifetime occurrence of an anxiety disorder other than PTSD or OCD (Barlow, 2002). These numbers are higher than for any other class of disorders in the National Comorbidity Survey, making anxiety disorders the most prominent mental health problem in the United States. In this chapter, I am focusing primarily on generalized anxiety disorder and social phobia, although, with some adjustments, treatments are similar for other anxiety disorders as well.

The current Western model for treatment of anxiety disorders involves medication and/or psychotherapy. Neither treatment is considered a cure, but rather an alleviation of the symptoms of anxiety that interfere with healthy functioning. The psychotherapeutic approaches suggested by the American Psychiatric Association are behavioral therapy, cognitive-behavioral therapy, and, in some cases, psychodynamic psychotherapy (APA, 1997). The specific elements included in the traditional psychotherapeutic approach to anxiety disorders follow (Roemer, Orsillo, and Barlow, 2002):

- *Psychoeducation:* Clients learn about the nature of anxiety and fear and the habitual physiological, cognitive, and behavioral responses that maintain the cycle.
- *Monitoring:* Clients learn to recognize cues for their anxiety response in order to implement new coping strategies and stress management techniques.
- *Relaxation:* Clients learn techniques for relaxation, possibly including visualization, diaphragmatic breathing, and progressive muscle relaxation.
- *Cognitive restructuring:* Clients learn to understand their patterns of thinking and counter distorted cognitions and inaccurate assessments of danger by questioning and challenging their interpretations and predictions.
- *Exposure/coping skills rehearsal:* This element is most useful for social phobia, specific phobias, panic disorder, and agoraphobia, where specific triggers for anxiety can be identified. Imaginal or in vivo exposure provides opportunities to practice cognitive restructuring and relaxation to reduce anxiety.

PHARMACEUTICAL TREATMENT AND THE PLACEBO EFFECT

Many cases of anxiety disorder appear in the general medical practitioner's office, leaving the primary doctor to administer treatment (Noyes and Hoehn-Saric, 1998), usually in the form of medication. Many anxiety sufferers hope that a pill will relieve their discomfort. This is a possibility for short-term treatment, though the rise in the use of medication for anxiety is alarming (Skaer et al., 2000). Historically, benzodiazepines have been prescribed to treat anxiety because they quickly get the symptoms under control. They are the most frequently prescribed medication for anxiety disorders (Stahl, 2002). They also have great potential for biological and psychological dependence, relapse when medications are withdrawn (Rivas-Vazquez, 2002; Noyes et al., 1988), and a number of other adverse reactions (Patten and Love, 1994). Buspirone, with its lighter load of side effects and low dependence potential, is another GAD treatment option for those who have not taken benzodiazepines and who can tolerate the longer onset of action. Antidepressants, especially tricyclics, can provide symptom relief as well. More recently some of the SSRIs (selective serotonin reuptake inhibitors) have shown some efficacy, particularly with social phobia, which also responds to monoamine oxidase (MAO) inhibitors (Blanco, Schneier, and Liebowitz, 2002).

The studies of pharmacological interventions for generalized anxiety disorder have not been able to provide valid conclusions about the efficacy of medications, due to the high rate of response to placebo in these studies (Roemer, Orsillo, and Barlow, 2002). This difficulty highlights the possibility that we are looking at a phenomenon beyond the physical effect of the medications. If the positive effects of anxiety medications can be attributed to the change they effect in brain chemistry, what internal process is spurred by the ingestion of a placebo to create the same brain chemistry changes? Research suggests that self-regulatory strategies, specifically meditation, relaxation, and biofeedback, contribute to reduction of both physiological and psychological components of anxiety (Kabat-Zinn et al., 1992). Combining these self-regulatory strategies that are an accepted part of anxiety treatment with therapy that consciously brings the client's beliefs (the impetus behind the placebo response) into the treatment process may provide a powerful alternative to the use of medications in alleviating symptoms.

PSYCHOSPIRITUAL PERSPECTIVES

Discussions of psychopharmaceutical approaches focus on eliminating or reducing symptoms as the goal for treatment. A psychospiritual focus shifts our attention to the possibility of a healing that goes beyond merely reducing symptoms. From that perspective a reduction of physiological indicators of anxiety may sidestep a needed healing process that the symptoms are calling to our attention.

Elio Frattaroli (2001) suggests we widen our field of understanding, noting that

> Mental illness cannot be just a chemical imbalance in the brain. Rather, it is a disharmony of body, brain, mind, and spirit within the whole person: an inner conflict of the soul. Such a disharmony may include a chemical imbalance in the brain as one of its elements, but the chemical imbalance itself is not the mental illness, nor does it cause the mental illness. (p. 9)

Rather than searching for temporary symptom reduction, we might look for what can shift the disharmony that Frattaroli is referring to.

Although numerous studies have shown psychological interventions to be helpful in treating GAD (Hoehn-Saric and McLeod, 1991), evidence does not support any specific technique as yielding any better results than what we can term the "common factors" of psychotherapy. Hoehn-Saric and McLeod list a number of studies that show improvement in symptoms with even minimal provider contact, including the administration of placebo, connective tissue massage, physical exercise, a pilgrimage to Lourdes, counseling by general practitioners, various relaxation and meditation techniques, temperature and muscle activity feedback, nondirective psychotherapy, cognitive-behavioral therapy techniques, and specifically targeted anxiety management training. Borkovec and Costello's study (1993) shows some advantage of applied relaxation and cognitive-behavioral therapies over nondirective psychotherapy in long-term gains, but all three were generally equivalent for immediate symptom reduction. In a later study Borkovec and colleagues (2002) found that a subset of clients had interpersonal issues that interfered with positive outcomes. This points us back to relational therapy and reminds us that psychotherapy at its best is not just a list of techniques and that immediate symptom reduction might not be the only goal of therapy.

What means can be used, then, to determine appropriate treatment? As Hubble, Duncan, and Miller (2002) ask, "If therapies work, but it has nothing to do with their bells and whistles, what are the common therapeutic factors?" (p. 6). They refer to Jerome Frank and Julia Frank's (1991) work in teasing out four features that are common to all effective therapies:

> (a) "an emotionally charged, confiding relationship with a helping person," (b) "a healing setting," (c) "a rationale, conceptual scheme, or myth that provides a plausible explanation for the patient's symptoms and prescribes a ritual or procedure for resolving them," and (d) "a ritual or procedure that requires the active participation of both patient and therapist and that is believed by both to be the means of restoring the patient's health." (Frank and Frank, 1991, pp. 40-43, cited in Hubble, Duncan, and Miller, 2002, p. 1)

These four features provide a useful template for tracking and understanding our work as therapists. Traditional therapies as well as psychospiritual therapies readily map on to these features.

We can work with any congruent conceptual scheme or rationale for the procedures we incorporate into our work as long as we believe they are a means of restoring the client's health. For many clients struggling with symptoms of any kind, including anxiety, the idea of understanding their discomfort from a larger, more spiritually informed framework is compelling. Often, clients are drawn to a psychospirtually oriented therapist because they want the transpersonal perspective. They may arrive to their first therapy session asking which chakras are involved in their distress. Then we can discuss their anxiety in terms of deficiencies in their first chakra functions using the psychospiritual narrative they are comfortable with (Judith, 1996). We then proceed with therapy basing our work on the conceptual scheme of the chakra system, determining treatment accordingly.

Whether we discuss spiritual issues with the client or not, we can include a transpersonal dimension in our understanding of even traditional psychotherapeutic conceptual schemes for explaining the client's symptoms. We can work with clients to find procedures that are appropriate and healing in each case, whether they are drawn from traditional psychology or spiritual traditions. Our clients are unique, and paying attention to the spiritual paths and beliefs that are part of their history and current worldview will help us determine the approach to take and how overt our psychospiritual perspective should be.

PSYCHOSPIRITUAL TREATMENT

Many traditional techniques used in the treatment of anxiety have origins in Eastern spiritual traditions. Neither clients nor therapists need to subscribe to a spiritual path in order to benefit from these transpersonal approaches. For example, relaxation techniques are an accepted part of anxiety treatment, the rationale being that they "reduce the physiological correlates of worry and anxiety by lowering the patient's overall arousal level" (Huppert and Sanderson, 2002, p. 151), as well as reducing the chronic tension associated with GAD. Among the best-known relaxation techniques introduced to the field of stress management were those of Jacobson, who developed them from a different source (McGuigan, 1993). However, Jacobson was not the first to bring the idea of relaxation to the field of psychology. Annie Payson Call's ([1891] 1998) book *Power Through Repose* may very well have been the first. Her plea for relaxation is aimed at the general population, but she addresses the specific problem of worry as follows:

> Never resist a worry. It is increased many times by the effort to overcome it. The strain of the effort makes it constantly more difficult to drop the strain of the worry. When we quietly go to work to relax the muscles and so quiet the nerves, ignoring a worry, the way in which it disappears is surprising. Then is the time to meet it with a broad philosophizing on the uselessness of worry, etc., and "clinch" our freedom, so to speak.
>
> It is not at the first attempt to relax, or the second, or the ninth that the worry will disappear for many of us, and especially for worriers. It takes many hours to learn what relaxing is; but having once learned, its helpful power is too evident for us not to keep at it, if we really desire to gain our freedom. (Section IX, ¶37 and 38)

She gives quite detailed instructions on techniques for gaining "natural repose," training the body both for rest and for motion without unnecessary tension. In the 1920s, Sandor Ferenczi used relaxation techniques in his version of psychoanalytic therapy. The humanistic psychology movement inherits his influence through the neo-Freudians in the United States, particularly Clara Thompson and Harry Stack Sullivan (Ferenczi, [1933] 1980).

Many of the relaxation techniques currently in common use in the treatment of anxiety—diaphragmatic breathing, muscle relaxation, visualization, and meditation—have a basis in yoga and Buddhist mindfulness meditation practice. They are usually taught without the religious connotations or any discourse on the spiritual principles from which they evolved (Patel, 1993). These techniques may be introduced for purely psychological and physiological reasons, without placing them in a spiritual realm. This neutral context places these effective techniques in the hands of therapists who are not spiritually inclined and allows clients to feel comfortable adopting them regardless of their interest in following a spiritual path.

Understanding that relaxation may have benefits beyond its generally accepted role in physiological stress reduction (release of tension and reduction of arousal level) is growing (Huppert and Sanderson, 2002). Anxiety tends to narrow or disrupt attentional focus. Relaxation widens the scope of attention, allowing the client to perceive more possible choices in response to anxiety-provoking situations. Relaxation may also act as a distraction from entrenched worry patterns, breaking clients out of their habitual anxious thoughts. In addition, relaxation exercises may bring to consciousness unexamined anxious thoughts that can then be verbalized and addressed. For example, as I led a relaxation exercise at the beginning of a movement therapy group session in a residential addictions program, one young man became increasingly restless and then ran out of the group room. In the midst of most clients' favorite part of our group, he had experienced a level of anxiety that he had been avoiding, first through drug use, and then through the many distractions of the program. In the quiet of relaxation, he came face to face with unacknowledged and unexpressed feelings that he could begin to process within the safe container of a residential program.

The overlap of psychospiritual techniques and Western psychology has been achieved by the efforts of transpersonal therapists bridging the two worlds through research (for example, see Shapiro and Zifferblatt, 1976). Relaxation is an important part of anxiety treatment, creating an opening for acceptance of many of the techniques of spiritual traditions, if not their belief systems. Even in the most traditional psychiatric textbook approaches to GAD, flexibility is recommended in choosing the relaxation technique to be used, and yoga, tai chi, and meditation are considered acceptable forms of relaxation training (Huppert and Sanderson, 2002). Jon Kabat-Zinn's work has been an important part of this trend, building on prior research and contributing both respected studies (Kabat-Zinn et al., 1992) and popular books (1990, 1994) that have brought mindfulness meditation into the mainstream.

Mindfulness has a role in psychotherapy beyond its place on a list of possible relaxation techniques. Mindfulness is "a way of integrating acceptance into change-based psychotherapies, emphasizing the non-judging, non-evaluative nature of mindful attention" (Roemer and Orsillo, 2002, p. 61). As with relaxation, mindfulness can help clients detach from habitual responses and widen awareness of possible perspectives and actions. This is part of a movement toward acceptance-based techniques, as psychotherapists and researchers realize the limitations of the change-based emphasis of traditional cognitive-behavioral therapy.

> Hayes, Strosahl et al. (1999) suggest that in order to alter the detrimental behavioral patterns motivated by experiential avoidance, clients should be introduced to the problems inherent in attempts at emotional or cognitive control, and a stance of acceptance and willingness should be practiced instead. (Roemer and Orsillo, 2002, p. 60)

In anxiety treatment, acceptance work directly addresses the function of worry as a means of avoiding uncomfortable inner experience. Worry acts as a distraction, keeping the client out of contact with private experiences (bodily sensations, emotions, thoughts, memories). If, through mindfulness, relaxation, or other techniques, we help clients experience the present moment, we need to be prepared to help them with attending to what they find there and accepting their experiences. "Acceptance is the developed capacity to fully embrace whatever is in the present moment. It requires a spacious mind, an open heart, and strength to bear one's experience" (Sanderson and Linehan, 1999, p. 200). We might say that the same requirements apply to the therapist.

Assisting clients with their healing processes is a form of spiritual midwifery. I believe that the common factors that Hubble, Duncan, and Miller (2002) speak of are truly the basis of the work that I do with my clients. My presence as a therapist is primarily informed by my connection to a spiritual source. I am able to form "an emotionally charged, confiding relationship" and create "a healing setting" (Frank and Frank, 1991, pp. 40-43) through the self-reflective and therapeutic work I continue to do on myself, which has its roots in a spiritual context. The conceptual scheme (my understanding of why we are doing what we are doing) and techniques brought to the therapeutic work with each client vary with the client's needs, expectations, and desires and with the therapist's intuitive sense. For many of us working from a psychospiritual framework, the underlying conceptual scheme centers on the healing of the therapist's presence, and willingness to remain present, for the whole person of the client they are sitting with, including the parts the client has disowned. Because the therapist's presence is such a pivotal aspect of the healing relationship we have with our clients, the commitment to work on ourselves is an important part of what it means to do psychospiritual psychotherapy.

In some cases, consciously working with spiritual issues, content, or techniques is an important aspect of the process. In private practice and workshop situations, those who find their way to me are usually aware of my background and interest in spirituality, so I am certainly not attempting to convert anyone. In situations in which clients may not have specifically come to me because of my transpersonal perspective, I ask about both their religious background and their current spiritual path, for these will have an impact upon our therapeutic work.

For those who do not have a current spiritual path, I might introduce a spiritual context in several ways. A somewhat indirect approach is what Seymour Boorstein (1996) calls "transpersonal bibliotherapy" (p. 285). When I suggest a book to my client, I avoid some of the transference issues that might arise from an attempt to teach spirituality within the session. The client can then explore independently and bring back thoughts and questions for discussion without confusing me for the ideas they are exploring. I may ask about an interest in meditation, provide information about meditation resources in our community, and discuss the different types of meditation available. Either way, I am an ally in spiritual exploration, rather than a spiritual teacher.

For many years now I have been introducing clients and students to what I call cognitive-spiritual therapy, which we might think of as cognitive-behavioral therapy grounded in spiritual principles. I use that term to describe the restructuring of conscious thoughts and actions based on spiritual principles that both appeal to logic and feel right intuitively to the client. Here again, I take care not to become the teacher of the principles, but rather a guide assisting my client's process of making sense of the reading and learning outside our sessions. To elicit the client's intuitive sense, I ask (based on Gilligan, 1997), "Does this (whatever we are working on, for example, the criticism of the internal judge, or a phrase that the therapist is introducing as a possible alternative) bring you closer to your center, to your connection with yourself, or does it take you farther away?"

Sometimes clients attempt to adopt spiritual ideas that are not yet authentic expressions of their deeper emotional and somatic states. For example, spiritual principles often encourage forgiveness. This can backfire when clients attempt to force themselves to forgive when they are just beginning to access their repressed rage. This "premature transcendence" or spiritual bypassing (Cortright, 1997) is one of several ways that spiritual principles can be distorted and become obstacles to the greater awareness that we strive for in psychospiritual therapy. It can lead to the repression of feelings deemed unacceptable within the spiritual parameters clients have chosen, as well as providing additional fuel for anxiety when they are unable to eliminate those feelings.

Stephen Gilligan's self-relations (SR) psychotherapy provides a model for understanding and working with the client's symptoms within a transpersonal context but without the hazard of further disconnection from what are viewed by the client as "unspiritual" feelings. These are the feelings that clients are often trying to avoid—the experiential avoidance mentioned earlier by Roemer and Orsillo (2002). Many spiritual teachers and texts, when taken superficially, lead people to believe that they should not be feeling the "negative" feelings or thinking the "negative" thoughts that are part of our human condition. Rather than acceptance, clients bring condemnation to those feelings, attempting to get rid of them by denial or judging themselves harshly for their inability to transcend them.

In SR therapy, we work together on connecting with the neglected self, which includes those intense feelings and needs that were met early in life with rejection or shaming. These parts of the client's being were disowned and now find disruptive or disturbing ways to make themselves known. Left unsponsored (without a mature presence to acknowledge them and help them find a means of acceptable expression), these somatic and emotional aspects find expression through symptoms. As therapists and sponsors, our job is to recognize that these symptoms are bringing our attention to an important aspect of the client that is attempting to emerge into the world. We understand the problem that brings someone to therapy not as an enemy to be overcome or a pathology to cure, but as a message from a disowned or neglected part of the self seeking acknowledgment and sponsorship into a form that can be of value.

Without these parts, we are not whole, but clients are not equipped to sponsor and integrate them alone. "Self-relations thus works to reactivate and maintain the presence and competencies of the cognitive self, accept and integrate the neglected experiences of the somatic self, and identify and differentiate from negative sponsors" (Gilligan, 1997, p. xvii). The therapist is in a position to accept and hold parts that clients perceive as unacceptable until they are able to create a bridge from the cognitive self to the feeling self. This provides a container for integrating both within the larger field that a psychospiritual perspective offers. The therapist is also able to notice negative sponsors and aid clients in identifying and separating from those voices that alienate them from their deepest selves.

Working with anxiety disorders from a SR perspective means approaching each client's symptoms with curiosity, wondering about what we can learn from the disowned part emerging at this time. "Self-Relations emphasizes the positive aspects of problems and symptoms. It sees such disturbances of the 'normal order' as evidence that 'something is waking up' in the life of a person or community" (Gilligan, 2002, p. 284). What is waking up may be personal, but it may also speak for or to the community. I see this most clearly in group settings. During an exercise designed to connect participants with feelings that are inaccessible to the conscious cognitive self, one person might touch into a deep well of sadness and anger about an issue that affects everyone in that group. Through the expression of an individual's feelings, attention and awareness of that sadness is opened to all of us witnessing and participating in the individual's process. The issue involved might be as specific as disconnection from a father figure, involving a personal story for one participant experiencing sadness at that moment, but invoking personal stories of their own from the rest of the people in the group.

The global anxiety I spoke of at the beginning of this chapter may also find expression, either within a group setting or individually. An important part of our work together may be sorting out what is personal and what is transpersonal, and addressing each appropriately. The voice of an individual may speak for the collective in terms that are more archetypal, as when feelings concerning environmental destruction or the ongoing violence in the world are the focus. These feelings may be associated with specific current events, but often they speak to an age-old struggle of which our current situation is merely a contemporary manifestation. An example of this is the strong feelings evoked in response to current violence in the world. A group participant might express grief and anguish about the many deaths in a particular war-torn region of the world, which might elicit a sense of the long history of violence in human experience and the timelessness of grieving the deaths that are part of war.

Again, it may be one individual in the group who connects with this, but often the feelings resonate in all the group members, as this voice speaks of something beyond the personal. Once the awareness of these feelings surfaces, each person in the group has the opportunity to find his or her own path to acceptance and possible responsive actions. The issues are now in the realm of consciousness, where the cognitive self can make choices, rather than have the feelings acted out in ineffective and disturbing symptoms. In addition, a sense of connection to community is present in this process, as each individual's awareness opens to the shared nature of the issues at hand.

Working in groups or individually, one of the basic skills to teach clients is centering in the body. This involves focus on breathing, but not necessarily a specific breathing technique meant to induce relaxation. We bring the breath into consciousness, but not with the goal of eliminating the feelings of the moment. Rather, we are bringing awareness and the caring touch of sponsorship to feelings that have been disowned, using the breath as a medium and a container.

> Centering brings our attention back to our core, back to the somatic self, back to a felt sense of experience. We remember that we are in bodies, and that our experience of the world and our relationships in it is mediated by these bodies. (Vega, 2004, p. 322)

The process of centering begins to build the bridge between the cognitive self and the neglected self by bringing attention to the somatic self and the feelings that exist right there in the moment. This is not a matter of remembering the past but of noticing an experience in the present that has history as well as immediacy. By reconnecting with the experience of the present moment and bringing awareness and focus to it, we are touching feelings that have been isolated and bringing them into the larger relational field. As Gilligan (2002) puts it, "the person is not the symptomatic experience but can be helped to 'be with it' in a way that provides a container within which it can be felt and expressed" (p. 244). Within that container healing occurs.

Case Example: Lawrence

The following case story offers an example of a client with generalized anxiety disorder and social phobia. Following the four features described by Frank and Frank (1991), I began by creating an emotionally charged confiding relationship within a healing setting, then choosing and applying procedures that both the client and therapist believed would be helpful. Working with cognitive-spiritual interventions and psychoeducation, hypnosis, breath awareness, and relaxation, we built a foundation for delving into unacknowledged longings and pain, as well as his sense of identity and spiritual purpose. Our work together gave him more than symptom reduction—it provided an opportunity to integrate neglected parts of himself and make life choices that reflected his values more completely.

Lawrence, twenty-nine, came in because his discomfort around others and fear of their judgments were keeping him from obtaining employment. He was extremely isolated, having contact mostly with his girlfriend and avoiding situations involving social interactions because of his fear that he would "do something stupid" and feel embarrassed. He was in danger of losing his unemployment benefits due to his inability to get past the terror involved in interview situations and the possibility that he might be hired and then be responsible in a job situation that would involve continually being watched and evaluated by an employer and co-workers. He was incapacitated by his anxiety about what would become of him, as well as by his overwhelming worries about various situations in his life concerning neighbors, his relationship with his girlfriend, his struggle with concentration and memory, and his angry reaction to simple things that go wrong in life.

Our first step was to establish the "emotionally charged, confiding relationship" in "a healing setting," the first two of Frank and Frank's (1991) four features of effective therapy. From there I introduced Lawrence to my conceptual scheme (the third feature), sharing my perspective through our conversations about his struggles in life. We approached Lawrence's discomfort through a number of procedures that I believed would help (the fourth feature), though to fulfill the requirements of that fourth feature, Lawrence also needed to believe these procedures would help, and this was one of our difficulties. Lawrence came to therapy with the fear that nothing could help him, that he was just too much of a loser.

Our early work together focused primarily on cognitive intervention, helping Lawrence to separate from the alienating voices of judgment ("I should have achieved more in my life by this time; I am just mean-spirited; I'm not worth anything; I'm boring," etc.). These were the judgments he was sure others must hold about him and that he held about himself. At first Lawrence was unable to disidentify from these judgments. My attempts to point out proof of the fallacies seemed to stimulate the intensity of the judgments, rather than reduce them. At one point I told Lawrence that I would move to another chair and take on that voice of judgment for him, which I proceeded to do, feeding back to him the criticisms he had been leveling at himself. Almost immediately, he began, for the first time, to argue in his own favor. I returned to my therapist chair and we laughed together about what had just happened, then moved into an exploration of where those judgments came from, asking whose voices from the past had he been hearing. This was the beginning of an observing witness who could notice when those alienating voices were active and acknowledge a center separate from them.

Given the critical nature of his internal voices, I was extremely careful to maintain a supportive and accepting attitude toward whatever Lawrence decided to do with his life, rather than become one more person with an agenda for his future. I focused on sponsoring the part of him that through his symptoms was insisting on support and acknowledgment for his deeper essential self. His anxiety and social discomfort seemed to provide him with a way to resist the push of family and culture to achieve and prove himself by successes in the external world. Until he could begin to love and acknowledge his neglected self's needs, I became the sponsor for that young, feeling self.

Using hypnosis, I guided Lawrence into breath awareness and states of relaxation that allowed his agitation to decrease. Following his own pacing and process, we explored imagery from his dreams, as well as images and metaphors from films and television that he often brought up in sessions, to help him find a larger perspective in which to hold the events of his childhood and his current life. I held a space of compassion and caring for Lawrence as he learned to touch the neglected child self deserving of love and sponsorship. As he became more willing to approach group situations, I suggested yoga classes, which he tried and found helpful in several ways. His anxious thoughts dissipated during the classes and he felt calmer throughout the day. His feeling of connection with his body increased, along with a sense of vitality. Finally, he found he was able to practice being with a group of people in a situation that relieved some of his usual anxiety by providing a specific focus for his thoughts that kept his mind occupied. At the same time his awareness that the others were also engaged in that focus, and therefore less likely to be watching and judging him, helped him to feel less exposed. When he brought up his confusion about his childhood religion and rejection of many of its beliefs, we explored together to find the parts of his religious experience that spoke to him. This helped him to reconnect more consciously with the aspects of divinity that felt comforting to him, choosing a particular prayer from his childhood to say as a regular practice.

Over time, Lawrence was able to begin some of the activities that interested him. He took classes in his field of interest, beginning to entertain the possibility of graduate school in the future. He volunteered at a local organization for a cause he believed in, and he went camping with new friends. He took small steps and brought into therapy the interactions that left him uncomfortable, allowing us to look at them together and do some reality checking with his interpretations, as well as planning and practicing his next steps. Sometimes when I suggested a possible scenario (e.g., "What if you told her how you feel about that?"), his anxiety would intensify. I guided him in caring for the frightened young self within him, using his breath to direct compassionate attention to the place in his body where he felt the anxiety centered.

As Lawrence was an avid reader, transpersonal bibliotherapy was a useful adjunct to our work. This enabled me to introduce transpersonal ideas and offer suggestions in an indirect way, allowing Lawrence to take in ideas that he might not have been comfortable hearing from me. For example, Cheri Huber's ([1993] 2001) *There Is Nothing Wrong with You* provided an introduction to cognitive-spiritual concepts and ways of reframing his thinking (focusing on goals such as compassion, gratitude, acceptance, and knowing the truth, rather than achieving material success and "perfection"). Huber is a Zen teacher who has written a number of wonderful books that translate basic Buddhist concepts into a simple and direct form. This one describes how the socialization process can generate self-hate and how to move toward self-acceptance. Another excellent book for cognitive-spiritual work, particularly in working with anxiety, is Bill Harvey's (2002) *Freeing Creative Expressiveness,* which covers some of the same territory as Huber but with a different style and a specific focus on developing the observing witness.

When we terminated therapy due to my leaving the area, Lawrence had gained many tools to use in situations that had been impossible for him to approach before. He had developed a relationship with the frightened parts of himself, and they no longer needed to block his way so completely. He was actively working on a few immediate goals (training in skills that could lead to a better job), as well as continuing to consider some future goals that he was not ready to tackle yet (graduate studies). His options had expanded considerably, and he was able to move in the world more freely.

CONCLUSION

The prevalence of chronic anxiety in our society today is a wake-up call. We are called to awaken to the condition of our world and find our individual responses. When we view anxiety as a call to pay attention to neglected aspects of the self, the potential for healing opens up, first in the individual, and then in the possibilities for addressing the larger situation. When the discomfort of worry and anxiety are extreme enough to bring someone into therapy, an opportunity to move beyond experiential avoidance presents itself. Our global situation as well as our personal stories become jumping-off points for bringing to consciousness those neglected parts that demand integration in order to deepen our spiritual connection as well as participate fully in ordinary life.

As long as we are lost in hopelessness, nothing can be done. As long as anxiety isolates individuals in their own personal hell of worry and fear about the future, life is frozen and no movement is possible. When we breathe into and accept fears, and pain, and suffering, response becomes possible—we are free to move, to take action, to make a difference.

In this chapter, I have outlined a number of approaches for entering into the healing work that anxiety symptoms may initiate. We create a healing relationship and a healing setting, and bring our psycho-spiritual perspective and context to the therapeutic work, creating the container for the work of healing. The healing procedures may in-

clude self-relations psychotherapy, centering and breathing awareness, hypnosis, meditation, and whatever other techniques emerge as
appropriate in each situation. Any of these can be the right path to
healing with the active participation of therapist and client and our
belief that they can restore health.

As therapists, we are called to awaken ourselves, in order to create
the healing relationships and settings to do this work. The collection
of techniques we offer is unlikely to open the door to healing without
the therapist's authentic presence. We can assist our clients and students in their transformative process to the degree that we accept our
own fears, pain, and suffering and bring our own connection with the
larger field to our work as spiritual midwives.

REFERENCES

American Psychiatric Association (1997). *Let's talk facts about anxiety disorders*
[brochure]. Washington, DC: American Psychiatric Association.

American Psychiatric Association (2000). *Diagnostic and statistical manual of
mental disorders* (Fourth edition, Text revision). Washington, DC: American
Psychiatric Association.

Barlow, D. H. (2002). *Anxiety and its disorders: The nature and treatment of anxiety and panic* (Second edition). New York: The Guilford Press.

Blanco, C., Schneier, F. R., and Liebowitz, M. R. (2002). Pharmacotherapy for social phobia. In D. J. Stein and E. Hollander (Eds.), *Textbook of anxiety disorders*
(pp. 309-321). Washington, DC: American Psychiatric Publishing.

Boorstein, S. (1996). Transpersonal techniques and psychotherapy. In B. W. Scotton, A. B. Chinen, and J. R. Battista (Eds.), *Textbook of transpersonal psychiatry
and psychology* (pp. 282-301). New York: Basic Books.

Borkovec, T. D. and Costello, E. (1993). Efficacy of applied relaxation and cognitive-behavioral therapy in the treatment of generalized anxiety disorder. *Journal
of Consulting and Clinical Psychology, 61,* 611-619.

Borkovec, T. D., Newman, M. G., Pincus, A. L., and Lytle, R. (2002). A component
analysis of cognitive-behavioral therapy for generalized anxiety disorder and the
role of interpersonal problems. *Journal of Consulting and Clinical Psychology,
70,* 288-298.

Call, A. P. ([1891] 1998). *Power through repose, 1891*. Whitefish, MT: Kessinger
Publishing Company.

Cortright, B. (1997). *Psychotherapy and spirit: Theory and practice in transpersonal psychotherapy*. Albany: State University of New York Press.

Ferenczi, S. ([1933] 1980). The principle of relaxation and neo-catharsis. In
M. Balint (Ed.), *Final contributions to the problems and methods of psychoanalysis*, Volume 3 (pp. 428-443). New York: Bruner/Mazel.

Frank, J. D. and Frank, J. B. (1991). *Persuasion and healing: A comparative study of psychotherapy* (Third edition). Baltimore, MD: Johns Hopkins.

Frattaroli, E. (2001). *Healing the soul in the age of the brain: Becoming conscious in an unconscious world.* New York: Penguin Putnam, Inc.

Gilligan, S. (1997). *The courage to love.* New York: WW Norton and Co., Inc.

Gilligan, S. (2002). *The legacy of Milton H. Erickson: Selected papers of Stephen Gilligan.* Phoenix, AZ: Zeig, Tucker and Thiesen Publishers.

Grof, S. (1985). *Beyond the brain.* Albany: State University of New York Press.

Grof, S. (2000). *Psychology of the future: Lessons from modern consciousness research.* Albany: State University of New York Press.

Harman, J. S., Rollman, B. L., Hanusa, B. H., Lenze, E. J., and Shear, M. K. (2002). Physician office visits of adults for anxiety disorders in the United States, 1985-1998. *Journal of General Internal Medicine, 17*(3), 165-172.

Harvey, B. (2002). *Freeing creative expressiveness.* New Paltz, NY: The Human Effectiveness Institute.

Hayes, S. C., Strosahl, K. D., and Wilson, K. G. (1999). *Acceptance and commitment therapy: An experiential approach to behavior change.* New York: Guilford.

Hillman, J. and Ventura, M. (1993). *We've had a hundred years of psychotherapy and the world is getting worse.* San Francisco: HarperCollins.

Hoehn-Saric, R. and McLeod, D. R. (1991) Clinical management of generalized anxiety disorder. In W. Coryell and G. Winokur (Eds.), *The clinical management of anxiety disorders* (pp. 79-100). New York: Oxford University Press.

Hubble, M. A., Duncan, B. L., and Miller, S. D. (2002). *The heart and soul of change: What works in therapy.* Washington, DC: American Psychological Association.

Huber, C. ([1993] 2001). *There is nothing wrong with you.* Murphys, CA: Keep It Simple Books.

Huppert, J. D. and Sanderson, W. C. (2002). Psychotherapy for generalized anxiety disorder. In D. J. Stein and E. Hollander (Eds.), *Textbook of anxiety disorders* (pp. 141-155). Washington, DC: American Psychiatric Publishing.

Judith, A. (1996). *Eastern body, Western mind: Psychology and the chakra system as a path to the self.* Berkeley, CA: Celestial Arts.

Kabat-Zinn, J. (1990). *Full catastrophe living: Using the wisdom of your body and mind to face stress, pain, and illness.* New York: Delta.

Kabat-Zinn, J. (1994). *Wherever you go, there you are.* New York: Hyperion.

Kabat-Zinn, J., Massion, A. O., Kristeller, J., Peterson, L. G., Fletcher, K. E., Pbert, L., Lenderking, W. R., and Santorelli, S. F. (1992). Effectiveness of a meditation-based stress reduction program in the treatment of anxiety disorders. *American Journal of Psychiatry, 149,* 936-943.

Kessler, R. C., McGonagle, D. K., and Zhao, S., Nelson, C. B., Hughes, M., Eshleman, S., Wittchen, H. U., and Kendler, K. S. (1994). Lifetime and 12-month prevalence of DSM-III-R psychiatric disorders in the United States: Results from the National Comorbidity Survey. *Archives of General Psychiatry, 51,* 8-19.

Macy, J. and Brown, M. Y. (1998). *Coming back to life: Practices to reconnect our lives, our world.* Berkeley, CA: New Society Publishers.

May, R. (1979). *The meaning of anxiety.* New York: Washington Square Press.

McGuigan, F. J. (1993). Progressive relaxation: Origins, principles, and clinical applications. In P. M. Lehrer and R. L. Woolfolk (Eds.), *Principles and practice of stress management* (Second edition) (pp. 17-52). New York: The Guilford Press.

Noyes, R., Garvey, M. J., Cook, B. L., and Perry, P. J. (1988). Benzodiazepine withdrawal: A review of the evidence. *Journal of Clinical Psychiatry, 49*(10), 382-389.

Noyes, R. and Hoehn-Saric, R. (1998). *The anxiety disorders.* Cambridge, UK: Cambridge University Press.

Patel, C. (1993). Yoga-based therapy. In P. M. Lehrer and R. L. Woolfolk (Eds.), *Principles and practice of stress management* (Second edition) (pp. 89-137). New York: The Guilford Press.

Patten, S. B. and Love, E. J. (1994). Neuropsychiatric adverse drug reactions: Passive reports to health and welfare. *International Journal of Psychiatry in Medicine, 24,* 45-62.

Rivas-Vazquez, R. A. (2002). Benzodiazepines in contemporary clinical practice. *Professional Psychology: Research and Practice, 34*(3), 324-328.

Roemer, L. and Orsillo, S. M. (2002). Expanding our conceptualization of and treatment for generalized anxiety disorder: Integrating mindfulness/acceptance-based approaches with existing cognitive-behavioral models. *Clinical Psychology: Science and Practice, 9*(1), 54-68.

Roemer, L., and Orsillo, S. M., and Barlow, D. (2002). Generalized anxiety disorder. In D. H. Barlow (Ed.), *Anxiety and its disorders: The nature and treatment of anxiety and panic* (Second edition) (pp. 477-515). New York: The Guilford Press.

Sanderson, C. and Linehan, M. (1999). Acceptance and forgiveness. In W. R. Miller (Ed.), *Integrating spirituality into treatment: Resources for practitioners* (pp. 199-216). Washington, DC: American Psychological Association.

Shapiro, D. H. Jr. and Zifferblatt, S. M. (1976). Zen meditation and behavioral self-control. *American Psychologist, 31,* 519-532.

Skaer, T. L., Robison, L. M., Sclar, D. A., and Galin, R. S. (2000). Anxiety disorders in the USA, 1990 to 1997—Trend in complaint, diagnosis, use of pharmacotherapy and diagnosis of comorbid depression. *Clinical Drug Investigation, 20*(4), 237-244.

Stahl, S. M. (2002). Don't ask, don't tell, but benzodiazepines are still the leading treatments for anxiety disorders. *Journal of Clinical Psychiatry, 63,* 756-757.

Vega, S. (2004). Movement practices for self-relations. In S. G. Gilligan and D. Simon (Eds.), *Walking in two worlds: Theory and practice of self relations.* Phoenix, AZ: Zeig, Tucker and Thiesen Publishers.

Chapter 4

Sacred Wounding:
Traumatic Openings to the Larger Self

Sharon G. Mijares

This chapter discusses alternative methods for treating posttraumatic reactions to violence and sexual abuse. Although abuse can never be condoned, the therapeutic response to overwhelming stress and abuse can actually open doors to transformation when treated within an integrative, psychospiritual paradigm. I compare traditional theory and treatment models with psychospiritual theory, responses, and treatment based upon the work of Carl Jung, Joseph Campbell, Stephen Gilligan, Roberto Assagioli, and mystical teachings from religious traditions. Three client narratives are presented to illustrate how trauma and psychospiritual treatment can lead to transformed identities.

INTRODUCTION

The cultural paradigm has a large influence on diagnosis and treatment of trauma. Although Western psychology has gathered considerable data regarding the effects of trauma on mind, body, and development, its primary focus has been on its pathology, ignoring the client's larger identity. For example, one limitation of mainstream psychotherapy is that it primarily focuses on the symptoms and ignores the client's larger identity.

The initial response from the therapist can have a large impact on how clients perceive themselves in relationship to the traumas. A typical therapist's response is one of reviewing the symptoms of trauma syndrome with the client and outlining a treatment plan focused on alleviating these symptoms. However, a therapist can acknowledge the trauma, educate in regard to symptoms, and also recognize the client's capacity to learn and grow in any circumstance. This is why increasing numbers of clients are choosing psychospiritual therapists and mind-body healers.

Many clients and therapists prefer an integrative treatment model because it also includes belief systems based on life's deeper meanings. A psychospiritual treatment model utilizes traditional approaches but also emphasizes theories and treatment paradigms based on the world's mythologies and religious traditions (Feinstein and Krippner, 1988; Mijares, 2003a). Traditional treatment models do not include this larger spectrum; hence, the client continues to be plagued with an identity of victimhood. Even the term *survivor* is more related to identity as victim, rather than one associated with the evolutionary capacity of heroic transcendence.

Paul Tillich, the German theologian, described how physics and consciousness combine in mystical unity. His student, Jean Houston, noted that "Many have had this experience, some by virtue and grace, others by years of search and inner discipline, still others *through some kind of trauma that lowered the particle resistance that keeps us so firmly entrenched in the foreground*" (Houston, 1987, p. 22 [italics added]). In other words, there is an opportunity for a quantum leap in consciousness. Trauma affects the victim's sense of time, place, and person. An adaptation is required. One can never be the same again. The victim has been forced into an archetypal experience, one that can open a previously entrenched consciousness to influences from the past that have the power to transform his or her life.

TRADITIONAL DIAGNOSTIC AND TREATMENT MODELS

The *Diagnostic and Statistical Manual of Mental Disorders* (DSM-IV-TR) (American Psychiatric Association, 2000) describes the crucial feature of post-traumatic stress disorder as the development of characteristic symptoms following exposure to an extreme traumatic stressor involving direct personal experience of an event that involves actual or threatened death or serious injury, or other threat to one's physical integrity; or witnessing an event that involves death, injury, or a threat to the physical integrity of another person; or learning about unexpected or violent death, serious harm, or threat of death or injury experienced by a family member or other close association. (p. 463)*

This description acknowledges physical, mental, and emotional responses that can occur when one's life, well-being, and safety (the integrity of one's body and identity) are threatened. Any event that endangers the integrity of one's being, a loved one, or others can cause trauma. Trauma research has particularly focused on war veterans and victims of violent assault (physical and sexual), child abuse, racial threats, and political terror (Herman, 1992; Yehuda, 2002). Following the bombing of the Alfred P. Murrah Federal Building in Oklahoma City and the terrorist attacks of September 11, 2001, trauma research and treatment have increasingly focused on the aftermath of terrorism.

Several psychotherapies are recommended for the treatment of PTSD. These include the following:

- *Exposure therapy* involves facing original emotions associated with traumatic experience; the client and therapist may go to the scene of the trauma in order to experience the original feelings as a step toward resolution (Foe and Cahill, 2002).
- *Cognitive-behavioral psychotherapy* (CBT) is concerned with core cognitions related to the trauma. The goal is one of cognitive restructuring, focusing primarily on fear-based cognitions (Bryant, Moulds, and Guthrie, 2001).
- *Stress inoculation training* (SIT) includes a variety of cognitive-behavioral techniques. Cognitive restructuring, thought stopping, guided self-dialogue, and behavioral techniques of breath control, relaxation skill building, and covert modeling are used

---

*Reprinted with permission from the *Diagnostic and Statistical Manual of Mental Disorders,* Fourth Edition, Text Revision, Copyright 2000, American Psychiatric Association.

to teach the client how to manage anxiety, fears, and avoidance behaviors (Foe and Cahill, 2002).

- *Eye movement desensitization reprocessing* (EMDR) is a technique of bilateral eye movements that was developed by Francine Shapiro in the late 1980s. The client is asked to describe the particular images, emotions, sensations, and cognitions associated with the traumatic event. The therapist then moves his or her fingers back and forth in front of the client's eyes while the client tracks the therapist's fingers, focusing on the traumatic memories. Implications of neuropsychological mechanisms are associated with bilateral eye movements that initiate integration and resolution (Christman et al., 2003).
- *Pharmacological interventions.* Although PTSD is one of the most prevalent of diagnosed mental disorders, it has the least research regarding psychopharmological treatment. Monoamine oxidase inhibitors (MAOIs) and tricyclic antidepressants have been widely prescribed. Some victims may have other mental disorders, and this is taken into account when prescribing pharmacological agents (Mellman, 2002). These interventions are used to support psychotherapy rather than to replace it. In particular, medications are prescribed to reduce "frequency and/or severity of intrusive symptoms . . . tendency to interpret incoming stimuli as recurrences of the trauma . . . reduction in conditioned hyperarousal . . . reduction in avoidance behavior . . . depressed mood and numbing . . . psychotic and dissociative symptoms . . . impulsive aggression against self and others" (van der Kolk, McFarlane, and Weisaeth, 1996, p. 512).

These criteria are *problem focused*. As previously noted, the therapeutic goal in traditional psychology is to reduce symptoms and return the client to pretrauma functioning. Its theoretical orientation and related treatments are not focused on a quantum leap in consciousness and lifestyle. Hence, an opportunity to facilitate the client's evolution is often missed. The client can never really be the same again; the heart, mind, and spirit have been affected. A complete life change is possible as a result of the ego's disorganization. The psychotherapist's orientation, combined with the client's level of receptivity and intuitive understanding, can open the door to the winds of change.

CROSS-CULTURAL PARADIGMS

Meaning making is a process of social construction. This does not mean that core truths are nonexistent, but rather that the meaning a particular culture gives to them both reflects and affects the consciousness of that culture. In discussing social construction and meaning making, Kenneth Gergen (1994) advises that

> any given theoretical view simultaneously serves to sensitize and to constrain; one sees more sharply but remains blind to that which falls outside the realm of focus. Thus it may be argued that any theory that commands widespread belief, that serves as a univocal view of reality within a given culture poses a threat to that culture. (p. 168; in Rosen, 1996, pp. 21-22)

It can be argued that the current model of psychopathology as illustrated by the DSM limits our clients and our culture. In regard to PTSD and the client—it supports an identity of psychopathology and victimhood. In regard to PTSD and the culture—the pathologizing of the client represents a loss of a broader and richer perspective for the therapist, the client, and the culture at large.

The growing awareness and compassion for victims of tragedy, terrorism, and crime is good. I do not discount the valuable work being done to help victims of trauma, but simply suggest that a therapist can utilize the knowledge gleaned from these traditional models of psychotherapy while holding a larger space for the client's healing and transformation. The following supports this wider perspective—one in which the client's dominant story can become one of new learning, discovery, and a richer life.

The late religious historian Mircea Eliade (1907-1986) researched patterns of initiation, rites of passage, and various rituals related to the mysteries of birth and rebirth from the Americas to Siberia. In discussing the making of a shaman (medicine man, healer), Eliade (1965) explained that "a man may become a shaman following an accident or a highly unusual event" (p. 88). In response to the psychopathology often attributed to shamanistic beliefs and behaviors he noted, "if shamanism cannot simply be identified with a psychopathological phenomenon, it is nevertheless true that the shamanic vocation often implies a crisis so deep that it sometimes borders on madness" (pp. 88-89). The shamanic experience differs from traditional psychopathological states in that "It has an initiatory structure and signification; in short, it reproduces a traditional mystical pattern" (p. 89). The shamanic crisis often brings one to a complete disintegration of consciousness. This chaotic state can be compared to the same chaos that precedes cosmological manifestation—in other words, an ordeal related to transformation. The shamanic crisis embodies themes of initiation (an event that takes one out of the ordinary) resulting in a transformed identity, which in turn contributes to the culture. The wounded becomes the healer. Traditionally the crisis is not perpetrated upon the future shaman by an outside force but arises from an internal state of consciousness. However, many modern-day versions of the wounded healer include imposed trauma.

One well-known example is evidenced in the life of the late Viktor Frankl (1905-1997). As a Jew he survived imprisonment in Auschwitz and Dachau and the loss of his possessions and family. During the traumatic imprisonment and torturous daily life he reconstructed his view of life and examined the importance of the meaning given to any event. Within five years following his release he had achieved a second doctorate, becoming an influential psychologist. His book *Man's Search for Meaning* (1959) was initially written in 1945, not long after his release from Auschwitz, and published in Austria in 1949. Since then it has sold millions—a testimony to the power of the human spirit to learn and develop under the most dire of conditions.

Canadian researchers Christopher Davis of Carleton University and Jolene McKearney of St. Francis Xavier University (2003) note that numerous studies (for example, Collins, Taylor, and Skokan, 1990, and Davis, Nolen-Hoeksema, and Larson, 1998) reveal that persons coping with loss or trauma often discover that their lives change in some unexpected and positive manner. Davis and McKearney also found that when subjects contemplated traumatic conditions, including their death (mortality salience condition), they tended to attribute increased meaningfulness to life and an enlarged worldview.

This has also been evidenced in the lives of the many Tibetan refugees, in particular the monks, who following the Chinese government's killing of over 100,000 monks and destruction of over 6,000 monasteries, escaped into India and went on to teach Buddhism to Western students. The Dalai Lama "understood their dispersion as an opportunity to share their form of Buddhism with the wider world and therefore preserve it" (Goss and Klass, 1997, p. 378). Their teachings of loving-kindness, compassion, and impermanence are having a positive impact on Western consciousness.

Tibetan teacher Pema Chödrön (1997) explains in her book *When Things Fall Apart* that

> suffering is inevitable for human beings as long as we believe that things last—that they don't disintegrate, that they can be counted on to satisfy our hunger for security. From this point of view, the only time we ever know what's really going on is when the rug's been pulled out and we can't find anywhere to land. (p. 9)

The recommended solution is loving-kindness to the self—to the one within who has been traumatized—and ultimately to others.

MYTH AND RELIGION: ARCHETYPAL THEMES OF ABUSE AND SELF-DISCOVERY

The victim of trauma is thrown out of the womb of safety and well-being. The world becomes a fearful and lonely place, for he or she has been exiled from the relational field. His or her innocence has been sacrificed, and he or she has been initiated into a world of darkness. Themes of exile and sacrifice are found throughout religious stories and mythological lore (Campbell, 1949, 1974; Jung, 1964). For example, the Old Testament tells us that the king of Egypt ordered all midwives to kill every male child born of the line of Israel. An Israeli woman hid her son (Moses) for three months, then placed him in a basket to be found and raised by Pharaoh's daughter. Jesus' life is similarly threatened as Herod orders the massacre of all male infants. The Bible tells us that his parents take him from the land of his birthplace into Egypt to protect his life. In the end he becomes the slain lamb of innocence, to be resurrected as a model for all.

A similar story is told of the Indian deity Krishna. The future Krishna's parents are imprisoned by King Kamsa to assure that all of their offspring are killed, for there is a prophesy that the eighth child of the Goddess Devaki (Krishna's mother) will kill the king. A goddess secretly takes Krishna away from his parents' jail cell. He is raised by cowherds until the time comes for Krishna to confront the wicked ruler and take his rightful place. Kamsa learns that he has been outwitted and orders the massacre of all male children. The theme in the story is one of exile, conflict, and the return to one's rightful place—the authentic self.

These stories suggest that the victim of trauma has entered an archetypal journey. An oppressive perpetrator or horrific event has disrupted the client's previous identity. An opportunity for a complete life transformation is at hand.

Case Example: Aiki

The following case example of acute trauma syndrome concerns a victim of a violent rape. It demonstrates how early and succeeding sessions with this woman helped to empower and transform her life. She was educated on the effects of PTSD, cognitions were explored, and she was trained in stress reduction exercises, but the therapy also encompassed the entirety of her life—including its spiritual dimensions.

One morning I received a call from a local women's center concerning a rape victim. The woman had survived a four-hour ordeal with an extremely violent and crazed rapist; her breast and knee had been injured and her sense of safety and well-being destroyed. The woman required both medical and psychological treatment.

The woman was in her midthirties. In this chapter, I will call her Aiki. Aiki had been born in Okinawa, Japan, and immigrated when she was seven years old. She was a married mother of two children. Although she had taken only a few university courses, she was very intelligent. In the description of the rape event, I learned that Aiki was willing to fight for her life. She had even bitten the testicles of the man, who, despite his own injury and profuse bleeding, continued his attack. She fought throughout this horrendous ordeal and eventually escaped.

Her early life history was particularly significant, as it demonstrated an instinctual tendency to defend herself and fight off attackers. Her mother had left her father when Aiki was around three years old. It was not culturally acceptable at that time for a wife to leave her husband (regardless of abuse), so Aiki's mother had been ostracized socially. As a result, schoolchildren taunted Aiki with sticks. She began carrying a sickle to defend herself against attacks.

When Aiki was seven, her mother moved with the children to the United States and married an American. Their lives changed dramatically. Aiki was introduced to Christianity and separated from her Buddhist roots. She grew up and, like her mother, married an American. She did not need to work, so she stayed home and raised her sons. The marriage had several problems and both partners had been unhappy for a long time. Although her employment experience was limited, she was an excellent artist, having spent years copying the works of the great masters.

As I listened to her story I had a great appreciation for the warrior nature within this woman. She had tremendous strength. Typically, therapists focus primarily on the rape. Although I educated Aiki on the traditional symptoms of acute and post-traumatic stress disorder, I was also interested in the overall lifestyle, the circumstances of her life. Aiki was lacking fulfillment in many areas. Her marriage had problems and she felt repressed in many areas. The rape acted as a catalyst for these unresolved issues to come to the forefront of her life.

Her style of processing the rape was intense in comparison to other women I had treated. In the beginning, she slept with a gun under her pillow (which caused me great concern). I related this to the little girl with the garden sickle and began to talk about that little girl and how she was still active in Aiki's life. I used and taught hypnotically induced relaxation exercises. She responded well to trance work. In fact, she did exceptionally well. Rather than focusing simply on the rape, we focused on all the areas of her life, including her childhood and marriage, and how these affected her life as a woman. I acknowledged her bravery as well as her fears, and explained that no matter what any woman did, or how she dressed, nothing gave anyone the right to violate or attack her. This always needs to be addressed. Women, like children, tend to blame themselves for the wrongs of others. Her own cultural heritage as a Japanese woman also had its influence: she did not have a felt sense of equality or power in her marriage and life.

Along with processing responses to trauma, the treatment focus included women's issues and her empowerment as a woman, improving the marriage, and getting beyond fears in order to step out into a career.

Her way of handling the rape was unique. She read every book available and became an expert in the area. A few months later, the local Sexual Assault Response Team (SART) asked me if I would recommend an appropriate client (rape victim) who would be willing to share her experience with SART for newspaper coverage of their five-year anniversary. I asked Aiki if she was interested in this venture and confirmed that her name would not be used. She readily expressed her gratitude for the entire rape response program. SART next asked her to speak at a large convention the following month. Later I learned that in front of local television cameras she stated,

"You were told my name was Alexandra. Why should I use a false name? I'm not the person who committed a crime! My name is Aiki . . ." (and she gave her full name). She was then asked to speak at the national conference. The audience included detectives, legislators, and medical staff. I was also invited. Aiki spoke against rape with such power that tears were in the eyes of male and female participants alike. The following month we were both honored by the district attorney's office. The DA then asked her to be the key speaker for a video to be shown in Canada and the United States. This client channeled her energy, emotions, and response to trauma in a positive direction. I had to let go of my ideas and expectations of more traditional responses.

I had a couple of individual appointments with her husband and a few sessions with both of them to address issues within the marriage. The focus here was twofold: first, to help him deal with his responses to the rape and, second, to shed some light on the various ways, both subtle and overt, that he had been neglecting his marriage and his wife. His neglect had its part in her being in the wrong place at the wrong time (the night of the attack). This was never directly presented to him, but it was obvious that she had been spending a significant amount of time away from the home as a result of loneliness. His appreciation and admiration of her grew as he saw her on television and realized her strength and beauty. It increased even more when she began to blossom in her career.

Aiki was terrified to go out into the world, as she lacked formal training and had limited experience in the working world. Here trance and breathwork proved helpful. She once again did well with trance work—often receiving images and feeling inner guidance. She began to formulate her career goals. These began in the area of managing an art gallery with a vision of promoting women's art. She joined my women's group, which focused on women's development, and met other artists. This led to training in faux finishing (artistic wall painting) from some recognized experts in this field. Her training as a classical artist was integrated into this work as she began to design panels and art on walls. The same warrior energy found in the young child defending herself against attackers and a woman fighting for her life against a rapist was channeled into creating a prosperous career.

I suggested breathwork because it induces rapid healing processes. The muscular armoring softens as a result of deeper inhaling and exhaling (Grof, 1987; Reich, 1972). The nervous system and brain are stimulated with deeper and faster breathing patterns. Contracted emotional and energetic states are released. After experiencing breathwork with Stanislav Grof, the founder of Holotropic Breathwork, John Mack (1993) explains,

> The transpersonal dimension of the work has a powerful spiritual impact, reconnecting the breather with primary religious experiences, a sense of sacred awe from which he or she may have been cut off since childhood. Powerful heart-openings and uplifting, luminous, or tran-

scendent experiences bring the breather to a higher sense of value and purpose and of connection to the universe. (p. 364)

This description is evidenced in Aiki's first encounter with breathwork.

I was somewhat concerned that unresolved trauma might surface, but I put my trust in the breathwork process and its capacity to both release and resolve trauma. She began a rather intense breathing pattern (in comparison to others I had worked with). Her entire body was quivering in response to this intensity. I simply sat alongside her and silently supported her process. An hour and a half later she described her intense cultural resolution of the rape along with an experience of spiritual awakening.

She had gone into a trance state in which she saw the bombing of Hiroshima, followed by the releasing of peace doves. She experienced cultural themes of suicide in that she picked up a sword (internal images) with the thought of killing herself for having dishonored her family. This was inwardly processed as she put the sword down and found peace within herself. Next she had a vision of the back of a Buddhist monk in saffron robes. He turned around and she saw her own face—outwardly sobbing as she recognized "I'm a Buddhist." The deep breathing session ended shortly after that experience. Her life had been affected on every level: improved self-image and marital relationship, career development, and spiritual dedication—all as a result of that rape. No one would wish such a painful and terrifying circumstance upon anyone, but, as previously noted, the response to trauma has the potential to transform one's life.

SELF-RELATIONS PSYCHOTHERAPY

Stephen Gilligan's self-relations (SR) psychotherapy focuses on re-creating a healthy relationship between the cognitive-egoic self and the somatic-feeling self as a means of reuniting with the larger universal field. SR psychotherapists recognize that "there exists a power and presence greater than the intellect and individual in the world" (Gilligan, 1997, p. 22) and incorporate the client's spirituality as part of the healing process (Gilligan and Simon, 2004). The theory incorporates teachings from Buddhism, Gandhi, Milton Erickson, and the martial art Aikido.

The significant element of the psychotherapy is that it encourages embracing and holding the neglected parts of ourselves, rather than struggling against them. This is called *sponsoring*. Often clients have learned to ignore the pain, rage, terror, and longings of their feeling selves. This is an internalized, introjected replication of the message often given to the victim by the perpetrator, that the victim's body, feelings, thoughts, and well-being are irrelevant. Sponsoring the unwanted, repressed, fragmented feelings and experiences of our neglected selves brings the possibility of healing, wholeness, and reconnection to the larger relational field. From this perspective, focusing on diminishing symptoms (the goal of traditional psychotherapies) tends to contribute to the problem by ignoring the neglected selves. I have found that self relations psychotherapy melds well with psychospiritual healing and my own training as a practitioner of Sufism.

I am a member of Sufi Ruhaniat International, an Inayati school of Sufism founded by Hazrat Inayat Khan (1882-1927). In particular, this school encourages a deep, experiential, lifetime study of the world's religious teachings. This has augmented my own psychospiritual knowledge while enabling me to utilize a specific healing technique and philosophy that adapts to the client's style and needs. Like other Eastern and indigenous traditions, Sufis use meditation, breathing practices, and intoning to facilitate alchemical and transformative healing. These practices have a deep effect upon consciousness and the body.

For example, the following represents a Sufi exercise encouraging relational healing. In my chapter in Stephen Gilligan and Dvorah Simons's (2004) anthology *Walking in Two Worlds: Theory and Practice of Self Relations,* I share an exercise used with many clients that helps them glean a felt sense of relationship with neglected parts of themselves. The client is asked to become more aware of his or her breath and to follow the feeling of breathing lower in the body using a natural (rather than forced) breath. He or she is encouraged to relax into the base of the breathing wave. (This is where exhale completes and the breath naturally begins the next inhale.) The client is then guided

> to enter the gentle darkness at the bottom of things and to use the awareness of breathing as a way to remain connected to the part that observes and witnesses all of the interactions within. Are there voices, sensations, or feelings on the "surface" of the depths that have been waiting to be heard and recognized? . . . breathe toward the self (or selves) in your depths with as much

love and thanks as you are in and out. Ask for help by aligning your breath to the breath that began the cosmos, the "Holy Breath," and feel your own potential for creation, which arises from "what waits in the darkness." (Douglas-Klotz, 1995, p. 23)

The following client example is an application of self-relations psychotherapy and Sufi practices (also found in Gilligan and Simon, 2004) such as those just described. It is a story of repressed memory recall related to childhood trauma.

Case Example: Kristen

The first time I met Kristen she requested hypnotherapy to explore possible abuse from a second grade school teacher. However, I did not feel comfortable with regression therapy in that she appeared to be emotionally vulnerable and I did not want her to be retraumatized. I recommended instead that we focus on her present state in order to promote spiritual, emotional, and cognitive development.

Kristen was very compassionate, sensitive, and feminine. She was also quite timid and unable to speak up for herself in a crowd. In order to manifest strength and wholeness in her life, Kristen needed to integrate other archetypal qualities, including both her masculine side and her earthy feminine nature (instinctual power). This was the foundation she needed in order to integrate any prior abuse issues. I therefore focused on developing ego strengths. Through trance and breathwork she was able to recognize and affirm her spiritual intuition, helping to cultivate ego strength through increased intuition and awareness. I also taught her Sufi breathing and intoning techniques. These were given to the client as homework assignments.

Her career goals included gardening and herbology; however, these goals were not pursued due to perceived obligations. Her husband's employment-related difficulties consumed his energies, and family care consumed hers. Kristen eventually discontinued individual psychotherapy but did remain a member of the women's group.

A few months later I received a phone call. Kristen had been paralyzed by debilitating feelings of terror while watching a television program on childhood abuse. Her husband had to carry her to bed due to bodily tremors that resembled seizurelike activity. She began seeing metaphorical images of schoolchildren with amputated legs and arms.

She responded well to an intense breathwork session. The nonordinary states of consciousness reached enabled her to process some of her experience and at the same time access transpersonal healing states. John Mack (1993) explains that

When we are able to access, or re-access, emotions that have been warded off in the body cells or in autonomic regulatory systems, then the human organism's previously blocked natural healing powers can become available. It is in this working through or integrative process that the greatest therapeutic value of nonordinary states may reside. (pp. 369-370)

While the client was in this state I hypnotically deepened her trance and encouraged her awareness of inner guidance. Kristen experienced a visual image that symbolically represented spiritual support. This image acted as an anchor[1] and continued to provide strength and support whenever she felt emotionally overwhelmed. Memories of familial childhood abuse came up and she readily processed them.

Her husband found employment in another state. They moved away and returned three years later. Kristen then experienced another episode of terror and intrusive images of abuse. Stress and confusion related to the relocation and financial security issues appeared to have triggered the unresolved trauma from second grade. Also, she was ignoring previous learning regarding self-sponsorship. All of her attention was focused on others. In neglecting herself she was replicating feelings related to childhood neglect, resulting in a reappearance of unresolved trauma. I recommended Pema Chödrön's (1997) *When Things Fall Apart* as bibliotherapy, believing that her Buddhist teachings concerning *maitri* (loving-kindness) toward the self provided a strong message of self-care.

The memories and associated feelings began to manifest in my office. Again, she was overwhelmed with waves of terror. I sat next to her on the couch and spontaneously took her hand. I could feel the intensity of the energy. Her body was evidencing the trauma it had stored for almost thirty years. She was flooded with childhood memories of abuse perpetrated by the schoolteacher and needed to stay present with this terrified part of herself.

As I held Kristen's hand I spoke to her adult self, "reminding her that she was a thirty-six-year-old mother of three children, and that this child, her neglected child self, needed love and compassionate healing" (Mijares, 2004). We gently breathed together as I reminded her of the presence of the higher Self. The session ended with the Sufi intoning and breathing practice described earlier in order to soothe and heal the energies released by the abreaction. In this compassionate atmosphere Kristen was able to sponsor and create harmony between her adult ego self and her neglected child self. It was the first time that she had actually remained present in both states and she has maintained this connection. This is the goal of self-relations psychotherapy.

Not long after, the family purchased a new home with vast gardens. The previous homeowner had been a master gardener, and now Kristen is also a master gardener. Her gardens are visited by many, and she is being noticed for her work. Her spirituality finds expression in being with and caring for nature. Three years have passed and she has not needed further treatment.

GROUNDING IN THE BODY: SOMATIC AWAKENING

As noted in the introduction, the late Italian psychiatrist Roberto Assagioli (1888-1974) stressed the importance of attending to the different parts of the personality, noting that a psychological foundation was needed in order to integrate and contain spiritual frequencies (Scotton, Chinen, and Battista, 1996). Many trauma victims turn to spiritual teachings and experiential practices hoping to avoid the feelings associated with the trauma. Churches, monasteries, and ashrams are filled with devotees seeking a better state of consciousness. However, far too often these devotees are attempting to experience a "spiritual awakening in an ill-prepared or undeveloped personality" (Scotton, Chinen, and Battista, 1996, p. 59). Self-relations psychotherapy deals with this by focusing on integrating the neglected self and building a relational self. This is an embodied, somatic process; therefore, attention to the body represents a fundamental condition for integrative healing (Mijares, 1995).

Research has tended to focus on the body's pathological response to abuse, for example, the effects of trauma (especially childhood trauma) on the body. Alterations have been noted in stress-related neurotransmitter structures. Neurotransmitters' corticotrophin-releasing factor and somatostatin have been found in increased amounts in people exhibiting PTSD (Bremner 2002; Bremner et al., 1997). Magnetic resonance imaging (MRI) and positron emission tomography (PET) indicate alterations in the hippocampus, associated with memory and learning (Bremner et al., 2003). These findings are often seen as permanent changes, and they support pharmacological treatments.

At the same time, however, other researchers are validating the plasticity (changeability) of the brain and its relationship to learning and neurological patterning. Research with PET has evidenced brain changes taking place in obsessive-compulsive disorder clients in response to Buddhist mindfulness training (Schwartz and Begley, 2002). Also, mindfulness-based cognitive therapy for patients with depression is receiving increasing attention (Segal, Williams, and Teasdale, 2002). Researcher Joseph LeDoux (2002) explains in his book *Synaptic Self: How Our Brains Become Who We Are* that "Most systems of the brain are plastic, that is, modifiable by experience, which means that the synapses involved are changed by experience" (p. 8).

Recent discoveries also indicate that the brain is part of the mind-body relationship; it does not run the whole show. The stomach has an intelligence of its own and sends and receives neurotransmitters (Gerson, Kirchgessner, and Wade, 1994). More recent discoveries indicate that the heart is also comprised of neuronal tissue and mediates with the brain (Pearce, 2002). Because somatic responses are rooted in personal history and archetypal experience, an integrative response is needed. The following example (Mijares, 2004) emphasizes the relevance of the mind, body, spirit relationship in psychotherapy.

Case Example: Alicia

Alicia had been diagnosed with chronic muscle fatigue and fibromyalgia. Her father had sexually violated her throughout her childhood. She wished he would die. Then he did die unexpectedly when Alicia was twelve years old, thereby adding guilt to mingle with her shame. Alicia entered adulthood with opposing coping styles: she attended religious services and joined a spiritual commune but also frequented bars and nightclubs and loved to drink and party. For years she successfully dissociated from any feelings associated with the abuse, but her body carried the memories and the psychic pain. It manifested itself in her illnesses (Morriss et al., 1999; Amir et al., 1997). Alicia found that late nights at local bars increased her physical pain, and that the pain diminished when she focused on meditative practices. Also, the pain increased when she neglected her childhood wounds and related feelings. Although her medical doctor had prescribed Zoloft at the onset of the illnesses, it appeared to have little, if any, impact on her self-sabotaging behaviors (for a while she bounced back and forth between these differing lifestyles as the patterns were deeply entrenched).

Because of her religious leanings, she related well to psychospiritual psychotherapy. I combined breathing practices, Sufi intoning, and hypnotherapy (Dolan, 1991; Hornyack and Green, 2000) with self-relations psychotherapy. The hypnotherapy enabled her to relax more deeply and to access inner guidance. The intoning and breathing practices, which resonate at deep cellular levels, facilitated alchemical transformation. (Mijares, 2004). I also invited her to join a women's group that focused on goddess stories and rituals that empowered women (Mijares, 2003b).

She began to appreciate her emotions and recognized that healing included reconnecting with the neglected child self within. I explained Jung's philosophy that childhood trauma blocks natural spontaneity and innate creative power (Jung, 1964); therefore, the wounding becomes the sacred place where one reconnects with life's deeper potentiality. Alicia had been dependent upon the Zoloft, afraid that she would fail in her therapeutic goals if it were discontinued. She also found it to be physiologically addictive.

Slowly she began to withdraw from the drug and was soon able to claim the psychological and spiritual changes as her own.

Since then she has entered into the healing field and heals by energetic touch. Alicia appears to be symptom free and no longer disturbed by fibromyalgia and chronic muscle fatigue. To quote Yvonne Dolan (1991), Alicia "has reclaimed her body," and she also appears to be walking the path of the wounded healer.

CONCLUSION

In this chapter I have shared an approach that integrates positive psychotherapies and applies spiritual practices. Obviously, clients differ and these experiential philosophies and exercises are not appropriate for all. Persons with limited intellectual exposure, impoverished emotional intelligence (lacking altruistic characteristics), and diminished spiritual intelligence and experience (Vaughan, 2002) may be unable to relate to psychospiritual paradigms. Therefore, the therapeutic goals of client and therapist must be matched with the style and needs of the client.

The formal and experiential training of the therapist provides the grounding the client needs in order to heal at a deep level. If the therapist is still within, he or she holds a sacred space allowing for the flow of transformational, creative power. The client can safely feel painful emotions and at the same time realize something more—the reclaiming of his or her life, psychologically and spiritually.

Increasing numbers of clients are seeking integrative approaches for healing trauma, and many professionals in the healing field are enriching their practices by training in supplementary forms of treatment. Other trainees have simply disregarded traditional training and directly entered alternative training modalities. My own practice is deeply influenced by Stephen Gilligan's Self Relations psychotherapy, but many programs specialize in integrative treatment models for healing trauma.

One such example is the Foundation for Human Enrichment, established by Peter Levine, co-author of *Waking the Tiger: Healing Trauma* (Levine and Frederick, 1997). At this time the foundation has nearly 2,000 students enrolled in Somatic Experiencing, a process that sees and treats the resolution of trauma in relationship to paths of ancient wisdom. Another program, Holotropic Therapy, was founded by Stanislav and Christina Grof in 1976. Since that time over 800 practitioners, representative of thirty-six different countries, have successfully completed the certification training program, utilizing hyperventilating breath and stimulating music to enhance nonordinary states of consciousness (Grof, 1987). Among the ranks of certified holotropic practitioners are psychiatrists, general medical professionals, psychologists, marriage and family practitioners, acupuncturists, and other professionals.

These treatment approaches support psychological and spiritual healing, but the most important element of spirituality has not been discussed. True spirituality manifests in love and compassion—at ever deepening levels. This is the core of psychospiritual therapy. If the therapist's heart has opened to these divine qualities, he or she can reflect them to the client. This sacred holding allows the client to absorb a deeper *felt* sense of healing.

NOTE

1. This is a term used in neurolinguistic programming (NLP). The technique is used to reinforce preferred emotional and behavioral states. For example, every time the client experiences the desired emotional state, he or she reinforces it with an external reference point, the anchor (visualizing or touching the crystal).

REFERENCES

American Psychiatric Association (2000). *Diagnostic and Statistical Manual of Mental Disorders* (Fourth Edition, Text Revision). Washington, DC: American Psychiatric Association.

Amir, M., Kaplan, Z., Neumann, L., Sharabani, R., Shani, N., and Buskila, D. (1997). Posttraumatic Stress Disorder, Tenderness and Fibromyalgia. *Journal of Psychosomatic Research,* 42(6), 607-613.

Bremner, J.D. (2002). *Does Stress Damage the Brain?* New York: W.W. Norton & Company.

Bremner, J.D., Licinio, J., Darnell, A., Krystal, J.H., Owens, M.J., Southwick, S.M., Nemeroff, C.B., and Charney, D.S. (1997). Elevated CSF Corticotropin-Releasing Factor Concentrations in Posttraumatic Stress Disorder. *The American Journal of Psychiatry,* 154(5), 624-629.

Bremner, J.D., Vythilingam, M., Vermetten, E., Southwick, S.M., McGlashan, T., Nazeer, A., Khan, S., Vaccarino, L.V., Soufer, R., Garb, P.K. (2003). MRI and

PET Study of Deficits in Hippocampal Structure and Function in Women with Childhood Sexual Abuse and Posttraumatic Stress Disorder. *American Journal of Psychiatry,* 160(5), 924-932.

Bryant, R.A., Moulds, M., and Guthrie, R.M. (2001). Cognitive Strategies and the Resolution of Acute Stress Disorder. *Journal of Traumatic Stress,* 14(1), 213-219.

Campbell, J. (1949). *The Hero with a Thousand Faces.* Princeton, NJ: Princeton University Press.

Campbell, J. (1974). *The Mythic Image.* Princeton, NJ: Princeton University Press.

Chödrön, P. (1997). *When Things Fall Apart.* Boston: Shambhala Publications, Inc.

Christman, S.D., Garvey, K.J., Kilian, J., Propper, R.E., and Phaneuf, K.A. (2003). Bilateral Eye Movements Enhance the Retrieval of Episodic Memories. *Neuropsychology,* 17(2), 221-229.

Collins, R.L., Taylor, S.E., and Skokan, L.A. (1990). A Better World or a Shattered Vision? Changes in Life Perspective Following Victimization. *Social Cognition,* 8, 263-285.

Davis, C.G. and McKearney, J.M. (2003). How Do People Grow from Their Experience with Loss? *Journal of Social and Clinical Psychology,* 22(5), 477-492.

Davis, C.G., Nolen-Hoeksema, S., and Larson, J. (1998). Making Sense of Loss and Benefitting from the Experience: Two Construals of Meaning. *Journal of Personality and Social Psychology,* 75, 561-574.

Dolan, Y.M. (1991). *Resolving Sexual Abuse: Solution-Focused Therapy and Ericksonian Hypnosis for Adult Survivors.* New York: W.W. Norton.

Douglas-Klotz, N. (1995). *Desert Wisdom: Sacred Middle-Eastern Writings from the Goddess Through the Sufis.* San Francisco: Harper San Francisco.

Eliade, M. (1965). *Rites and Symbols of Initiation.* New York: Harper and Row.

Feinstein, D. and Krippner, S. (1988). *Personal Mythology.* Los Angeles: Tarcher.

Foe, E.B. and Cahill, S.P. (2002). Specialized Treatment for PTSD. In R. Yehuda (Ed.), *Treating Trauma Survivors with PTSD* (pp. 43-62). Washington, DC: American Psychiatric Publishing, Inc.

Frankl, V. (1959/1984). *Man's Search for Meaning.* New York: Washington Square Press.

Gergen, K.J. (1994). *Toward Transformation in Social Knowledge* (Second Edition). Newbury Park, CA: Sage.

Gerson, M.D., Kirchgessner, A.L, and Wade, P.R. (1994). Functional Anatomy of the Enteric Nervous System. In Leonard R. Johnson (Ed.), *Physiology of the Gastrointestinal Tract* (Third Edition) (pp. 381-422). New York: Raven Press.

Gilligan, S.G. (1997). *The Courage to Love.* New York: WW Norton and Co., Inc.

Gilligan, S.G. and Simon, D. (Eds.) (2004). *Walking in Two Worlds: Theory and Practice of Self Relations.* Phoenix, AZ: Zeig, Tucker and Thiesen Publishers.

Goss, R.E. and Klass, D. (1997). Tibetan Buddhism and the Resolution of Grief: The *Bardo-Thodol* for the Dying and the Grieving. *Death Studies,* 21, 377-395.

Grof, S. (1987). *The Adventure of Self-Discovery.* Albany: State University of New York Press.

Herman, J.D. (1992). *Trauma and Recovery.* New York: Basic Books.

Hornyack, L.M. and Green, J.P. (2001). Healing from Within: The Use of Hypnosis in Women's Health. In *Contemporary Hypnosis* (pp. 49-65). London: Whurr Publishers, Ltd.

Houston, J. (1987). *The Search for the Beloved*. New York: Penguin-Putnam.

Jung, C. (1964). *Man and His Symbols*. New York: Doubleday and Co., Inc.

LeDoux, J. (2002). *Synaptic Self: How Our Brains Become Who We Are*. New York: Viking.

Levine, P.A. and Frederick, A. (1997). *Waking the Tiger: Healing Trauma*. Berkeley, CA: North Atlantic Books.

Mack, J.E. (1993). Nonordinary States of Consciousness and the Accessing of Feelings. In S. Ablon, D. Brown, E.J. Khantzian, and J.E. Mack (Eds.), *Human Feelings: Explorations in Affect Development and Meaning* (pp. 357-371). Hillsdale: New Jersey: The Analytic Press.

Mellman, M. (2002). Rationale and Role for Medication in the Comprehensive Treatment of PTSD. In R. Yehuda (Ed.), *Treating Trauma Survivors with PTSD* (pp. 63-74).Washington, DC: American Psychiatric Publishing, Inc.

Mijares, S. (1995). Fragmented Self, Archetypal Forces and the Embodied Mind. *Dissertation Abstracts International,* 56(11), B (University Microfilms No. 9608330).

Mijares, S. (Ed.) (2003a). *Modern Psychology and Ancient Wisdom: Psychological Healing Practices from the World's Religious Traditions*. Binghamton, NY: The Haworth Press, Inc.

Mijares, S. (2003b). Tales of the Goddess: Healing Metaphors for Women. In Sharon G. Mijares (Ed.), *Modern Psychology and Ancient Wisdom: Psychological Healing Practices from the World's Religious Traditions* (pp. 71-98). Binghamton, NY: The Haworth Press, Inc.

Mijares, S. (2004). At Every Moment a New Species Arises in the Chest. In Stephen Gilligan and Dvorah Simon (Eds.), *Walking in Two Worlds: Theory and Practice of Self Relations* (pp. 180-191). Phoenix, AZ: Zeig, Tucker and Thiesen Publishers.

Morriss, R.K., Ahmed, M., Wearden, A.J., Mullis, R., Strickland, P., Appleby, L., Campbell, I.T., and Pearson, D. (1999). The Role of Depression in Pain, Psychophysiological Syndromes and Medically Unexplained Symptoms Associated with Chronic Fatigue Syndrome.

Pearce, J.C. (2002). *The Biology of Transcendence: A Blueprint of the Human Spirit*. Rochester, VT: Park Street Press.

Reich, W. (1972). *Character Analysis* (Third Edition). Toronto: Doubleday.

Rosen, H. (1996). Meaning-Making Narratives: Foundations for Constructivist and Social Constructivist Psychotherapies. In H. Rosen and K.T. Kuehlwein (Eds.), *Constructing Realities: Meaning-Making Perspectives for Psychotherapists* (pp. 3-51). San Francisco: Jossey Bass.

Schwartz, J.M. and Begley, S. (2002). *The Mind and the Brain: Neuroplasticity and the Power of Mental Force*. New York: HarperCollins.

Scotton, B.W., Chinen, A.B., and Battista, J.R. (1996). *Textbook of Transpersonal Psychiatry and Psychology*. New York: Basic Books.

Segal, Z.V., Williams, J.M.G., and Teasdale, J.D. (2002). *Mindfulness-Based Cognitive Therapy for Depression*. New York: The Guilford Press.

van der Kolk, B.A., McFarlane, A.C., and Weisaeth, L. (Eds.) (1996). *Traumatic Stress: The Overwhelming Experience on Mind, Body and Society*. New York: The Guilford Press.

Vaughan, F. (2002). What is Spiritual Intelligence? *Journal of Humanistic Psychology*, 42(2), 16-23.

Yehuda, R. (Ed.) (2002). *Treating Trauma Survivors with PTSD*. Washington, DC: American Psychiatric Publishing, Inc.

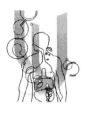

Chapter 5

Eating Disorders
As Messengers of the Soul

Anita Johnston
Kyrai Antares

INTRODUCTION

There was once a man who had black and white cattle. He
loved his cattle and treated them as though they were his children. Every morning they would give him white frothy milk.
Suddenly, the cattle stopped producing milk, and after three
mornings of no milk, the man decided to stay up all night to find
the problem. In the wee hours of the morning he saw the most
amazing sight. A rope dropped down from the heavens, and
with it, the most amazing women he had ever seen. They
climbed down the rope and filled calabashes with his white, de-
licious milk!

The man no longer cared about his milk; he was so taken by
these women. He ran toward them and grabbed one. The others
fled. She struggled with him until he proclaimed his desire to
marry her, at which point she stopped struggling and agreed to
marry him—under one condition. She told him she owned a pre-
cious basket with an exquisitely woven lid that fit perfectly on the

bottom. She was willing to marry him if he agreed not to open the basket until she said so. He agreed and they were married.

One day while she was out milking the black and white cattle, he decided to look into the basket, assuming that all that was hers was now his, and vice versa. He was surprised to find nothing in it. When she returned, he confessed that he had peeked into the basket and had found it empty. With great sadness she told him if only he had waited she would have shown him how to see what was in the basket. And she took her basket and left him.*

The old Kikuyu storyteller says, "Tsk, tsk, tsk. Mankind still thinks those things of the spirit which cannot be seen are nothing."

With eating disorders, many clients, family members, and professionals, as well, are like the man in the story. They focus on the obvious behaviors regarding food, weight, fat, and body image, and fail to perceive the more invisible aspects, the hidden hungers that fuel the disordered eating behaviors. They are unable to recognize that, for those who struggle with eating disorders, more than their bodies are not being adequately fed. Their souls—the invisible, nonphysical aspects of themselves that are much more than the body and personality—are starving. According to Marion Woodman (Woodman and Sharp, 1993), when we confuse spiritual food or soul food with actual material food, the soul is left starving and the body is abandoned.

Some years ago, scientists discovered how to calculate the total mass of a galaxy by observing how it interacted with other galaxies. They were stunned at the results. They knew that a galaxy needed to have a certain mass for it to behave the way it did. Their bewilderment arose when they added up all the visible matter (planets, stars, asteroids, moons, etc.). The sum of everything observable within the galaxy could account for only about 10 percent of the total mass of the galaxy. What was the rest? Where was the rest? It had to be there. Why could they not see it? They had no choice but to admit that the rest was unknown and invisible. They did not know what to call it, so they termed the mysterious 90 percent *dark matter.*

---

*The Black and White Cattle story is a folktale from the Kikuyu Tribe of East Africa. This retelling is based on a version by storyteller Laura Simms (1991) *Women & Wild Animals.* Minocqua, Wisconsin: North Word Audio Press.

If this is true for the entire galaxy, might it not also be true for everything within the galaxy? If we apply this idea to psychology, then all visible behaviors, all body manifestations, everything we could possibly "know" about a client could, at most, be only 10 percent of the total body-mind-spirit dynamic. The rest, 90 percent of the client, would be unknown and invisible to us. If the visible eating disorder symptoms are at most only 10 percent of the whole, then the traditional offerings in the treatment setting (fixing symptoms, determining brain chemistry, modifying behaviors, setting goals, exploring cognitive distortions) do not allow room for the bigger mystery: the true origin and meaning of the eating disorder. Such interventions, then, may be incomplete or ineffective.

Just as the man in the story at the beginning of this chapter devalued what was invisible and it cost him everything he held dear, we as helpers cannot afford to devalue or ignore the client's own psychospiritual, albeit not yet revealed, reality. If we, as therapists, can respect and acknowledge the mysterious and rich phenomenological and existential world of the client, instead of working only with what we know and what we can see, we may then be able to enter into a true therapeutic relationship with the whole client. Therapy then becomes a process of revealing the unseen, unknown, and as yet unstoried, mystery.

How do we best assist the client in identifying and integrating the unseen hungers of the soul that remain out of conscious awareness and manifest as disordered eating behavior? As Carl Jung (Meaney and Berger, 1957) said, "The unconscious *really is* unconscious." One of the ways we clinicians can gain access to this mystery, to the part of the psyche that remains in the dark and not yet revealed, is through the language of the soul: metaphor. This is the language of myth, poetry, imagery, and storytelling.

In this chapter, we propose a psychospiritual approach for reconnecting clients with the needs and hungers of the soul by viewing the eating disorder as a messenger—a messenger from the soul who speaks in metaphor through the body, the heart, and the mind.

TRADITIONAL ETIOLOGY

Since the late nineteenth century, theories of disordered eating have varied greatly, tracing the appearance of symptoms to "perversion of the will," developmental disturbances, an oppressive patriarchal culture, biochemical imbalances, genetic predispositions, maladaptive cognitions and perceptions, sexual abuse, parental preoccupation with weight and size, and many other factors (Streigel-Moore and Cachelin 2001; Wilson, Fairburn, and Agras, 1997). Some theories have yielded a corresponding model of therapy or treatment approach.

Cognitive-behavioral theory, for example, is based on the idea that distorted thinking patterns and related patterns of maladaptive behavior cause and maintain eating disorders. Therapy involves identifying, challenging, and replacing those thoughts and behaviors (Wilson, Fairburn, and Agras, 1997). One medical viewpoint on eating disorders is that these are physical illnesses that can be treated with a combination of medication, nutritional rehabilitation, and psychosocial support. Although psychotropic drugs were once thought to be a stand-alone treatment approach, enough research has been done to show that medications may have a role to play in helping some people with eating disorders but should not be an exclusive mode of treatment (Garfinkel and Walsh, 1997). Another medical theory is that disordered eating is genetic and runs in families (Streigel-Moore and Cachelin, 2001).

The addictions theory holds that eating disorders are incurable diseases, much the same as alcoholism. In this system, "being in recovery" depends upon continued abstinence, the development of a social environment supportive of abstinence, spiritual renewal, and relapse prevention (McCrady, 2001).

Many current treatment approaches tend to follow the medical, behavioral, or addiction models, all of which focus primarily upon symptom removal. Success in treatment is measured by weight gain or loss, or abstinence from purging behaviors. This approach fails to address the issues underlying the person's eating disorder and leaves the patient vulnerable to relapse, much as it is with a gardener who simply cuts off the top of a weed and fails to remove the roots.

Other treatment approaches go deeper and address the possible issues underlying eating disorders. Narrative therapy, for example, works to externalize the disordered eating and separate it from the individual (Freedman and Combs, 1996). This modality encourages clients to explore the stories of their lives that as of yet have not been lived—to give name and face to those inner aspects held prisoner by the disordered eating.

Insight-oriented psychotherapists focus on such issues as psycho-dynamics, childhood development, family dysfunction, trauma, or sexual abuse to help understand the problem. Such approaches tend to view dysfunction or trauma as critical to the later development of an eating disorder. Empirical studies exploring the link between trauma and disordered eating have yielded differing and controversial results (Fallon and Wonderlich, 1997). To understand women for whom trauma is not a significant factor, we must dig wider and deeper to find the roots of disordered eating.

Jungian psychotherapists work with masculine and feminine ar-chetypal forces that exist deep within the collective unconscious of the culture and within our psyches, regardless of gender. The work of Jungian analyst Marion Woodman suggests that women who struggle with disordered eating may need spiritual and therapeutic support that includes the divine feminine, the Goddess, the archetypal Mother who can nurture and nourish them (Woodman and Sharp, 1993).

Feminist sociocultural theories of eating disorders emphasize pres-sures from patriarchal cultures as playing a primary role in etiology. These pressures include rejection of a woman's natural curves, obses-sion with fat and dieting, and the unrealistically thin body ideal por-trayed by the media. Feminist spirituality theorists address problems inherent in the patriarchal religions' use of the image of a male God as a model of divine existence and as a model for human behavior for women (Christ and Plaskow, 1979).

THE ROOTS OF DISORDERED EATING:
TOWARD A NEW ETIOLOGY

Our view is that the roots of disordered eating extend beyond pathological psychodynamics, family dysfunction, and trauma and go deeper than the pressures and omissions of the patriarchal culture and religions. We believe that eating disorders are not only a conse-quence of a patriarchal culture, which values the masculine principles of logical, linear thinking and goal-directed behavior over the feminine principles of emotion, intuition, and connection, but also are a result of the internal conflict this creates in those innately predisposed toward the feminine principle. In their attempts to internalize this cultural imbalance, these women feel compelled to reject their inherent feminine nature, their emotions, and their female bodies. Most important, they reject their intuition, which we define as "the voice of the soul."

We propose that girls and women who struggle with disordered eating are typically highly intuitive, emotionally sensitive individuals. As children they had an ability to perceive subtle realities that others could not. They could read between the lines, see the bigger picture, sense hypocrisy, and intuit when things were not okay. Like the woman in the Black and White Cattle story, they could see what was invisible to others. Their perceptions, however, were often in conflict with the perceptions, beliefs, and needs of parents, teachers, and other family members. When they expressed their views or concerns, they were ignored, rejected, ridiculed, or in some cases abused. Their rich, though invisible, inner lives were devalued and dismissed, much like the contents of the basket in the story. Because their survival and self-esteem depended upon a sense of belonging and acceptance, they needed to find a way to diminish that which was causing the conflict and rejection—their intuition (Johnston, 1996).

Unlike the woman in the story, these girls began to believe that their ability to "see the invisible" meant something was wrong with them. Steeped in a culture that valued the material over all else, inundated by thousands of images of unrealistically thin women as the modern beauty ideal and the ceaseless promotion of diet products in the media, they decided that what was really wrong with them was physical—the size and shape of their bodies. Although this belief created more emotional pain, at least in their minds the solution was simple and clear: lose weight.

The disordered eating can then be viewed as not a problem but a creative solution to the constant pressure to conform to a way of being in the world that is in direct contradiction to their inherent nature. Glasser (2000) asserts that what is commonly referred to as mental illness is actually need-meeting behavior. The disordered eating may actually serve an important purpose by relieving pressure, providing a solution, and giving a sense of power—albeit only temporarily.

As these girls and women began to focus on weight loss as the solution, it became their goal. This goal then effectively distracted them from the more complicated problem of learning how to cope with their sensitive, intuitive nature, with being "thin skinned" in a world that valued being "thick skinned." To accomplish this goal, they believed they needed to focus on their physical appearances rather than the instinctual needs of their bodies, to value the rational properties of their minds over intuitive ways of knowing, and to reject their emotions in favor of their intellects.

They stopped listening to their intuition—the voice of the soul—and in doing so forgot the language of the soul—metaphor. They came to understand their struggles with food as literal rather than symbolic, their hungers as physical rather than spiritual. Some made repeated attempts to fill their spiritual and emotional emptiness with comfort food. Others began restricting or purging, for fear that if they began to attempt to feed the hunger they would never be able to stop. Unable to recognize and respond to their "soul hunger," they became filled with confusion, terror, and despair as they realized no amount of food could satisfy their immense hunger. The disordered eating that arrived as a solution became its opposite, prohibiting these women from truly living the lives they desired.

As women struggling to break free from disordered eating are affirmed within the therapeutic relationship and find it safe and desirable to embrace and apply their natural gifts to their lives, they may begin to give active story to the unlived life—to bring the previously forbidden aspects of themselves into their active life stories. Freedman and Combs (1996) refer to this as clients "unpacking" themselves: letting out emotions, talents, ideas, goals, and dreams that had been stuffed down and disallowed. The parts of them that have been silenced will begin to speak, and they will set themselves free.

UTILIZING THE LANGUAGE OF METAPHOR WITHIN THE THERAPEUTIC SETTING

If we listen carefully to the story the client tells us, with an ear for the invisible/symbolic message that is contained within her struggle with food, fat, and body image, we can understand that this struggle holds deep meaning for her and is serving an important function. Use of the metaphoric language of imagery and storytelling can help ferret out what those needs are. The following is an example of how we can use metaphor and imagery in a therapeutic setting:

Imagine yourself standing in the rain on the bank of a raging river. Suddenly, the water-swollen bank gives way. You fall in and find yourself being tossed around and pulled under by the rapids. Your efforts to keep afloat are futile. You are drowning. By chance, along comes a huge log and you grab it and hold on tight. The log keeps your head above water and saves your life. Clinging to the log, you are swept downstream and eventually come to a place where the water is calm. There in the distance, you see the riverbank and want to swim to shore. You are unable to do so, however, because you are still clinging to the huge log with one arm as you stroke with the other. How ironic. The very thing that saved your life is now getting in the way of your getting where you want to go. People on shore who see you struggle are yelling, "Let go of the log!" You feel like a fool for being unable to let go.

Deep down you know you do not have the strength and confidence to make it to shore, so immediately abandoning the log may not be the very best thing to do. Instead, very slowly and carefully, you let go of the log and practice floating. When you start to sink, you grab hold again. Then you let go of the log and practice treading water, and when you get tired, hold on once again. After a while, you practice swimming around the log once, twice, ten times, twenty times, a hundred times, until you gain the strength and confidence you need to swim to shore. Only then do you completely let go of the log (Johnston, 1996).

The clients can then begin to imagine their eating disorders as something that helped to keep them afloat during emotionally difficult or chaotic times when they had no other available resources. They can appreciate how it came to be what Bulik and Kendler (2000) call "an integral part of the identity; a central integrating factor of his or her sense of self" (p. 1755). Through this metaphorical revisioning and retelling of their "eating disorder story," they can begin to release some of the shame associated with the behavior. In addition, they can get a glimpse of the therapeutic process as one wherein they can gradually develop alternative coping mechanisms to replace the disordered eating.

Case Example: Melanie

Melanie, who struggled with disordered eating for seven years, began her recovery process in traditional clinical and hospital settings. She found them to be lacking the spiritual dimension of healing and self-discovery and, therefore, to be what she calls "surface treatments." Melanie and her therapist now incorporate imagery and story into their sessions. Melanie states:

> The disordered eating once controlled everything. I thought of myself as my body. Because I thought my body was all that defined me, I used the disordered eating to try to get my body how I thought it was supposed to be, thinking this would make me how I wanted to be.
>
> Now, my therapist and I watch movies together every week. As we watch the films, we discuss the characters (which ones we resonate with, which ones remind us of parts of ourselves), the themes, the stories, the symbols. It helps me to see the characters and themes that are playing in my life. I am starting to enjoy investigating and expressing them. This continuous exercise helps me to see my life as kind of like a movie, and myself as the director.
>
> The more I see myself as a spiritual entity directing the story of this life for learning and growth, the less attractive and useful the harmful manipulation of my body seems. When I think back to the time when all I knew of me was my body, it seems absent of meaning—a meaning that I now cannot imagine living without.
>
> Anorexia was the most difficult thing I have ever gone through, but it made me who I am today. I wouldn't have it any other way.

Meaningful stories have heroes and villains, challenges and triumphs, highs and lows, ascents and descents. Without one there could not be the other. As Melanie discovered the role her struggle with disordered eating played in her life story, she was able to see it as a way to learn more about herself. By viewing the struggle with disordered eating as an important part of her personal story, it could cease to be a source of regret or shame or evidence that something was wrong with her. Instead, it could become a valued source of newfound strength, an opportunity to grow and learn more than she had ever imagined possible. Her terrifying and difficult journey into the dark valley could become a rich tale of victory.

As the client becomes more proficient with the language of metaphor, she and her therapist can engage in the process of translating the original, literal interpretation of her struggle with food, eating, and her body, rather than simply attempting to eliminate it. She can begin to recognize it as a symbolic message from her deeper self and eventually come to understand it from the transpersonal, Jungian perspective, as "a message that has a purpose for our mental health and [can] teach us something if we are willing to experience it. We do not cure it, it cures us" (Gilliland and James, 1998, p. 82).

RECONNECTING

The body protects us and guides us. Its symptoms are the sign-posts that reconnect us to our own lost soul.

(Woodman and Sharp, 1993, p. 21)

The gateways through which the soul's influence can flow into life are the five senses of the body and the emotions and thoughts of the personality. When one becomes overidentified with one's body, emotions, or thoughts, the connection to soul becomes blocked and awareness of one's greater self is lost. Life becomes empty, superficial, and limited. A deeper hunger for a life that is rich, meaningful, and fulfilling can show up as disordered eating.

In the following sections, we offer practical ideas and imagery to encourage clients to expand their self-images to include the soul—to see themselves as greater than the functions of their bodies or expressions of their personalities. As they recognize their bodies, thoughts, and feelings as portals to their souls and not all of who they are, deeper meaning can take shape in their lives, new stories about who they are can unfold, and the function of their disordered eating can reveal itself. As they use the needs of their bodies, hearts, and minds to bring them into alignment with the needs of their souls, they can receive true nourishment and the need for disordered eating can diminish.

Body

Women and girls who struggle with disordered eating are at war with their bodies. They believe their bodies have betrayed them, and they perceive their appetites as enemies ready to ambush them at every turn. Their minds engage in a battle plan to "outwit" and override physical hunger signals, and their emotions rise in fury if they are caught "off guard" when the body retaliates and "overeats." They swear to undo the damage done, to gain the upper hand, or to punish via further food restriction, dieting, purging, or excessive exercise. This hopeless war ceases as clients develop identification with the aspect of themselves that is greater than thoughts, emotions, and body; they strengthen their awareness of their essential selves and become more fully present. A step toward this objective is to become a witness to the body and its functions.

In working with the physical body, clients are encouraged to develop proprioceptive awareness: learning and responding appropriately to the body's signals of hunger and satiety. "Soul hunger" has been confused with physical hunger. The more clients become aware of the physical sensations that accompany physical hunger and fullness, the more they will know when the hungers of the soul are being mistaken as hungers of the body.

Using the metaphor of two tanks, Tank A and Tank B, can help clients begin to distinguish between the hungers of the body and the hungers of the soul. Tank A is the tank to fill with food, sleep, massage, etc,. when physical nourishment is needed. Tank B is to be filled with attention, appreciation, relationship, quiet time in nature, acknowledgment, meditation, prayer, etc., when emotional or spiritual nourishment is needed. No amount of food can fill Tank B. No amount of attention, affection, or quiet time will ever fill Tank A.

When the signals from these two tanks become crossed, we may eat or want to eat when we are not physically hungry, continue to eat after we are physically full, or fear our seemingly insatiable appetites. In order to distinguish between the two tanks, we begin by learning physical hunger and satiety cues. With this skill comes the ability to rule out the physical need for food when a hunger arises. If physical hunger is not present, one can be sure the hunger signal is coming from Tank B, and then take appropriate steps to obtain emotional or spiritual nourishment.

When clients are encouraged to listen to their bodies with the "inner ear" of their souls, they can begin to value the wisdom of the body. As they learn the language of metaphor, they are able to hear their bodies with increasing accuracy and build trusting relationships with their bodies.

Heart

Many girls and women who struggle with disordered eating also struggle with recognizing, accepting, expressing, and managing their emotions. They are often afraid that if they allow themselves to fully experience their anger, they will become *angry individuals*; if they dare to feel loneliness, they will become *lonely forever*; and if they experience sadness, it will *never leave them*. Envisioning feelings as fluid waves of energy that flow through all of humanity can help these clients come to view their feelings as natural, ever-changing aspects of who they are, not the sum total of who they are. If they can see their emotions as having a course as natural as the waves in the ocean that cyclically come in, peak, and pass, they can come to understand feelings as a natural force that flows freely through us and can actually help to raise our self-awareness. If emotions are blocked they may cause increased tension and eventually emerge in a disturbing manner. As women come to understand that feelings are neither "good" nor "bad," "right" nor "wrong." Although it is not possible for people to control their feelings, it is possible to work with them by altering the perceptions about emotions and how they are expressed.

Part of gaining freedom from disordered eating is developing an ability to work with feelings: to identify, accept, and express feelings so they can flow freely. This can be frightening in the beginning because many women with disordered eating issues have repressed or denied their uncomfortable emotions for many years. When they begin to allow for emotional expression, the potency of the experience can seem overwhelming, similar to a dammed river suddenly allowed to flow unobstructed. It is important that clients are assured that while this initial stage may be intense, it will gradually become more manageable as they become more skillful in their expression.

Emotional work naturally follows the development of proprioceptive awareness. As clients learn their hunger and satiety cues, it becomes easier for them to recognize emotional eating. If they note the absence of physical hunger in the face of food cravings or fears, they can examine Tank B and ask themselves, "What am I really hungry for?" If they are not able to answer that question, viewing their food phobias or cravings as metaphors can give them clues as to their deeper emotional or spiritual hungers. For example, sweet foods can represent a craving for more sweetness in one's life or a desire to be "sweeter," while crunchy, salty foods often express anger and frustration. Warm foods can indicate a longing for emotional warmth, spicy foods may represent a need for more stimulation or excitement, and, for many women, chocolate is symbolic of sex and romance (Johnston, 1996).

When women begin to identify, accept, and express their feelings—flow with them rather than fight them—they can understand that emotions have the potential energy to carry them to their innermost truths, to their greatest desires of the heart, to their deepest hungers. Through feelings, the soul comes to life.

Mind

Many spiritual traditions propose that the mind is a wonderful servant but a terrible master. In contrast to this ancient wisdom, we live in a culture that encourages us to overidentify with and overvalue our mental thought processes. Like most of us, many women who struggle with disordered eating have not been encouraged to examine and question the thoughts or stories about who they are that are told to them throughout their lives by family members, peers, authority figures and, perhaps most important, by themselves. The internal stories told by themselves, even if first told by someone else, solidify as they are retold in the mind. A belief is actually manufactured. This manufacturing, the meaning ascribed to what other people said, may cause more trauma than the original event. The original event remains in the past while the story remains current. These stories and thoughts, regardless of accuracy, truth, or their lack thereof, become real in the mind and continually contribute to the formation of a self-image that includes and is sometimes founded upon self-destructive thoughts The mind can create belief systems that stand in direct contradiction to a healthy view of the self. Consequently, many beliefs (I am too fat; I am ugly; I am not good enough) remain entrenched in the identities of many women and stand as a substantial challenge in the recovery process.

To engage the mind as a tool for uncovering the mystery of disordered eating, one must assume a position of *not-knowing*. This evokes curiosity rather than judgment. In approaching a "who-dunit" murder mystery, for example, if one automatically assumes the maid is the culprit because she has been behaving in a peculiar, disorderly manner, one may overlook the butler who actually committed the crime, not recognizing the maid as simply a red herring. With eating disorders, issues regarding food and fat are often red herrings, distracting us from the real culprits—misguided thoughts about who we are, those false interpretations given to the events of our lives, the untrue stories told about who we are.

A client, for example, may notice that thoughts about her mother can trigger a binge. Further investigation reveals that because her mother scolded her frequently as a small child, she came to believe that she was never good enough to get the nurturing she desired. Because of this story, whenever she felt needy she believed she needed to grasp at any form of nurture she could get, even if it was physical rather than emotional food. If this story (which she created with the mind of a small child who could not imagine any other reason for her mother's criticism) remains unexamined with her current, more developed, adult thought processes, it continues to be a large part of her identity and her mind will continue to collect evidence to substantiate it. If, however, the client can witness her thoughts and question the meaning she ascribed to her mother's behavior, she may realize many other possible reasons for her mother's constant criticisms besides her not being "good enough." She can then realize that her mother's past behavior does not cause the bingeing, but the current story she continues to tell herself about what that meant holds the power. Freedom from the disordered eating comes when she realizes that although she cannot change her past, she can change the story she tells herself about it. She can change her present experience of her past.

Many women and girls report having "fat attacks," where they suddenly feel twenty pounds fatter overnight. Even though they *logically* understand gaining twenty pounds overnight is not possible, they believe it to be so. Trying to block, argue with, or let go of their thoughts usually results only in further obsessions about food and fat and body parts. By learning to step back and observe the thoughts, they can then say to themselves, "Oh, look where my thoughts are going," then question, "What's that about?" or then ask, "What is the feeling I am trying not to feel?" Once clients have fully learned to be in witness, the thoughts can let go of them.

The journey toward recovery begins with the recognition that "fat attacks" or urges to binge are messages from a greater part of the self, and these messages are very creatively designed to gain attention. If these thoughts are taken too literally, however, the deeper meaning of this communication will be lost. As clients begin to use their mental processes as tools to get to their innermost truth, rather than automatically believing whatever thoughts or stories come into their minds, they can then begin to respond to these experiences much the way they might respond to the red light that goes on in their cars to let them know they are running low on fuel. They can recognize that their higher selves are trying to send them messages, albeit in symbolic language, that something needs to be attended to, that they are veering off course, or that their souls are in need of nourishment.

CONCLUSION: REMEMBERING THE SPIRIT

When a baby elephant is captured and taken to the circus, it is attached to a large tree with a strong rope. The baby elephant, with its instincts fresh and strong, struggles with all its might against the restraint of the rope. It struggles until it cannot physically continue. It struggles so hard that it would break a small rope, or even a small tree. But only a small rope and tree are needed to restrain an adult elephant, for the adult, being captive for so long, has lost contact with its inherent nature of freedom. (Amritanandamayi Devi, 2003, p. 4)

Disordered eating is similar to the rope that ties the elephant to the tree. It ties women to a limited view of themselves. However, their inherently intuitive nature and their ability to find meaning in and use struggle to their advantage are not lost. The journey to wellness can take one deep into the instincts, emotions, and thoughts as a participant as well as witness. As the process completes itself, the needs of the body, mind, and heart come into alignment with the yearnings of the soul. The disordered eating arrives in the lives of these women as a redirecting metaphor to help them find their way onto the path that feeds the soul's purpose. In that light, every time an urge to engage in disordered eating behavior arises, it can be experienced by these women as an alarm clock, awakening them to the hungers of the soul.

The psychospiritual perspective creates the potential for disordered eating to be a breakthrough, instead of a breakdown. It sees the crisis as having spiritual significance, as an opportunity for growth. When clients are invited to move through their struggles toward what they may become, they are no longer limited by a diagnosis. They may become a heroine waiting for the call to adventure, or a magician ready to cast a spell, or a leader ready to emerge and come into power.

Carl Jung (1989) said, "The Gods visit us through illness" (p. 297). We meet those parts of ourselves which cannot be met any other way. Mijares (2003) states:

> In many native cultures, a symptom of psychospiritual distur-
> bance is perceived as an indication that something greater is
> about to occur in the individual's life. Illness or psychic distress
> is a sign that some challenge needs to be met, or an ordeal under-
> taken. It is, simply put, a wake up call announcing that there is
> something more to attend to than the mundane circumstances in
> one's life. (p. 5)

Disordered eating can be seen as an intense preparation for the rest of one's life. Some people are fortunate enough to come to a crisis in order to ignite forces within them that they had previously not ac-knowledged.

As the hungers of the soul are attended to through the body and the thoughts and feelings of the personality, the spirit is remembered, and the life comes into harmony with the soul. As therapists, we are sometimes privileged enough to have the opportunity to observe, guide, marvel at, and play our small but important part in this healing process. Along the way, a sacred reconnection can be made. The rope can be severed, the basket opened, the log released. The soul's nature can be revealed.

APPENDIX

An obvious need exists for clinics that specialize in the treatment of women struggling with disordered eating integrate psychospiritual paradigms of healing. Following is a description of two such clinics.

Anita Johnston's 'Ai Pono Intensive Eating Disorder Clinics in Honolulu and Maui utilize myth, storytelling, and symbolism when working with clients. Her philosophy and methods used in the clinic are further illuminated in Dr. Johnston's book, *Eating in the Light of the Moon*. The clinic incorporates concepts of soul work and the sacred feminine into the treatment process. Clients are encouraged to develop life skills for tending the body, heart, mind, and soul as a means of healing their food and body image issues.

Carolyn Costin's residential treatment facility, *Monte Nido,* in Malibu treats severe cases of eating disorders. In addition to traditional treatment approaches, they use meditation, yoga, body/soul work (reconnecting the body and soul), and herbs, vitamins, minerals, and amino acids.

Another example of an integrative model for treating eating disorders is the *Healthy Within Clinic* in San Diego. This clinic was established by Dr. Divya Kakaiya who utilizes yoga, acupuncture, and principles of mindfulness in treating women and girls struggling with food issues. These holistic modalities have been found to be helpful in relieving stress and migraines, reducing carbohydrate cravings and edema, creating a gentle partnership with the body, and shifting the focus off of calorie burning and on to total health. Dr. Kakaiya has found that acupuncture has been helpful in preventing relapse (particularly with bulimia). The goal of the clinic is one of total health, including mind, spirit, and body.

No doubt, many more positive approaches for working with eating disorders are available—the authors encourage readers to investigate what is offered in their areas.

REFERENCES

Amritanandamayi Devi, M. (2003). *Immortal bliss.* San Ramon, CA: Mata Amritanandamayi Center.

Bulik, C. and Kendler, K. (2000). "I am what I don't eat": Establishing an identity independent of an eating disorder [Electronic version]. *American Journal of Psychiatry,* 157, 1755-1760.

Christ, C.P. and Plaskow, J. (Eds.) (1979). *Womanspirit rising: A feminist reader in religion.* New York: HarperCollins.

Fallon, P. and Wonderlich, S. (1997). Sexual abuse and other forms of trauma. In D.M. Garner and P.E. Garfinkel (Eds.), *Handbook of treatment for eating disorders* (Second edition) (pp. 394-414). New York: The Guilford Press.

Freedman, J. and Combs, G. (1996). *Narrative therapy: The social construction of preferred realities.* New York: W.W. Norton.

Garfinkel, P.E. and Walsh, B.T. (1997). Drug therapies. In D.M. Garner and P.E. Garfinkel (Eds.), *Handbook of treatment for eating disorders* (Second edition) (pp. 372-382). New York: The Guilford Press.

Gilliland, B. and James, R. (1998). *Theories and strategies in counseling and psychotherapy* (Fourth edition). Needham Heights, MA: Allyn and Bacon.

Glasser, W. (2000). *Counseling with choice theory.* New York: HarperCollins Publishers.

Johnston, A. (1996). *Eating in the Light of the Moon: How Women Can Transform Their Relationships Through Myths, Metaphors, and Storytelling.* Carlsbad, CA: Gurze Books.

Jung, C. G. (1989). *Memories, dreams, reflections.* New York: Vintage Books.

McCrady, B. (2001). Alcohol use disorders. In D.H. Barlow (Ed.), *Clinical handbook of psychological disorders* (Third edition) (pp. 376-433). New York: The Guilford Press.

Meaney, J. W. (Director/Photographer) and Berger, M. (Editor) (1957). *Jung on Film* [motion picture]. Zurich, Switzerland: Public Media Video.

Mijares, S. (2003). *Modern psychology and ancient wisdom: Psychological healing practices from the world's religious traditions.* Binghamton, NY: Haworth Integrative Healing Press.

Simms, L. (1991). *Women & Wild Animals.* Minocqua, WI: North Word Audio Press.

Streigel-Moore, R. and Cachelin, F. (2001). Etiology of eating disorders in women. *The Counseling Psychologist, 29,* 635-661.

Wilson, G., Fairburn, C., and Agras, W. (1997). Cognitive-behavioral therapy for bulimia nervosa. In D.M. Garner and P.E. Garfinkel (Eds.), *Handbook of treatment for eating disorders* (Second edition) (pp. 67-93). New York: The Guilford Press.

Woodman, M. and Sharp, D. (1993). *Conscious femininity: Interviews with Marion Woodman.* Toronto: Inner City Books.

Chapter 6

Getting Focused in an Age of Distraction: Approaches to Attentional Disorders Using the Humanology of Yogi Bhajan

Gurucharan Singh Khalsa

Any therapy that cannot create self-esteem is a failure. You may help a person to any point, but it is the self-esteem and the personal energy from that self-esteem that makes someone practice the disciplines needed to break through the deficiencies to the efficiency, regardless of what their environments are.

Yogi Bhajan, 1986, p. 4

We live in an age of distraction. Getting and keeping a focus on what is important, meaningful, and effective is a challenge. Perhaps it should not be surprising that disorders of attention and impulse such as attention deficit disorder (ADD) and attention deficit hyperactivity disorder (ADHD) have gained such prominence in both the professional and public arenas. Without the ability to voluntarily focus attention, our rapidly changing, high-density information environment can grab that attention and scatter it along a hundred mental and emotional pathways. Left untreated, these disorders often result in significant dysfunctions. ADHD is associated with short-term memory impairment, pervasive disorganization, and a trail of unfulfilled dreams and ambitions. Other features of the ADHD pattern include depressed or anxious moods, poor decisions, and lowered self-esteem. Social relationships suffer from a lack of intimacy or stability.

All of this can coexist with brilliant talents, a high IQ, and great status and responsibility. Unruly attention mixed with impulsiveness forms an emotional maelstrom of hope and frustration, brilliance and foolishness, fuzzy goals and impulsive efforts. Although the focus of the standard treatment approach is an expanding array of stimulant and neurotransmitter drugs combined with multimodal counseling and supports for organizational skills, effective complementary approaches are available that use the psychospiritual techniques in Humanology—the applied psychology of Kundalini yoga and meditation founded by Yogi Bhajan (Bhajan and Khalsa, 1998). This alternative leads to a stronger sense of self, enhanced self-efficacy, and a refined ability to direct one's attention and awareness.

A GROWING NEED—PREVALENCE AND CHANGING DIAGNOSIS

The prevalence of ADHD/ADD is estimated to be 5 to 7 percent of school-age children in the United States and has been shown to persist into adolescence for up to 80 percent of those diagnosed earlier and into adulthood for at least 50 percent of cases (American Psychiatric Association, 2000; Barkley, 1998; Weiss and Murray, 2003). Symptoms in those with hyperactivity and impulsiveness seem less prominent in adulthood but this may be due to successful coping mechanisms and socialization. Males are diagnosed three to nine times more frequently than females, although this may move toward equality in adults as the hyperactivity lessens and the attentional symptoms dominate (Weiss and Murray, 2003).

For many years the focus of ADD concern, research, and diagnosis was on young male children who demonstrated disruptive behavior, poor performance, and socialization and learning problems. Within the past decade studies have extended to adult populations. At first there were protestations that it does not exist, that it goes away after childhood, or that the symptoms were purely the result of stress and societal factors. It is now firmly established that the disorder adversely affects a significant group of adults (Faraone, 2000; Faraone et al., 2000).

Recent research is extending to women (Hinshaw, 2002; Hinshaw et al., 2002; Rucklidge and Kaplan, 2000), documenting the characteristic ways attentional disorders appear in children and adults, and establishing normative data comparing women to women instead of to men. In women ADHD is often missed when they are young and emerges as a concern only as they encounter job problems, deal with the same syndrome in their children, or suffer under depression and low self-esteem from frustrated accomplishments. They often present with patterns of learned helplessness, a sense of being overwhelmed, and with relentless self-blame for any problem. They are mired in time- and money-management difficulties and may even show symptoms reflecting PTSD from repeated social traumas in the classroom and beyond (Adelizzi and Goss, 2001). The results of these studies suggest potential widespread underdiagnosis of ADD in women because of a normative bias that came from describing the effects of the syndrome almost exclusively in terms of young males.

Public and professional awareness of ADHD's impact on learning and social skills in children and its continued effects through adulthood have made ADHD and related attentional syndromes one of the more widely studied childhood disorders by professionals from school counselors to psychiatrists (DuPaul, 2003). Along with this has come recognition that, even though genetic and neural mechanisms are clearly involved, the symptoms exist on a multidimensional scale. One can have it a bit or a lot. It can persist as a central issue or a peripheral one that sporadically flavors all the rest. John Ratey (1997) aptly calls this spectrum of symptom intensities "shadow syndromes."

Shadow syndromes refer to a subsyndromal set of behaviors that fits only part of the DSM syndrome or consists of characteristics from several different syndromes. This speaks to all those people who need help but are the "walking wounded," doing well enough to function with excellence in some areas and disastrously in others. This patchwork collection of behaviors speaks to both our individuality, biologically and spiritually, and to the nature of the attentional syndromes.

If we include these shadow syndromes, though they would miss the full categorization of the DSM, a large percentage of "normals" would be included, and that percentage seems to be rising.

The DSM guidelines are just that—guidelines. As symptom-oriented guidelines, they helped establish a more effective conversation among therapists by avoiding conflicting and often irresolvable theoretical orientations in the absence of clear etiology and measures for many syndromes. Practitioners are well aware that the DSM does not cut the problems at its causal joints; 20 to 50 percent of patients do not fulfill all the needed checklists for a syndrome, even when they clearly have it. They are included in a general no-man's land called "not otherwise specified" (NOS). The average patient who fits a personality disorder also fits six to ten of the other categories (Helmuth, 2003). So it is best to remember that syndromes are verbs not nouns. They exist only in context, in an individual, in interaction, relative to purposive living and moderated by the consciousness and other resilient capabilities of that individual.

Given all this, we must be careful when assessing a child or adult for this syndrome. Difficulties with attention can arise from many sources and not be the central feature of the problem. Many other disorders often co-occur with ADHD, such as conduct disorder, bipolar disorder, depression, oppositional defiant disorder (50 percent), substance abuse, learning disorders, Tourette's syndrome, anxiety, psychotic disorder, and retardation (Murphy and Barkley, 1996).

The best approach is to use a multisource and multi-instrument assessment that includes a thorough interview with the client, parents, spouse, caretakers, and teachers as appropriate. For complete certainty the best approach is direct observation of a child in multiple settings, rating scales for behavior from multiple sources, and a history that reflects behavior over time (Anastopoulos and Shelton, 2001). Equal concern has been raised about underdiagnosis, as with women and adults, and overdiagnosis, mistaking normal developmental opposition and learning, annoying as it can be, as a signature of these disorders (Marshall, 2000).

The core characteristics needed to match the DSM-IV-TR category for ADHD are to show "a persistent pattern of inattention and/or hyperactivity-impulsivity that is more frequently displayed and more severe than is typically observed in individuals at a comparable level of development" (APA, 2000, p. 85).* This should be apparent before age seven, show significant impairment in at least two separate contexts for at least six months, and not occur exclusively as the normal course of another mental disorder. A nine-point checklist is used for inattention and for hyperactivity, of which at least six points are needed for a diagnosis. The manual recognizes three main diagnostic subtypes of ADHD: one with inattention as primary, one with impulsivity as primary, and one with mixed features.

For individuals diagnosed with the full ADHD symptoms, their lives show the results in a wide range of well-documented problems: higher levels of both anxiety and depression (20 to 30 percent), more frequent and serious driving accidents and violations, higher use of drugs and smoking, and poorer health (Barkley et al., 2002). Adults show more job changes and difficulties (70 percent), unstable or isolating relationship styles (50 to 70 percent) (Friedman et al., 2003), and disorganized finances, projects, and home environments. They leave a consistent record of missed appointments, forgotten priorities, and risky behaviors they seek as sources of stimulation. They have higher divorce rates, lower levels of completed education, and more accidents (Young, Toone, and Tyson, 2003). It is a significant problem for the individuals, their families, and for society, yet fewer than half receive any kind of help or treatment.

ETIOLOGY

As the number of people being diagnosed with ADHD vaults to new heights, the pressure is on for researchers to explain the origins of the problem and to guide new approaches to treatment. Is it bad genes, neuronal malfunction, traumatic environments, or toxic insults to the body? The good news is in the many new discoveries and new research tools. The bad news is we do not have a solid answer yet. We do have a well-developed framework to guide ongoing research on etiology. The research paints a complex picture with three key components that create and maintain the syndromes.

---

*Reprinted with permission from the *Diagnostic and Statistical Manual of Mental Disorders,* Fourth Edition, Text Revision, Copyright 2000, American Psychiatric Association.

The first component is the ADHD brain. The ADHD brain is distinctly different from the brains of those who do not have the disorder. Various brain imaging techniques, such as computerized tomography (CT), positron-emission tomography (PET), magnetic resonance imaging (MRI), and Single Photon Emission Computerized Tomography (SPECT), allow us to see how brain function and structure is altered in ADHD. Results on both men and women show similar areas of the brain are involved. ADHD affects the prefrontal cortex, which is a key to our capacity to inhibit unwanted impulses and thoughts. It shows diminished function in the right orbital prefrontal cortex. The amygdaloidal complex that mediates impulsiveness and anxiety is more active. In SPECT studies the actual metabolic activity of the brain can be traced. When someone with an ADHD brain tries to concentrate, the activity of the prefrontal cortex in the right hemisphere decreases. This is just the opposite of what happens in the non-ADHD brain.

When Ritalin is given as a stimulant drug, the ADHD brain increases its prefrontal activity—just the opposite of the normal control brain. These functional differences are some of the most consistent findings. Structural differences in the size of the right frontal lobe, corpus callosum, right caudate, and putamen are found inconsistently and are at best small (Rubia, 2002). It is unclear whether the brain irregularities reflect a causative trait for ADHA or whether they reflect the operating physiological state when ADHD functions are active. The areas that are affected suggest abnormalities in the regulation of dopamine and serotonin levels.

ADHD can develop in many recognizable subtypes and variations. Four areas of the brain are affected differently in each of the subtypes.

1. Diminished prefrontal cortex activity corresponding to disinhibited impulses and thoughts
2. The overactive anterior cingulate gyrus that mirrors the capacity for sporadic episodes of hyperfocus
3. The activity in the temporal lobe areas that occurs with volatile moods and temper
4. The overactive limbic areas, especially the hypothalamus, that can induce lowered energy and motivation

These areas and others can act together in various combinations to produce the many types of ADHD behaviors that we see clinically

(Amen, 2001; Aman, Roberts, and Pennington, 1998). Ideally, these studies will allow us to identify the particular type a person has and choose an appropriate strategy for treatment. Much is yet to be learned in this rapidly growing area of research.

The second component of the etiology of ADHD is the genome. ADHD has the most heritability, between 70 and 90 percent, of any mental disorder. This fact has led to the first whole-genome scans to identify the specific genes that may be involved (Fisher et al., 2002; Bakker et al., 2003). The first papers to report on this discovery identified genes on chromosomes 5, 6, 7, 15, 16, and 17.

They also found no support for a major cause of ADHD from a single gene. Instead, "the high heritability of ADHD is probably accounted for by multiple loci with small-to-moderate effect sizes" (Fisher, 2002, p. 1188). This means each gene may contribute 1 to 3 percent risk of developing the syndrome. Researchers are still searching for genes that could give a 10 percent or higher effect. It also suggests that many shadow syndrome variants can exist from the many possible gene combinations. The genes involved are known to produce proteins that release neurotransmitters that affect the dopamine system. The genes overlap significantly with the genes for autism and dyslexia, which implies a common fault that diminishes the brain's executive decision, planning, and inhibitory functions.

This leads us to a third component of the ADHD puzzle: the environment. The environment can trigger genetic expression and development. It is now possible to show the exact pathway a stressor follows to turn on the expression of a single gene. In other words, the environment is in a dynamic relationship with the genes. The outer environments can shape the terrain of the local cellular environment, which can in turn change the gene regulators and other mechanisms that express the proteins that direct our metabolism. This is an amazing step forward for the field of epigenetics. Some clinicians are so optimistic that they imagine a new version of the DSM based on causal webs linking brain function, genetic expression, and environment to symptomatic behaviors. Environmental factors are significant contributors to the development of ADHD. Lifestyle factors, from maternal smoking during pregnancy to chronic family conflict, contribute to ADHD. Nutritional supports to physical activity can be used to positively shape the intricate matrix of the nervous system, hormones, cellular messengers, and genetic expression. These lifestyle practices can moderate the development and expression of attentional syndromes. We still have much to learn about the relative significance and specific effects of each factor.

TREATMENT APPROACHES WITH HUMANOLOGY

The core of the Humanological treatment approach to ADHD and attentional syndromes is to give individuals techniques to awaken a strong sense of their consciousness as a primary reality within themselves. Through these experiences they can begin to harness the power of their minds and thoughts, enhance their innate capacity for resilience under challenge, and choose effective habits that integrate body, mind, and spirit. This approach uses innate strengths. Humanology focuses on the person, the primacy of consciousness and spirit, and understanding each symptom in the context of the person's purpose, social interactions, and physical, mental, and emotional habits. A successful treatment not only reduces symptoms but also strengthens the ability of individuals to make voluntary choices about their feelings, thoughts, and actions. It builds their caliber and character to act effectively under challenge. It gradually develops the facility to identify and apply the neutral mind and intuition. The therapeutic process establishes a relationship between the individuals and their minds. They can successfully choose to act from their awareness, not from reactions to internal and external circumstances.

A practitioner uses a carefully tailored combination of Kundalini yoga and meditation, humanological dialogue, and positive lifestyle choices for each client. The client is guided to experience and use the power of the mind to balance the entire mind/body complex as a unified process. We work equally through the body with exercise and through the mind with meditation. Ideally the person learns to act consciously in the present moment to create his or her future, not out of reactions determined by the past, the environment, mental impulses, or our genes. This capacity develops as the consciousness establishes a disciplined and refined relationship to the mind.

In over thirty years of teaching, Yogi Bhajan, the founder of Humanology, has explained literally thousands of specific Kundalini meditations and exercises. He demonstrated how these can be used to balance the many facets, aspects, and projections of the mind and improve the health of the body. The techniques can develop the subtle levels of chakras and meridians as well as balance the actions of nerves, hormones, and the immune system. Equally, many techniques enhance effectiveness of the therapist's faculty for conscious communication and for the ability to release and resolve the subtle energies in the client's mind and body.

At a conference on Humanology for psychologists in Italy, Yogi Bhajan stated the goal of the approach this way:

> Kundalini Yoga and Humanology is not theory, but a practical way to balance our life against an unbalanced world and is a systematic way to get rid of our weaknesses and follow the path of strength. It's a wonderful science and it has stood practically thousands of years. It's as good as it was, is and shall be. I welcome you to the land of yogis where mind is creative, balanced, tolerance is infinite, and compassion is always illuminated like that of the star of God. Where lotuses shine like stars in the space where everything is nothing but divine. I'm talking of the man so united, so together, where angels take privilege to serve, Mother Nature takes the privilege to bless and divine God follows your path through to completion. That is the wonderful and exalted story of man, when he creates the balanced union between the brain hemispheres and his lotuses so he has his temperament and his physical, mental and spiritual capacities merged in such a sweet balance that all is attracted to it. That is the concept of a healthy, happy and bountiful holy man or a woman. When this state of mind and consciousness is established practically through developing the applied mind, even needs come to have the privilege to serve him or her and struggle and hassle in such a life is story of the past. (Bhajan, 1986, pp. 25-26)

He enjoins us to evoke what is uniquely human in our approach to therapy and to rely on the innate strengths that come from consciousness, conscious consciousness, choice, and the spirit:

> A human being has absolutely nothing in its nature that forces it to react. . . . Our human capacity is to take in the whole environment, then act accordingly, consciously, intentionally. We

have the sensitivity for spontaneous assessment and the caliber to act according to that assessment. Many unnecessary pains, unhappiness and diseases come from the tremendous mental stress caused by the urge to react unconsciously. . . .

A human being is fundamentally a social animal. . . . [To treat a person,] first understand the environments . . . then in the light of that information, identify and include the physical, mental and emotional temperament of the person. . . . What suffers is the human being plus the environments that provide nurturing, nourishment, identity and his future orientation—his hope. All this is in danger and suffers. . . .

Integrate all this into a diagnostic overview. . . . The resulting approach will be creative, helpful, understood and will give the person some immediate relief as you help them [with therapeutic exercise, meditation, food, lifestyle and dialogue]. (Bhajan, 1986, p. 3)

This approach for ADHD creates environmental supports for goal-oriented organizing and coping as do other effective programs. Kundalini yoga exercise and meditation and healing foods are used extensively. These techniques are pathways that reshape the nervous system (Peng et al., 2003). The nervous system is highly neuroplastic and responds almost immediately with growth and learning to rhythmical patterns and stimulation (Schwartz and Begley, 2002). The use of sounds in some meditations interrupts the internal dialogues that reify anxious and depressive moods and disordered thinking. Repeating them also affects many of the central areas of the brain including the hypothalamus, striatal areas, cingulate gyrus, and amygdale cortex, all of which are involved in proper regulation of attention, impulsiveness, and executive functions (Lazar et al., 2000).

The client is trained to identify and redirect unintended thoughts that hijack attention using meditation techniques that direct the thoughts' sensory components. In counseling dialogues the many subpersonalities that are constantly created by the mind are integrated, eliminated, or aligned to transform shame, guilt, and other destructive emotions into constructive emotions. Primary caretakers or partners are included in recognizing and coping with ADHD behaviors and separating syndrome patterns from intentional insults or assaults.

Programs are designed for individuals according to the blend of symptoms, the qualities of their minds and temperament and their environments. The following two cases should demonstrate some of the unique exercises and approaches that are used. In these cases I emphasize the use of exercises and show how the programs using them are tailored to the individuals.

Case Example: Karen

When I met Karen she was seeking an alternative to dealing with her depression. She had been taking Wellbutrin for a number of years with some positive results, but she was suspicious of the long-term effects and did not like the idea of being drug dependent for the rest of her life. Karen was thirty-four, an active, energetic, and expressive person. She was the executive in charge of sales and marketing at a dynamic software company that had over 100 employees near a metropolitan area. Her feelings of depression were not constant and seemed to increase when job setbacks occurred and when she began a strong internal dialogue of self-criticism.

Her family physician had prescribed Wellbutrin without a psychological evaluation. Although it was prescribed for depression, it can also help ADHD by affecting serotonin and, indirectly, dopamine (Oades, 2002). However it coincidentally masked her real problem. Normally clinical depression will be more pervasive and enduring. Her body became animated and changed along with her interest in what she described. She did not show the graduated slowing of movements that often accompanies long-term depression. When she described the features of her company's software, she seemed to forget she was depressed as she engaged. She told me of her repeated failures in personal relationships. Her previous mates would complain that she did not seem present, or that she would talk only when she wanted and then wander on as if she was not listening. Her work relationships were a mixture of appreciation and disappointment. Appreciation came from her dedication and frequent insights. Her ability to identify a new market and take the risks to initiate a new approach to a sales campaign was legend in her office. Disappointment came from her equally mythic reputation for interrupting people in meetings, "taking over" with an idea she had, whether or not it was in line with the discussion, and missing deadlines for presentations. This combination of brilliance and brinkmanship led her colleagues to fool her by setting a strategic presentation three days earlier than actually needed and announcing a three-day "postponement" on the day she was scheduled. That way she was ready and so were they. Of course, that worked only once.

As a child she was often bored and restless and received extra tutoring to write legibly—much to her embarrassment and critical comments from her parents and friends. She had no history of drug use. She dealt with stress by immersing herself in online multiple-player games and by surfing the modest New England coastal waves spiced with spontaneous jaunts to the greater awe-inspiring and risky waves off of Costa Rica and Hawaii. She did this almost entirely alone where she could "escape the expectations and the letdowns. Where I can consume the waves and the waves consume me."

On rating scales she was strong and frequent on six items on fluctuating inattention and five items on impulsivity on the DSM-IV-TR criteria. All the symptoms were active over the previous six months and were clearly present in her childhood. She was certainly ADHD, although the hyperactive symptoms had diminished considerably as she aged, leaving only impulsive decisions and actions when she became frustrated or stimulated in conversations. I presented this to her. She had heard of ADD/ADHD but never applied it to herself, feeling that depression was the problem and that if she just overcame that she would be able to have more energy, act faster, and accomplish more. I explained the standard treatment approaches with methylphenidate and dextroamphetamine. I connected her to a psychiatrist/neuropharmacologist to advise her if she chose to taper off Wellbutrin or try the new drugs. In a flash she read several books on ADHD and treatment. She knew that symptoms could be reduced by 80 to 90 percent by the use of Ritalin, Adderall, or other drugs that had a range of only mild side effects if used properly.

However, she wanted something more. She said, with typical insight, "Maybe this is a challenge I can use. What happens if I take this on by my own efforts and counseling? Can I succeed? If I did I would feel better about myself and learn something about myself at the same time." I explained that it would mean a significant effort and that the same challenges for consistency will be there for any approach using exercise, meditation, and guided conversations between her and her mind. We agreed she would enlist an exercise coach to help her keep to her goal for three months. She was already an avid user of lists and Palm Pilots to help her remember things. When I asked to see her list, she had two Palm Pilots, one old, one new, and had not finished transferring the records yet. She had to go back and forth between them. I smiled. Truly ADD.

We engaged in a full program to help Karen learn tools to focus her mind, redirect her impulses, improve relationships, and learn what the challenge of ADHD can teach her about herself. Karen progressed rapidly over a period of six months. She kept that job for more than four years, established an ongoing relationship that became an engagement, and has no signs of depression. She no longer uses Wellbutrin or any stimulant drugs. She devotes an hour a day in the morning and fifteen minutes before bed to a regular exercise and meditation practice. More than that, to paraphrase her speaking to a public class, she had an

> awakening in myself. Before, I often felt guilty. I felt trapped in the moment. Now I am grateful for each moment. I trust myself and watch my

mind. When I need to be more present and look to the future I can do it—with effort, but I can do it. I learned to be still inside. I can feel my spirit and my heart. I relax. There is nothing more to do. For a doer getting to that nothing is doing a lot.

The Program

I pointed out that Karen already self-medicated with exercise, but she did not understand that she could get that self-medicated surfing effect in a fifteen- to forty-five-minute walk when properly done. In as little as ten minutes, exercise can significantly alter all the primary neurotransmitters in the brain that seem to be involved in ADHD with both disinhibition of impulse and distractions and a deficit of reward to inhibit distracting stimuli in preference for a specific goal. As a Harvard psychiatrist and specialist in ADHD summarizes,

> The three major neurotransmitters—norepinephrine, dopamine, and serotonin—that have preoccupied researchers concerned with mood, cognition, behavior, and personality are all increased by exercise. . . . Dopamine, the key neurotransmitter involved in the feelings of reward and motivation, and attention is increased in the intensive phase of exercise and in prolonged exercise . . . exercise increases . . . the abilities to handle stress and aggression and to become more attentive and social. (Ratey, 2001, p. 360)

We designed a program for Karen that had a strong exercise base, enhanced with specific meditations and supported with work on her internal conflicts. For the regular exercise program we used Breathwalk—a way of walking that combines conscious breathing patterns with mindful attention, preparatory triggering exercises, and the mental use of primal sound scales (consisting of specific phonemes). The Breathwalk techniques are fully described in the book *Breathwalk* (Bhajan and Khalsa, 2000; <breathwalk.com>). This form of exercise has the advantage of creating an immediate experiential change so practitioners stay motivated and keep using it on their own. It elevates mood very quickly as it simultaneously develops attentional skills. The more than twenty programs in Breathwalk lead to a wide variety of states. Some programs have the effect of focusing attention, whereas others relax attention. Some programs target anxiety; others lower depression. All give the general benefit of exercise plus immediate, tangible changes in direct perception: sharper visual and auditory perception, enhanced spatial and movement sensitivity, and a blend of arousal and relaxation. This immediate reward is especially useful to motivate ADHD clients and increase a sense of personal efficacy to easily change their own mental and emotional states.

Karen began with this Breathwalk program and mastered it in a short version, for twenty minutes, a long version, forty-five minutes, and a "booster" version of ten minutes. She Breathwalked each morning and used the short booster during the day when she felt it appropriate and needed to refocus or become more present. Over the course of treatment she mastered four other Breathwalk programs for quick energy and focus, for full sensory presence and joy, for increased rapport, and for breaking depression. I also had her create a journal for the changes she noticed in the Breathwalks. She recorded from multiple perspectives changes in her senses, impulses, flow of thoughts, sense of self-presence, and clarity of goals. She was able to track her ability to watch the thoughts and feelings of her mind without reacting. This was helpful when she developed a new narrative about herself in the therapeutic dialogues.

The Eagle Breathwalk Program*

Each Breathwalk program has five steps. Here are instructions for one of them.

Step 1: Awakener exercises. Each program begins with four or five specific exercises that target a combination of bodily systems, meridians, and chakras, and levels of arousal that enhance and align with the primary purpose of the particular breathing and meditation patterns. For this program the exercises are as follows:

> *Step 1-1:* Stand straight and breathe slowly, four times a minute or less, as you stay aware of each sensation of the breath and the thoughts and feelings that pass through the body.
> *Step 1-2:* Stand with arms out parallel to the ground, palms up, and breathe as before for three minutes.

Step 1-3: Stand with the arms over the head, palms together, elbows straight. Breathe as before for three minutes.

Step 1-4: Standing, inhale as the arms go out to the sides, wrists bent, fingers up. Exhale back to the center of the chest, palms together. Three minutes.

Step 1-5: Standing, cross hands over the heart center. Inhale as the head turns left, exhale as it turns right. Continue smoothly for two to three minutes.

Step 2: Align the body and mind by scanning each area of the body mentally, adjusting the walking form and becoming fully present.

Step 3: Vitality intervals. Begin to Breathwalk by inhaling through the nose in four equal distinct segments synchronized with the footsteps, one step for one inhaled segment. Exhale in four equal segments in the same manner. Focus the mind on primal sounds: either the sound of the breath itself, or on repeating the sounds *sa, ta, na, ma,* mentally synchronized with the steps. Alternate this directed breathing pattern in a designated series of intervals with regular walking. Total time varies from fifteen to forty-five minutes.

Step 4: Balance. Relax the breath, slow the walk, pay attention to your senses and do a stretch (the Triple Balance Stretch). Two minutes.

Step 5: Integrate. Standing or sitting, become aware of all the sensations generated in the body. Sense the surface of the skin all over the body until you can consciously feel it in all areas at once. Gradually expand the feeling of the sensory bubble of the skin as if that bubble expands outward as far as you can. Be aware of all the senses, thoughts, and feelings without restriction.

At the end of the Breathwalk, Karen was able to focus, become calm, and neutrally explore the thoughts and feelings that normally flood her mind. Many people separate activity and exercise from meditation. In Kundalini yoga they are often integrated. People with ADHD find it difficult simply to sit and be mindful. Several instructors at mind/body clinics that employed the relaxation response or mindful sitting told me that over 60 percent of their clients discontinue treatment after a brief period. Efforts to relax can frequently have the opposite effect as the mind is suddenly engulfed with thoughts and feelings that had veiled themselves in the background.

A better approach is to stimulate the nervous system first to increase arousal and engage the areas that regulate attention and executive functions. Then, use meditation and dialogue to help the person separate his or her awareness from all the objects that course through that awareness. In this state a person can redirect the inner narratives to quell self-criticism and choose what information to focus on.

The Breathwalk is both exercise and meditation. At the end, during the integration step, Karen has many more resources available to her. She can easily be still, watch her mind without reacting, and begin to cultivate new choices that strengthen her sense of control and open the ability to better connect to people and things around her.

This very human moment is also a perfect therapeutic moment. It is a good time for her to write in her journal, to do a meditation, or to conduct a self-guided exploration of the moment-to-moment way she consciously or automatically directs her mind to deal with each thought. At this time she can cultivate a choice about how to react to each thought and feeling. She can perceive the impact and consequence of each thought as if it creates a world. Does that world fit her own consciousness of her self, of what she values, and of what her soul wants? The constant jumble of impulsive actions gives way to a few moments in which a single decision about a thought is engaged fully, with a deep and satisfying sense of personal engagement and choice.

Karen experienced this, though briefly at first. Those experiences helped us create a useful therapeutic dialogue around the sense of herself that came in those moments. Instead of understanding her world through the disappointments that nagged at her, she started to take on a new perspective where the task became less about suppressing unwanted behaviors and more about recalling this awakened sense of a choosing self. She was gradually victorious over her reactive mind. She could find this sense of her self when she first began to think in a scattered way, or a depressed way, or when her thoughts intensified to seize her for a spate of hyperfocused activity.

As she gained experience, she could put into words her desire to explore this sense of self. She told me that when she could quell her thoughts, she could sense something more, something almost spiritual or sacred that was part of her. She wanted to connect with that more. When she did connect with it, she felt she could quickly recognize which thoughts and beliefs were authentically hers and which were not. Her sense of being a bit of an imposter as she tried to handle people and their seemingly impossible expectations began to give way to more self-acceptance and self-trust. She developed a profound and intimate relationship to the renewed sense of spirit. It began to be a "larger voice" with which she could view herself with acceptance as she repeatedly rallied her efforts to shift disorder to the background and herself to the foreground.

We tracked those times when, like many with ADHD, she would swing into a hyperfocused work mode. All other projects and relationships would disappear from her scope. She would be productive, creative, and fully attentive. However, other things would suffer from the inattention and she was drawn to the new or exciting parts of the project, often leaving the other necessary project parts to find their own manager. Hyperfocus would end as abruptly as it began, giving anyone she was with cognitive whiplash. They would feel abandoned, cut off, or disrespected. When she heard these comments from her colleagues or friends she would respond by affirming a list of her good intentions and start to withdraw inside.

We used a few dialogical techniques to identify the parts of her that carry out this action. Dealing with the hundreds of fragments of the psyche and subpersonalities is a specialty of Humanology as it is in NLP (neurolinguistic programming) and other emerging cognitive therapy techniques. We would establish stillness and a tangible feeling of presence. Then she would identify the parts of her that were active with unwanted thoughts and feelings. The strengths of each part, comfortable or not, were aligned with her core awareness. With meditation she could diminish thoughts that were not useful, true, or effective. She began to recognize what she called her "master self that just is." We used a wide range of guided interactions with these subpersonalities that helped her regain a sense of time, reduced her disturbing reactions to her ubiquitous sequential incongruities, and helped her remember goals.

She began to see her ability to hyperfocus as a positive ability that she could use to explore her mind and spirit if she could engage it voluntarily, and at least sometimes disengage it when unwanted. We added a very classical, effective Kundalini yoga meditation in Humanology that is central to healing many disordered nervous system processes and many mental and emotional pathologies. This meditation is called Tershula Kriya—the "thunderbolt of Shiva." The name refers to the three-pronged trident carried by the Mahan ("greatest") yogi, Shiva. That trident means he conquered the action of the three minds—negative, positive, and neutral (Bhajan and Khalsa, 1998; Bhajan, 2003)—and the qualities or forces ("gunas") that create our experience of the world. This meditation gives the practitioners command of themselves beyond the mind's vicissitudes. Clinically, it helps a practitioner, be bigger than or other than the mind and its processes.

Karen began this in earnest as an exercise to hyperfocus voluntarily, to go beyond hyperfocus. We talked about it as "paying attention to that awareness in her that was paying attention to attention."

Tershula Kriya Meditation*

Sit with the spine straight, hips balanced, and chin slightly in. The eyes are closed looking straight. Bring the elbows next to the ribs, forearms extended in front with the hands at the heart level, right over left, palms up. The hands are approximately ten degrees higher than the elbows, with wrists straight. The thumbs are extended out to the sides with the fingers of the two hands, crossing each other at an angle (see Figure 6.1). You mentally chant these sounds as you hold the breath in or out: *har har wha-hay guroo.* Inhale through the nostrils, pull back on the navel, and suspend the breath. Mentally chant the mantra for as long as you are able, without strain, while retaining the breath. While chanting, visualize your hands surrounded by white light. Exhale through the nostrils and visualize lightning shooting out from your fingertips (see Figure 6.2). Hold the breath out, as you contract the lower pelvis and pull the navel point in. Again mentally recite the mantra as long as you are able.

Inhale deeply and continue for up to sixty-two minutes (we used fifteen to thirty-one in the case). It is helpful, for balance, to do this in a cool room, as it can heat the body significantly (Bhajan, 2003).

FIGURE 6.1. Tershula Kriya Meditation Body Position

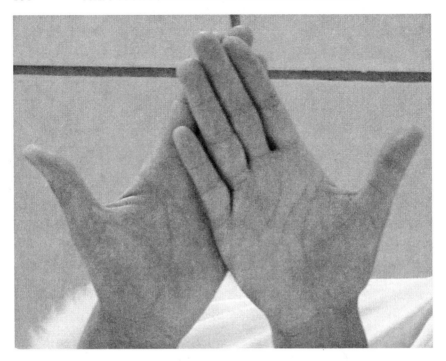

FIGURE 6.2. The Position of the Hands in the Tershula Kriya Mediation

Karen found it difficult at first to coordinate the visualization, breath, posture, and mental sounds in a single smooth pattern, but she persisted. After two weeks she was confident and gradually increased the time successfully to either fifteen or thirty-one minutes, depending on her available time. The results were profound. By not fighting the hyperfocus she formed a new relationship to it. Her feelings of appreciation for her unique mental qualities grew stronger than her bad feelings about herself. She gained much more control of her ability to "lock onto" a topic in meetings, a project at work, or an activity with others. As her confidence increased so did her social interactions with others. She was able to identify her internal state and either alter it or put in positive organizational supports to ensure she would follow through in ways meaningful to others—and ultimately to her.

The meditation experiences and her success in consciously altering her attention and energy levels interacted with the dialogical processes. She ultimately came to terms with her neurological temperament. She could recognize her rising symptoms such as increased intensity of her impulses, racing or jumping thoughts, and suddenly aggressive self-criticism. At the first wave of the mind's increased ADHD symptoms, she learned to locate her sense of her self, shift her breath pattern, and consciously become present to act from her conscious awareness. She looks on the challenge of ADHD as a gift that has given her a deeper understanding of herself and of the value and effect of a conscious relationship to her mind. She also increased her involvement in her church in social activities and prayer. She said she realized that the self she could sense in her most quiet moments in meditation was always there and that she now had neither shame to present herself to her spirit nor neediness. This was a very new feeling of self-dignity and strength.

Case Example: Brendan

Brendan is perhaps more typical of the ADHD syndrome. He was fourteen years old with a history of problems in school. He had withdrawn his efforts from many classes and gravitated to listening to hours of hip-hop music and to social groups that had already experimented with a spectrum of drugs. His parents were very supportive, however, and met with him and school counselors for both learning skills and antidrug efforts. The counselor identified Brendan's ADHD as the type that was hyperactive dominant. Indeed, while talking with Brendan he constantly writhed, wiggled, and vibrated parts of his body as if he was seeking a new physical form to live in. His eyes would drift askance as he talked, so you could not be sure who he was talking to.

The parent and counselor decided to use Ritalin as a treatment and as a way to separate out ADHD symptoms from other masking problems. Unfortunately, Brendan's response to the Ritalin was minimal at best. The family had changed his diet as well. The roles in the family had started to rigidify around the "sick one" and the "caretaker," which was the mother in this case. The family narrative that blamed her first husband, Brendan's biological father, for the bad gene supported Brendan's many attempts to divert responsibility for his actions to others or to circumstance.

For all of Brendan's difficult behaviors and transgressions, he was still respectful of his mother and had no quarrels with his stepfather except short fights over who cheated at basketball. The stepfather was a high-tech engineer and was looking for a way to use neurofeedback to help. I encouraged his exploratory efforts, especially to identify the areas of the brain that were most active in Brendan's subtype of ADHD. Knowing this could also help us specify the kinds of meditations and exercise that would be most effective.

Brendan was back and forth about pursing neurofeedback. He did not want to seem too strange or sick to his friends. He had an introduction to yoga watching his parents do it and once while going to a yoga camp with them in the Caribbean. He found it a little boring, but some of his friends knew about it and thought it was okay.

The Program

They decided to try an approach with Kundalini yoga and the Humanological perspective. They also wanted to do something as a family with him. They were worried and did not want to "lose him" or have him at greater risk as he went through the full hormonal rage of adolescence. We designed a simple support program to work along with the efforts already initiated by the counselor using medications, learning strategies, and organizing tools. The program emphasized stimulating exercises, especially with the breath, that would help him address his hyperactive energy directly. He needed to feel effects immediately or he would lose motivation. The meditations we started with required effort and allowed him to have immediate physical feedback about his attention and his energy level. The program encouraged many ways for the family to be supportive and to connect through action with him to build confidence and social skills.

Every day at least one parent, sometimes both, would do two Kundalini yoga exercises with Brendan, go for a short twenty-minute Breathwalk (using a different more energetic pattern than previously discussed), and then look at the lists that would help him organize during the day.

The two exercises, described briefly in the next sections, are very powerful and help adjust the temporal and limbic overloads his brain seemed to give him. The Tershula Kriya that Karen used would not work as well for Brendan, since he has much higher impulsiveness and somatized hyperactivity. In terms of the subtle structures called chakras, which is part of Kundalini yoga and the humanological perspective, impulsivity always involves an imbalance in the first three chakras. The nervous and subtle energy associated with them needs to be enhanced and moved through the body to the sixth and the fourth chakras. As this bodily change occurs, cognitive and emotional changes begin. The ability to be more empathic and see the cues given by others improves. As this experience was expressed in small, new behaviors, it was reinforced with therapeutic dialogues to nurture new self-perception. Unintended thoughts, untoward emotions, and impulsiveness all gradually lessen. With practice the basic neurological patterns can be changed and a new sense of character and self-presence developed.

Exercise One: Swimming the Ocean of Thought*

Sit with a straight spine. Close your eyes. Move the arms as if swimming, extending arms alternately in a constant motion (see Figure 6.3). Imagine you are in a vast ocean, night is falling, a storm is coming, and you are swimming. You cannot see the shore, so you use your intuition and swim with power, joy, and determination. Your survival depends on it! Breathe automatically in synchrony through the nose. Continue for eleven minutes. End with a deep inhale, holding one arm forward, one back. Exhale. Inhale with arms switched. Relax. Then come into a baby pose sitting on the heels with the forehead on the ground, arms back along the sides (see Figure 6.4). Relax and imagine you have made it safely to shore and all is fine. Allow gratitude to flow into every cell and let go. Seven minutes. End with an inhale that you hold as you move the spine in all directions. Then rise up slowly (Bhajan, 2000).

Exercise Two: Sat Kriya—Consolidating the Self

Sit on the heels and stretch the arms over the head so that the elbows hug the ears (see Figure 6.5). Interlock the fingers except the index fingers, which point straight up (see Figure 6.6). Begin to chant the two sounds *sat* and *naam*. (*Sat* rhymes with *but*.) Chant them emphatically in a constant rhythm about eight times per ten seconds. Chant the sound *sat* from the navel; point and pull the umbilicus in and up. As you say *naam* relax the abdominal muscles. Continue for at least three minutes, then inhale and squeeze the muscles tightly from the buttocks all the way up the back, past the shoulders. As you hold the breath, mentally sense the energy and sensations the entire length of the spine, from bottom to the top of the skull. Ideally, relax for twice the length of time that the kriya was practiced. Practice this with little or no food in the belly, no psychotropic drugs, and build up the time gradually (Bhajan, 2003).

---

*Exercises one and two are copyright Yogi Bhajan 2004. All rights reserved.

FIGURE 6.3. Body Position at the Beginning of Swimming the Ocean of Thought

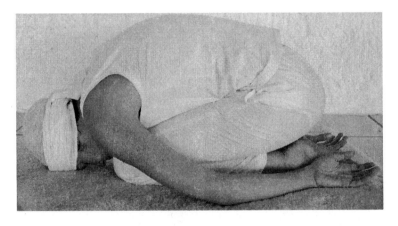

FIGURE 6.4. Body Position at the End of Swimming the Ocean of Thought

FIGURE 6.5. Body Position for Sat Kriya

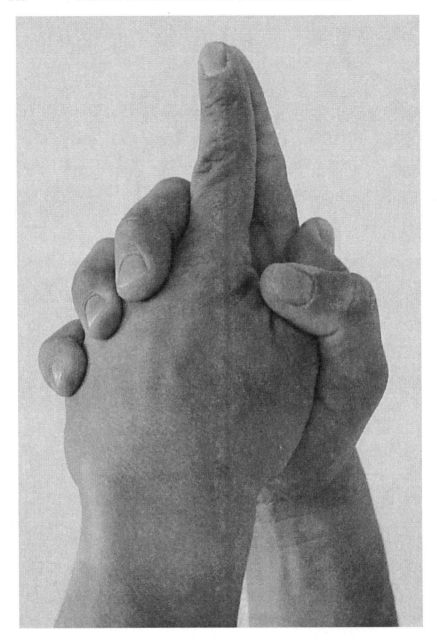

FIGURE 6.6. Position of the Hands in Sat Kriya Pose

The family committed to do the exercises together for three months. This allowed for more family contact and communication outside of the context of school or therapy. The parents felt they had a better awareness of Brendan's daily state and felt closer to him. Negative reactions among family members noticeably decreased. They all felt more connected and more able to be realistic about the ongoing efforts needed.

In addition we role-played various interactions as a family. As each member played his or her own role and that of the other members, new narratives emerged. The parents learned to reframe their perspective on Brendan as they acted with each other in new and varied configurations. The way they would speak about Brendan and the family incorporated several new perspectives: a long-term developmental view, a spiritual gift view, and a learning and growth view in which Brendan is "given" to them with his unique energy to help their fulfillment. They also learned about the biological perspective that emphasizes how changeable—neuroplastic—our neural wiring and brain is. Exercise, social interactions, and small victories in habits wove an emotional atmosphere of hope and progress in the family.

Brendan improved significantly in a month. Interestingly, the parents chose to learn a much wider range of Kundalini yoga kriyas than I had asked. They said the exercises helped them handle their own stress and helped them to have a nonreactive, connected stance with Brendan. This shifted the entire family dynamic. Brendan began to do the two exercises on his own as well and began to think of it as a special skill that gained him more trust and freedom to be on his own with his friends and in other activities. They noticed that if he skipped the exercises for more than five days his hyperactive movements would begin to exaggerate, especially in the morning.

The dialogues with Brendan helped him to use his meditation experience as he learned he can select one thought or task at a time. We created several structured approaches to put all the supports in place to act on those tasks—lists, asking for help, placing certain items in easy-to-see locations so he could remember them as he leaves for the day. I guided him in several directed meditations so he could consciously hear his internal narratives such as, "I am all messed up" or "I'm totally hopeless." Once heard, he learned to consciously alter each voice and separate from them. He became quite adept, "like a sound booth guy," at replacing distracting narratives with something useful or something that would bless and uplift him. This and the exercise practice formed the beginning of his confidence that he could direct himself and not let everyone, including himself, down. He has continued to increase his ability to direct himself. He has learned many other techniques since then and is active in soccer and composing melodies on his computer. He has been much more successful at projects in school and puts in place the supports and organizing tools he thinks he needs as he begins the new projects.

The two cases are quite different and show how this approach provides a practical complementary or alternative approach that empowers the person with ADHD to change with exercise, Breathwalk, Kundalini yoga, and meditation.

CONCLUSION

The capacity to effectively direct our attention and to act consciously, not impulsively, is critical in the globally connected, information-saturated world we have created. Childhood behaviors that might have been tolerated in the past are less acceptable by society. Adult impulsiveness and inattention can be preludes to simple mistakes which, in this technologically amplified environment, can have complex and long-lasting consequences. ADHD and attentional disorders make daily tasks and goals difficult and often derail the fulfillment of the individual's potential and career. Perhaps this is why we have seen the amount of methylphenidate chloride (e.g., Ritalin, Concerta) prescribed in the United States increase by more than 500 percent between 1991 and 1999, and prescriptions for amphetamines (e.g., Dexedrine, Adderall) increase by more than 2,000 percent (Sax and Kautz, 2003).

The psychospiritual approach using exercise, meditation, and therapeutic dialogue is a powerful alternative for many and a valuable adjunct for any treatment program. The powerful and unique exercises in Kundalini yoga and Humanology provide an example of this rapidly growing approach. This approach focuses on individuals as whole persons, on their environments, and on the resources they can call on within themselves. This natural approach builds self-esteem and provides a wide array of practical techniques that are adaptable to the various types of attentional disorders.

REFERENCES

Adelizzi, J.U. and Goss, D.B. (2001). *Parenting Children with Learning Disabilities.* Westport, CT: Bergin and Garvey Publishers.

Aman, C.J., Roberts, R.J. Jr., and Pennington, B.F. (1998). A Neuropsychological Examination of the Underlying Deficit in Attention Deficit Hyperactivity Disorder: Frontal Lobe Versus Right Parietal Lobe Theories. *Developmental Psychology,* 34(5), 956-969.

Amen, D.G. (2001). *Healing ADD: The Breakthrough Program That Allows You to See and Heal the 6 Types of ADD.* New York: Berkley Publishing Group.

American Psychiatric Association (2000). *Diagnostic and Statistical Manual of Mental Disorders* (Fourth Edition, Text Revision). Washington, DC: American Psychiatric Association.

Anastopoulos, A.D. and Shelton, T.L. (2001). *Assessing Attention-Deficit/Hyperactivity Disorder.* New York: Kluwer Academic/Plenum Publishers.

Bakker, S.C., van de Meulen, E.M., Buitelaar, J.K., Sandkuijl, L.A., Pauls, D.L., Monsuur, A.J., van't Slot, R., Minderaa, R.B., Gunning, W.B., Pearson, P.L., and Sinke, R.J. (2003). A Whole-Genome Scan in 164 Dutch Sib Pairs with Attention-Deficit/Hyperactivity Disorder: Suggestive Evidence for Linkage on Chromosomes 7p and 15q. *American Journal Human Genetics,* 72, 1251-1260.

Barkley, R.A. (1998). *Attention Deficit-Hyperactivity Disorder: A Handbook for Diagnosis and Treatment* (Second Edition). New York: Guilford Press.

Barkley, R.A., Murphy, K.R., DuPaul, G.J., and Bush, T. (2002). Driving in Young Adults with Attention Deficit Hyperactivity Disorder: Knowledge, Performance, Adverse Outcomes, and the Role of Executive Functioning. *Journal of the International Neuropsychological Society,* 8, 655-672.

Bhajan, Y. (1986). Transcript of lecture to psychologists in Rome, Italy. January 24-26. Archives of KRI. Edited for use by Gurucharan Singh Khalsa, pp. 3-4; 25-26.

Bhajan, Y. (2000) *Self Experience: Kundalini Yoga As Taught by Yogi Bhajan.* Espanolo, NM: KRI Publishers.

Bhajan,Y. (2003). *The Aquarian Teacher.* Espanola, NM: Kundalini Research Institute Publisher.

Bhajan, Y. and Khalsa, G. (1998). *The Mind: Its Projections and Multiple Facets.* Espanola, NM: Kundalini Research Institute.

Bhajan, Y. and Khalsa, G. (2000). *Breathwalk: Breathing Your Way to Vitality for Body, Mind and Spirit.* New York: Broadway Books.

DuPaul, G.J. (2003). Assessment of ADHD Symptoms: Comment on Gomez, et al. *Psychological Assessment,* 15(1), 115-117.

Faraone, S.V. (2000). Attention Deficit Hyperactivity Disorder in Adults: Implications for Theories of Diagnosis. *Current Directions in Psychological Science,* 9(2), 33-36.

Faraone, S.V., Biederman, J., Spencer, T., Wilens, T., Seidman, L.J., Mick, E., and Doyle, A.E. (2000). Attention-Deficit/Hyperactivity Disorder in Adults: An Overview. *Biological Psychiatry,* 48(1), 9-20.

Fisher, S.E., Francks, C., McCracken, J.T., McGough, J.J., Marlow, A.J., MacPhie, I.L., Newbury, D.F., Crawford, L.R., Palmer, C.G.S., Woodward, J.A., Del'Homme, M., Cantwell, D.P., Nelson, S.F., Monaco, A.P., and Smalley, S.L. (2002). A Genomewide Scan for Loci Involved in Attention-Deficit/Hyperactivity Disorder. *American Journal of Human Genetics,* 70, 1183-1196.

Friedman, S.R., Rapport, L.J., Lumley, M., Tzelepis, A., VanVoorhis, A., Stettner, L., and Kakaati, L. (2003). Aspects of Social and Emotional Competence in Adult Attention-Deficit/Hyperactivity Disorder. *Neuropsychology,* 17(1), 50-58.

Helmuth, L. (2003). In Sickness or in Health? *Science,* 302, 808-810.

Hinshaw, S.P. (2002). Preadolescent Girls with Attention-Deficit/Hyperactivity Disorder: I. Background Characteristics, Comorbidity, Cognitive and Social Functioning, and Parenting Practices. *Journal of Consulting and Clinical Psychology,* 70(5), 1086-1098.

Hinshaw, S.P., Carte, E.T., Sami, N., Treuting, J.J., and Zupan, B.A. (2002). Preadolescent Girls with Attention-Deficit/Hyperactivity Disorder: II. Neuropsychological Performance in Relation to Subtypes and Individual Classification. *Journal of Consulting and Clinical Psychology,* 70(5), 1099-1111.

Lazar, S.W., Bush, G., Gollub, R., Fricchione, G., Khalsa, G., and Benson, H. (2000). Functional Brain Mapping of the Relaxation Response and Meditation. *Neuroreport,* 11(7), 1-5.

Marshall, E. (2000). Duke Study Faults Overuse of Stimulants for Children. *Science,* 289(5480), 721.

Murphy, K.R. and Barkley, R.A. (1996). Adults with ADHD: Comorbidity and Adaptive Functioning. *Comprehensive Psychiatry,* 37, 393-401.

Oades, R.D. (2002). Dopamine May Be "Hyper" with Respect to Noradrenaline Metabolism, but "Hypo" with Respect to Serotonin Metabolism in Children with Attention-Deficit Hyperactivity Disorder. *Behavioural Brain Research,* 130, 97-102.

Peng, C.K., Henry, I.C., Mietus, J.E., Hausdorff, J., Khalsa, G., Benson, B., and Goldberger, A.L. (2004). Heart Rate Dynamics During Three Forms of Meditation. *International Journal of Cardiology,* 95(1), 19-27.

Ratey, J.J. (2001). *A User's Guide to the Brain: Perception, Attention and the Four Theaters of the Brain.* New York: Pantheon Books, Random House.

Ratey, J.J. and Johnson, C.J. (1997). *Shadow Syndromes.* New York: Pantheon Books.

Rubia, K. (2002). The Dynamic Approach to Neurodevelopmental Psychiatric Disorders: Use of fMRI Combined with Neuropsychology to Elucidate the Dynamics of Psychiatric Disorders, Exemplified in ADHD and Schizophrenia. *Behavioral Brain Research,* 130, 47-56.

Rucklidge, J. and Kaplan, B. (2000). Attributions and Perceptions of Childhood in Women with ADHD Symptomatology. *Journal of Clinical Psychology,* 56(6), 711-722.

Schwartz, J.M. and Begley, S. (2002). The Mind and the Brain: Neuroplasticity and the Power of Mental Force. New York: Harper Collins Publishers.

Weiss, M. and Murray, C. (2003) Assessment and Management of Attention-Deficit Hyperactivity Disorder in Adults. *Canadian Medical Association Journal,* 6, 168.

Young, S., Toone, B., and Tyson, C. (2003). Comorbidity and Psychosocial Profile of Adults with Attention Deficit Hyperactivity Disorder. *Personality and Individual Differences,* 35(4), 743-755.

Chapter 7

Dissociative Identity Disorder and Psychospiritual Perspectives

Colin A. Ross

Dissociative identity disorder (formerly called multiple personality disorder) is the most chronic, complex, and disabling of the dissociative disorders (Putnam, 1989; Ross, 1997). It is usually linked to severe childhood trauma, which can involve any combination of physical, sexual, and emotional abuse; neglect; loss of primary caretakers; and family violence and chaos. On the planet as a whole, the burden of chronic childhood trauma consists mainly of war, famine, disease, poverty, natural disasters, and cultural disintegration. In North America, these forms of suffering are less common than they are in other parts of the world, so mental health professionals here tend to focus on intrafamilial trauma. I favor a broad definition of trauma, one that includes suffering caused by the failure of parents to bond, connect with, and nurture their children. Errors of omission by the parents can be as harmful and painful as errors of commission—the active acts of abuse we usually think of as "trauma."

In this chapter I describe some of the spiritual conflicts that occur in people with dissociative identity disorder. Most of the peer-reviewed literature focuses on psychological and secular concerns, with few exceptions (Bowman et al., 1987). Therefore I welcome this opportunity to discuss spiritual aspects of a disorder I have studied for two decades (Ross, 1984, 1989, 1994, 1995, 1997, 2000a,b, 2004).

HOW MANY SOULS ARE IN THIS BODY?

Individuals with dissociative identity disorder have other "people" inside. The alter personalities may differ in name, age, gender, hair color, or any other imaginable attribute. One alter personality, A, may be aware of another alter personality, B, or may have complete amnesia for periods when B is in executive control of the body. When A has amnesia for B, but B is aware of A, this is called *one-way amnesia*. When A and B are mutually amnesic for each other, this is called *two-way amnesia*. When A and B are mutually aware of each other, this is called *co-consciousness*.

By convention, the alter personality who is in executive control most of the time is referred to as the *host personality*. Often, the host personality has the name, age, and gender that correspond with the birth certificate, and has been the host personality since childhood. In other cases, however, the host personality can change, and he or she need not necessarily have the age or gender of the physical body. The complexities of dissociative identity disorder are illustrated by the following case example.

Case Example #1

A forty-two-year-old man with dissociative identity disorder had a number of different alter personalities. One, a heterosexual sixteen-year-old female alter personality, had voluntary sexual relations with a sixteen-year-old boy. The host personality, a forty-two-year-old married heterosexual male, had complete amnesia for this behavior. Further, the host personality believed that homosexuality is sinful and against God. The sixteen-year-old female alter personality believed that she lived in a sixteen-year-old female body and did not grasp the difference between vaginal and anal intercourse. She had a negative hallucination that resulted in her not seeing or being aware of her male genitalia, and two-way amnesia existed between this alter personality and the host.

From a psychological perspective, the host personality never had sex with the sixteen-year-old boy. However, from an objective behavioral perspective, the man was a pedophile and had committed a crime. From his own spiritual perspective, the host personality was unaware of the sexual activity and had not committed a sin. Treatment directed at removing the two-way amnesia barrier between the host personality and the sixteen-year-old alter personality would cause the host personality to experience guilt, remorse, shame before God, and suicidal ideation.

Alternatively, leaving the two-way amnesia intact would likely result in future pedophilic offenses. This would cause harm to the victims and might result in the forty-two-year-old man being caught, arrested, and incarcerated. Imprisonment could in turn cause even greater guilt and risk of completed suicide, even with the two-way amnesia still in place. The host personality might punish himself more severely than the criminal justice system—in effect, he might impose capital punishment on himself in order to relieve his guilt and pay for his sins.

Clinical and spiritual dilemmas similar to this one are common in dissociative identity disorder. They have stimulated several authors (Braude, 1995; Hacking, 1995) to write at length about the philosophical implications of dissociative identity disorder, especially for the definition and meaning of personhood. Can spiritually separate and distinct moral agents reside in the same body? Can two or more souls be in the same body? This possibility is allowed by theologies that accept the reality of possession by discarnate entities.

In my opinion, the question of whether more than one "person" is living in the body of an individual with dissociative identity disorder is meaningless. All the different people or souls are fragmented aspects of a single person. In a successfully treated case, the fragments are integrated into a unified, single identity. The illusion of separate identities is not a spiritual fact. It is a symptom of a psychiatric disorder. It is no more "real" than paranoid delusions or germ phobias, which are also psychiatric problems. The person with dissociative identity disorder has only one soul; the person with paranoid delusions is not being persecuted by Martians; and it is not necessary to wash your hands 100 times a day to decontaminate them.

In my opinion, nothing can be learned from dissociative identity disorder about fundamental spiritual questions, such as the unity or divisibility of the soul, survival after bodily death, or the nature of

God. These are important problems, and they have engaged great minds from all civilizations, but dissociative identity disorder is not relevant to their solution.

COGNITIVE ERRORS ABOUT GOD

People with dissociative identity disorder often come from rigid fundamentalist families. They both endorse and reject the beliefs of their parents, and they have a great deal of unresolved ambivalence and conflict about their spiritual values. No matter how rigid the family background, however, people with this disorder commonly feel abandoned and betrayed by God. As children, they were often emotionally abandoned, abused, and neglected by their parents. Their feelings about God are in part a projection onto God of feelings about their parents. This is not the whole story, however.

The individual with dissociative identity disorder often feels singled out by God for abuse and neglect. God could have intervened but instead chose not to, on purpose. The cognitive therapy for this error in thinking involves pointing out how many children die from disease, famine, natural disasters, and war every year on our planet. The individual believes that God selected him or her for a special degree of neglect. Actually, God equally "neglects" everybody. The discussion then turns to free will and the certainty that human beings have finite minds and therefore cannot understand God's plan or motives.

The purpose of this discussion is not theological; it is therapeutic. The analysis works therapeutically only if it is consistent with the person's basic belief in the existence of God and free will. Once the error of thinking is corrected, the anger at God for special, targeted neglect of the self dissipates, as does the underlying shame—it is no longer true that the self is undeserving of God's love. At this point, the discussion may shift to another aspect of the person's theory of God: why God sends him or her so much abuse and misfortune. This is the active aspect of God's malevolence, the passive aspect being his failure to intervene. The same error of thinking underlies both aspects of God's malevolence.

Linked to this conflict is the question, "Why have I not received God's grace?" This question can be asked in a variety of ways using a variety of different terms.

My response is often to ask in return whether God is in a particularly crabby mood today. Maybe God just got up on the wrong side of bed today, I say. Once we agree that this is an inaccurate view of God, I then propose an alternative view: God is always willing to give us his grace. Who receives it and who does not depends on us, not on God. He loves all of his children equally. I then suggest that the person's self-blame and self-hatred are blocking the receiving of God's grace. The person does not feel worthy of grace. This feeling and its attendant core belief are directly linked to the belief that the self caused and deserved abuse and neglect by both the parents and God.

In the terminology of my trauma model (Ross, 2000b), we are dealing with *the locus of control shift,* which is the self-blame for abuse and neglect that arises from normal egocentric childhood cognition. I deal with the locus of control shift in the same therapeutic manner, whether the content of the conversation is secular or religious, and whether the abuse and neglect were by human beings or by God.

COGNITIVE ERRORS ABOUT SUICIDE

People with dissociative identity disorder are often suicidal. The suicidal ideation has two aspects: on one hand, it is a kindly euthanasia designed to relieve the suffering of the self. On the other hand, it is an angry, violent, hostile murder of a human being. My method for disrupting the kindly euthanasia justification for suicide is to focus on the angry, destructive drive behind the thinking. The person is really more like a battering spouse than like a kindly veterinarian. Murder of the self is "okay" only when the self has been devalued and is regarded as subhuman. This anger at the self is derived from self-blame for childhood abuse and neglect, which returns us to the locus of control shift.

Not uncommonly, a theological or spiritual element is present in the "suicide as kindly euthanasia" viewpoint. The person may hear a dead loved one calling him or her to the afterlife. Or, without an auditory hallucination, the person may want to join a loved one in heaven. I first point out that this is a completely normal, natural feeling; of course, anyone would miss and want to be with an absent loved one, whether the loved one is overseas or in heaven.

Next I clarify that the person believes in an afterlife and heaven and hell. I then ask what the person believes concerning suicide. I point out the risk: no matter what the person's belief, suicide could result in going to hell. If that is true, then suicide will not result in being re-united with the dead loved one. This argument provides only a preliminary caution.

I then look at my watch and ask what time it is in heaven. The person in therapy usually looks puzzled and does not know what I mean. I then point out that heaven is in Eternity, which lies outside time. I ask whether people grow older in heaven. Since they do not, time does not exist in heaven. This means that, from the perspective of the loved one in heaven, the person will arrive in heaven at the same time, whether he or she dies from suicide next week or from natural causes at age ninety-four. This reasoning cancels one rationale for suicide: "I'm doing it for my loved one."

I then ask whether the person believes that the loved one in heaven can watch what is going on here on earth. Either way, I ask what the loved one would say if I could phone him or her in heaven. Would the loved one vote yes or no for suicide? Would the loved one want the person to have a life, be happy, and live out his or her allotted years on earth? Does the dead loved one love the person in therapy? The answers to these questions are always yes. Therefore suicide is a selfish act that goes directly against the wishes of the loved one.

Rather than being delighted that the person had arrived in heaven so early, the loved one would more likely be upset and disappointed. This would spoil the reunion. This line of argument is most powerful when the dead loved one is a child. The power is augmented if the person in therapy has other surviving children. How would the dead child feel about his or her mother or father abandoning the remaining living children?

I might ask, "How much do you miss your dead child?" The pain and loss of the person in therapy would be imposed on the person's surviving children if he or she committed suicide, and in fact it would be double, because they would have lost both a parent and a sibling.

This gift to them would increase their risk for suicide, which would in turn be passed on to the person's grandchildren.

I might ask, "Is this really the gift you want to give your grandchildren?" I am trying to get the person to see the suicide plan from the perspective of an outside family member. If the response is that the family members would be better off without the parent, I ask how the surviving children on earth would vote. If the person's children love him or her, I ask whether the children are delusional. Since they are not, the self must be lovable. I am trying to get the suicidal person to see himself or herself from the perspective of loving children.

I know that there is great love for the dead child, because otherwise the child in heaven could not be used as a rationalization for suicide. I am shifting the shame and guilt away from self-blame for events in the person's childhood to healthy, preventative shame concerning suicide. In conclusion, I will point out that a suicide means one more victory for child abuse. I and the other patients in the cognitive therapy group will not celebrate the suicide or be happy about it. We will conclude that child abuse and self-hatred have claimed one more victim.

As for cognitive errors about God, I blend the spiritual aspects of suicide into the regular work of therapy. I do not shift roles or manner—I am still Dr. Ross doing cognitive therapy. The principles, tasks, and strategies of therapy are the same whether the content is secular or sacred.

SPIRITUAL ALTER PERSONALITIES—GOOD AND EVIL

I have spoken with countless different types of alter personalities. For instance, after speaking with the host personality of a woman in her thirties about her paternal incest, I then spoke directly with her father, who lived in her body. He told me to leave his daughter alone; he was under the impression that she currently lived with him in his home and was eighteen years old. He thought the current year was 1986. The father was most disconcerted when I pointed out that he was using an adult female body to converse with me. The actual father was still alive and, like his daughter, was much older than he had been in 1986.

The demographic qualities of the alter personalities are not literal or objective facts. Although I have spoken with demons, Satan, a variety of transcendental entities, dead relatives, a few animals, and countless children, none of these beings were literally separate creatures. Bearing that in mind, the pantheon of alter personalities preserves, gives expression to, and makes manifest the full range of human potentialities, from the banal to the evil to the sacred. The spiritual plane of human life operates in people with dissociative identity disorder.

Within the same person, one alter personality may pledge allegiance to Satan, look forward to the next human sacrifice ritual (whether it is objectively real or not), and plan suicide as a way to be with Satan in hell. Another alter personality may express abhorrence for these beliefs and be a devout Christian. A cosmic battle between good and evil is fought within the psyches of dissociative individuals. It is full of conflict, drama, and suffering. The suffering and conflict are real, even if the historical facts alleged by the person to be true are not.

From a treatment perspective, it does not matter if the demon is really a demon, and it does not matter if the demon has really participated in Satanic human sacrifices led by the person's father. The demon plotting to attend a sacrifice at the upcoming solstice is an expression of a simple human need: to be special in Dad's eyes, to have a place in his world, and to be loved by him. The "good" Christian host personality is using a double defense against the pain of not being loved and nurtured by Dad, and of not being special in his eyes.

The first layer of the defense is to make the longing for attachment to Dad the feeling of another entity. The second layer is to transform the entity into a demon and the father into a Satanist. The Christian host personality can thereby disown and disavow the pain of the unfulfilled positive attachment to the father. Rather than an exorcism, the demon needs empathy and acceptance, which will transform it into a scared, lost, lonely child. That is the effect of Christian love on demons of this type.

MEMORIES OF SATANIC RITUAL ABUSE

During the first half of the 1990s, thousands of patients with dissociative identity disorder from all over the United States described growing up in Satanic human sacrifice cults. To this day no evidence exists to prove the reality of any of these allegations made by patients in treatment. A great deal of energy was expended in books, television programs, and the courts arguing whether the memories were real and whether the accused parent or the therapist should be sued and should pay damages in civil lawsuits. On one hand, the "crime" was child abuse; on the other, it was implantation of false memories and creation of iatrogenic dissociative identity disorder.

The dispute was focused on disagreement about the reality of the allegations. This meant that memory was on trial. Despite all the sound and fury on the subject, no guidelines were provided in the professional literature on how to proceed therapeutically. To help remedy this deficit, I wrote a book, *Satanic Ritual Abuse: Principles of Treatment* (Ross, 1995). The basic purpose of the book is to describe in detail a set of therapeutic principles, goals, tasks, and techniques that are the same, no matter what percentage of the memories is assumed to be accurate. As long as the "memories" are contained within the treatment process—as long as no allegations are made in public—then their historical accuracy is a minor consideration in treatment.

For instance, if the memories are real, then the person has very good reasons for an ambivalent attachment to his or her parents. If the memories are false, on the other hand, they certainly embody and symbolize a highly conflicted, ambivalent attachment. Either way, the goal is to resolve the polarized, conflicted attachment pattern, with its attendant black-and-white thinking and polarized feelings and behavior.

In terms of spiritual principles, in my opinion, nothing can be learned from the Satanic ritual abuse memories of people with dissociative identity disorder. Real or not, they prove nothing about the human condition, religion, or God that cannot be learned from study of the Third Reich or of civilization in general.

EXORCISM AS A PSYCHOTHERAPY TECHNIQUE

Exorcism is viewed by many mental health professionals as a culturally primitive procedure based on superstition. Despite that widespread belief, I have met many people with dissociative identity disorder who have undergone exorcisms by Christian clergy and therapists. This is not simply a theoretical issue in North America. A demonic possession model of dissociative identity disorder is endorsed by Friesen (1991), for instance, and allowed by Crabtree (1985). Most of the time, exorcisms of demons in dissociative identity disorder cases are unsuccessful, as noted by Fraser (1993) and Bowman (1993).

Often, exorcisms fail to expel the entity and instead cause anger, resentment, increased internal conflict, and alienation from the church carrying out the exorcism. This is to be expected if the demons are disavowed psychological elements of the person.

In my view, the question of whether a demon really is present is similar in structure to the question of whether Satanic ritual abuse memories are real. Within the therapy, there is no way to tell, and in any case, it does not make any difference. The classical Catholic techniques for discernment, such as application of holy oil and invocation of Jesus, in my opinion, simply do not work. A "demon" will respond the same way if it really is a demon or if it only thinks it is discarnate. Similarly, levitation, if it occurred, would not prove a demonic influence because it could be caused by secular paranormal mechanisms.

An entity departing in response to an exorcism does not prove it was discarnate because the person could simply have responded to a culturally acceptable suggestion. Failure to depart, conversely, could be due to the tenacious efforts of an actual demon, or the fact that the demon is psychological in nature and serves defensive functions. In the end, no valid and reliable technique for discernment exists.

I participated in a study that provides the conceptual solution to this aspect of dissociative identity disorder (Bull, Ellason, and Ross, 1997), and I provided presubmission feedback on a second paper that follows up on the first (Bull, 2001). In our study we devised operationalized definitions of good and bad outcomes for exorcism rituals. We then studied the outcomes of two types of exorcism rituals in a series of dissociative identity disorder cases. The bad outcomes involved increased conflict, symptoms, acting out, and alienation. They resulted from exorcisms that were coercive, dramatic, nonnegotiated, and unilateral.

The good outcomes involved a reduction in conflicts, symptoms, acting out, and alienation from the church. They resulted from exorcisms that were negotiated, noncoercive, undertaken with the consent of the person and the demon, and experienced more as a voluntary departure. They were carried out through conversation in the therapist's office. No unusual equipment or behaviors were employed. The following vignette, a case treated in the mid-1980s, illustrates the therapeutic use of "exorcism."

Case Example #2

A married woman in her forties had dissociative identity disorder. Her personality system was quite simple and consisted of her adult host personality and three alter personalities, one of whom was her dead grandmother (Ross, 1994). The grandmother had been the patient's primary caretaker during her childhood and adolescence. Her current family life was stable, and her husband was supportive of her, the diagnosis, and the treatment. In direct conversation, the grandmother explained and justified her harsh child-rearing practices, which included some physical abuse.

Teenage girls, the grandmother explained, are likely to be sexually promiscuous, which could bring shame to them and their families, and also result in pregnancy. To prevent her granddaughter from walking on this path, the grandmother forbade all jewelry, makeup, dating, and "provocative" behavior. After the patient was an adult, and after the external grandmother was dead, the internal grandmother continued her harsh attacks on the host personality's character and behavior, which contributed to her depression.

The host personality agreed that two of her alter personalities were psychological constructs, and they were treated to stable integration. They joined her in a secular integration ritual. However, the patient believed that her dead grandmother was a discarnate intrusion by her actual grandmother. She would not agree to integrating the grandmother because the grandmother was not a part of her self. From the patient's perspective, we had two souls in treatment.

After a course of "couple therapy" for the grandmother and granddaughter, both agreed that it was time for the grandmother to move on to heaven. The therapist performed a departure ritual in which the two said good-bye to each other and the grandmother exited from the host personality's body, leaving behind a single personality. Just as she was departing, the grandmother reported seeing the souls of dead loved ones waiting for her in a shining light in heaven.

Technically, this was an exorcism, not an integration. The successful outcome is the same whether one believes that the dead grandmother was a discarnate entity or a psychological construct. Debating the ontological status of the grandmother with the host personality would have been countertherapeutic.

My conclusion from my clinical experience and research is that exorcism is a universal, time-honored therapeutic ritual. The utility and outcome of exorcism rituals for dissociative identity disorder cannot help us solve spiritual problems. Used in an empowering, empathic, and restrained manner, it can be very helpful as a therapeutic process. Used in an invasive, violent, dictatorial fashion, it can be destructive. The problem is not with exorcism as such, but rather with the way it is carried out. This is equally true of all other techniques used in psychotherapy.

THE BATTLE BETWEEN GOOD AND EVIL

One might mistakenly infer that this chapter is written from an agnostic viewpoint. The opposite is true: if there is no higher spiritual meaning to life, then the long, painful work of recovery is pointless. If there is no meaning to human life, then how can there be value in therapy? What would be the point of the exercise? The spiritual properties of chronic, complex dissociative disorders are illustrated by the following case example.

Case Example #3

A woman in her thirties had experienced childhood sexual abuse. In her early adolescence she disclosed paternal incest to her mother, but she was amnesic for the conversation when she awoke the next morning. This event was corroborated by her mother. The woman had a complex inner world with numerous traumatized children, different subregions, and groups of identity states related to different types of trauma.

The child parts included little girls with no skin, children hidden at the back of dark caves, and other children living in rooms that mimicked rooms in the external world where abuse had occurred thirty years earlier. The healing of the inner children involved the assistance of a figure named the Angel Lady. The children were drawn out from their internal hiding places during the therapy, the adult self developed empathy for them, and their role in the reconstructed trauma narrative was clarified. They were then integrated.

Integration occurred in several different ways. Some parts dissolved spontaneously, and others were integrated during therapy rituals. The rituals involved preparatory therapeutic work, then it would be time for an "Angel Lady ritual," as we called them. The adult self would become quiet and introspective for a few minutes, and would report on what was going on internally every once in a while.

During these rituals, the Angel Lady would do one of several things. She might bathe a traumatized child in healing light, then escort the child to a safer, less lonely place in the inner landscape. At times, she would escort a group of children to heaven. On other occasions, the Angel Lady would communicate with the adult self by showing her things, such as love, empathy, and forgiveness for children who had committed the "crime" of being abused. The Angel Lady sometimes taught the adult self lessons through an internal telepathic "knowing." She would directly communicate a viewpoint or thought to the adult self. All of these events were the culmination of a great deal of hard work in therapy.

The adult self believed that the Angel Lady was a spiritual guide, not a part of her self. The Angel Lady brought a healing power to the therapy that was transcendent and divine. During an Angel Lady ritual, I always felt that a higher healing principle was at work. Secular principles of trauma and dissociation could not account for the qualities of this inner figure, to my mind. The Angel Lady brought energy and power to the recovery process I have never seen in secular identity states.

In the end, there was no way to determine whether the Angel Lady was more than a psychological element of the client. From a therapeutic perspective, it did not matter. Discarnate or not, the Angel Lady provided structure for higher spiritual principles in the client and provided the adult self hope, purpose, and direction for her healing.

The battle between good and evil on this planet is played out in the souls of people with dissociative identity disorder. Most have been subjected to childhood physical and sexual abuse, as well as neglect, severe verbal and emotional abuse, and failure of attachment, empathy, and nurturance by their parents. The conflict between good and evil is played out at two levels in the inner world. There is the complex inner drama of the alter personalities, who often hate one another and try to murder one another, often not realizing that they are in the same body. Through identification with the aggressor, they endorse and act out on themselves and others the cruelty they experienced as children. Yet they long for healing and peace and can be very kind.

The conflict between good and evil also takes place apart from the structure of the dissociative identity disorder. Simply as human beings, these individuals are full of contradiction, conflict, paradox, and unresolved ambivalence. The dissociation does not cause these problems; rather, such a psychological strategy reduces ambivalence and conflict. Another "person" holding an opposing viewpoint is more tolerable than holding both viewpoints oneself. The pious married person can feel angry about his or her extramarital affairs but need not feel guilty, because "someone else" is committing the adultery. The pious alter personality has forgotten the maxim, "Let him who is without sin cast the first stone."

CONCLUSION

The themes, myths, conflicts, depravity, and transcendent spirituality that fill the world's religions, literatures, and cultures are alive and well in dissociative identity disorder. Working with these individuals as a therapist can be stressful and tiring, but never empty or meaningless. Indeed, the therapeutic conversation has more depth, complexity, urgency, and spiritual import than most conversations in the world. Done well, it provides a microcosm of healing and recovery from which our planet could learn at the macrocosmic level.

REFERENCES

Bowman, E.S. (1993). Clinical and spiritual effects of exorcism in fifteen patients with multiple personality disorder. *Dissociation,* 6, 222-238.

Bowman, E.S., Coons, P.M., Jones, R.S., and Oldstrom, M. (1987). Religious psychodynamics in multiple personalities. *American Journal of Psychotherapy,* 41, 542-543.

Braude, S.E. (1995). *First person plural: Multiple personality and the philosophy of mind* (Revised edition). London: Rowman and Littlefield.

Bull, D.L. (2001). A phenomenological model of therapeutic exorcism for dissociative identity disorder. *Journal of Psychology and Theology,* 29, 131-139.

Bull, D.L., Ellason, J.W., and Ross, C.A. (1997). Exorcism revisited: Some positive outcomes with dissociative identity disorder. *Journal of Psychology and Theology,* 26, 188-196.

Crabtree, A. (1985). *Multiple man: Explorations in possession and multiple personality.* Toronto: Collins Publishers.

Fraser, G.A. (1993). Exorcism rituals: Effects on multiple personality disorder patients. *Dissociation,* 6, 239-244.

Friesen, J.G. (1991). *Uncovering the mystery of MPD.* Nashville, TN: Thomas Nelson.

Hacking, I. (1995). *Rewriting the soul: Multiple personality and the sciences of memory.* Princeton, NJ: Princeton University Press.

Putnam, F.W. (1989). *Diagnosis and treatment of multiple personality disorder.* New York: Guilford.

Ross, C.A. (1984). Diagnosis of multiple personality disorder during hypnosis: A case report. *International Journal of Clinical and Experimental Hypnosis, 32,* 222-235.

Ross, C.A. (1989). *Multiple personality disorder: Diagnosis, clinical features, and treatment.* New York: John Wiley and Sons.

Ross, C.A. (1994). *The Osiris complex: Case studies in multiple personality disorder.* Toronto: University of Toronto Press.

Ross, C.A. (1995). *Satanic ritual abuse: Principles of treatment.* Toronto: University of Toronto Press.

Ross, C.A. (1997). *Dissociative identity disorder: Diagnosis, clinical features, and treatment of multiple personality* (Second edition). New York: John Wiley and Sons.

Ross, C.A. (2000a). *BLUEBIRD: Deliberate creation of multiple personality by psychiatrists.* Richardson, TX: Manitou Communications.

Ross, C.A. (2000b). *The trauma model: A solution to the problem of comorbidity in psychiatry.* Richardson, TX: Manitou Communications.

Ross, C.A. (2004). *Schizophrenia: Innovations in diagnosis and treatment.* Binghamton, NY: The Haworth Press.

Chapter 8

Alternative Treatments for Borderline and Narcissistic Personality Disorders

Manjit Kaur Khalsa

INTRODUCTION

Relationships can be difficult. Many people have experienced the pain of conflict, separation, and even divorce at some time in their lives. But some people experience extraordinary difficulties because of an intense disturbance in the fundamental nature of their personalities. Clinically, these disturbed patterns are known as personality disorders.

We all know people with these disorders: they seem exceedingly insecure, and while some tend to get irrationally and fiercely angry, others can be excessively arrogant and grandiose.

Case Example: Stephen

Stephen is a tall, handsome man who easily engages you with his eyes. The first time I met him he told me about his relationship with his former therapist. With his head in his hands, Stephen explained that his therapist had recently died. He told me that his therapist had been more of a father to him than anyone else he had ever known. He explained,

> When I first met him, I was crazy, wildly going from one woman to another. I was always insecure, and always furious about something. I was unable to control my moods at all. A few months ago, at the end of

one of my tirades, my therapist told me, "I know you are really angry, but please try to understand that even though you feel so completely controlled by your emotions, it's just your personality at play—you can *choose to change* and find your way." Maybe he knew he was dying because he softly added, "Always try to remember this for me." I believe that he loved me—I felt I was more than just a patient to him. I miss him terribly now that he's gone. To honor his memory, I am trying to honor his request. I *choose* to change.

Stephen's story illustrates some of the difficulties experienced by people with personality disorders. In this chapter, alternative methods for treating borderline and narcissistic personality disorders are examined. These methods support Stephen's belief that change is possible.

Historically, people with these diagnoses have remained in therapy for lengthy periods of time, and the results of the treatment were mixed, at best (Goldstein, 1990). Today several psychospiritual approaches combine the best techniques of modern psychology with various aspects of Eastern thought. We will examine two of these approaches in some detail: dialectical behavioral therapy and Humanology. Available research indicates some promising results (Linehan, 1993a).

PERSONALITY DISORDERS

Our *personality* can be defined as the stable set of traits or characteristics that makes each of us unique. All of us have personality traits—they are part of being human and how we define ourselves to ourselves and to others. However, when these psychological traits become inflexible or maladaptive, they cause distress and impairment and, at this point, they become personality disorders.

The American Psychiatric Association's *Diagnostic and Statistical Manual of Mental Disorders* (Fourth Edition, Text Revision) defines personality disorders in this way: "The essential feature of a Personality Disorder is an enduring pattern of inner experience and behavior that deviates markedly from the expectations of the individual's culture" (2000, p. 686).*

---

*Passages in this chapter are reprinted with permission from the *Diagnostic and Statistical Manual of Mental Disorders,* Fourth Edition, Text Revision, Copyright 2000, American Psychiatric Association.

Although there are ten distinct categories of personality disorder, an alternative view, a dimensional perspective, suggests that personality disorders can be understood as extreme points along a dimensional personality trait continuum. For example, at times we might demonstrate obsessive-compulsive behaviors by "needing to control everything in sight." At other times we may express narcissistic tendencies when we "fervently wish that the world revolved around our every need." In fact, these patterns are reflective of the major psychological themes that run through modern culture: fear of abandonment, difficulties in intimacy, and fear of asserting one's real self. When these become extreme, they become personality disorders.

This chapter examines alternative treatments for two types of personality disorder: the borderline personality disorder and the narcissistic personality disorder. Historically, personality disorders have been considered very difficult to treat (Ronningstam, 1998). After all, they are the visceral, enduring characteristics of our personalities. Beginning in the 1990s, however, alternative therapies have been improving treatment (Linehan, 1993a).

Some of these alternatives combine elements of Eastern spiritual thought with the best of modern psychological techniques. They are called psychospiritual therapies, and they address the meaning of life and the very deep core identity of the personality. From this greater depth of self, new, more adaptive personality traits can emerge.

EMERGENCE OF THE PSYCHOSPIRITUAL THERAPIES AS TREATMENTS FOR PERSONALITY DISORDERS

For much of the twentieth century, available psychoanalytic treatments produced mixed results. Practitioners were often "baffled, drained, and frustrated" (Goldstein, 1990, p. 4). By the 1970s and 1980s, using an object relations model, Kernberg (1984) began to make some progress. Similarly, cognitive-behavioral therapists were having some success in abating the very serious suicidal complications of severe borderline personality disorder (Linehan, 1993a). These early theorists deserve much credit—they improved treatment, saved many lives, and created a platform on which new ideas could be built. By the early 1990s, treatment methods had begun to mature and evolve. Cognitive-behavioral therapy had become even more precise and effective. Another new treatment, with its roots in the psychoanalytic traditions, the *psychology of the self,* had matured and was gaining solid recognition. Eastern spiritual thought was also beginning to affect the field of psychology, and today a growing set of treatments combines psychological theory and Eastern spiritual thought. These new psychospiritual therapies have several elements in common.

1. Symptoms that were previously seen as pathological—as an illness to be relieved, or as a set of symptoms to be removed or fixed—are now seen as opportunities for transformation.
2. The whole person—the interplay between body, mind, and spirit—has become an important consideration.
3. Most of these therapies are eclectic, in that they use a variety of techniques, often taking the best of modern psychotherapy and combining it with Eastern traditions, such as yoga and meditation.

One of these therapies, dialectical-behavioral therapy (DBT) has received widespread recognition. This therapy was devised by Marsha Linehan at the University of Washington. Numerous research studies have demonstrated DBT's ability to create significant improvement and lasting change for people with borderline personality disorder (Linehan et al., 1992, 1991; Linehan, 1993b). It is widely recognized as a premier treatment, and I will briefly review it here.

Dialectical-behavioral therapy is usually classified as a cognitive-behavioral approach, but it is actually quite holistic in nature as it combines biological, psychological, and spiritual elements. Linehan balances a very detailed, active cognitive-behavioral focus with corresponding warmth and emphasis on acceptance of the client's current psychological state, just as it is. She also focuses on "dialectics"—the synthesis of opposites. An example of this reconciliation of opposites is the simple therapeutic notion of accepting clients as they are, while trying to teach them how to embody the valuable features of their inconsistent beliefs and to resolve any contradictions between them. This synthesis then acts as a beginning for the next cycle. In this way, truth is seen as a process that develops over time in transactions between people. Truth is approached as the middle between extremes. This emphasis on strategic synthesis, according to Linehan (1993a), "flows directly from the integration of a perspective drawn from Eastern (Zen) practice with Western psychological practice" (p. 19).

For Linehan (1993a), "Zen mindfulness skills are central to DBT. . . . They are the first skills taught. . . . They are psychological and behavioral versions of meditation skills taught in Eastern spiritual practices" (p. 144). Mindfulness is participating in the present moment, with full attention, without judgment or internal dialogue.

Another Eastern idea central to DBT is the "wise mind," which focuses on the inherent wisdom of the client: "The therapist trusts that the patient has within herself all of the potential that is necessary for change. The acorn is the tree" (Linehan, 1993a, p. 33).

How effective are these techniques? Most other therapies anticipate a lengthy course of treatment, often lasting for years. Linehan found significant differences over the course of a *one-year* program when DBT was compared to "treatment as usual." For example, DBT subjects reported better control of their emotions, better interpersonal skills, less anger, and less anxious rumination. The superiority of DBT as compared to treatment as usual, was maintained both six and twelve months after the end of the one-year program (Linehan, 1993a).

Through her research and success, Linehan has brought her version of psychospiritual therapy into the mainstream of psychological thought. She used replicable methods and made scientific testing of her theories relatively easy. This is a good model for new theorists to follow.

HUMANOLOGICAL THERAPY

Another evolving psychospiritual therapy is called *Humanology*. This evolving therapy draws from the Eastern disciplines of Kundalini yoga and meditation taught by Yogi Bhajan and the healing tradition and philosophy of Sikh Dharma. Humanology shares certain features with the dialectical behavioral therapy described previously: self-transformation is seen as a choice, Eastern practices are used directly in the therapies, and the orientation is to work with the whole person—mind, body, and spirit.

Humanology emphasizes the idea that to be truly human is to allow the light of the soul to come through the thoughts of the mind. Humanology uses this guiding principle, a wide array of dialogue techniques, and the disciplines of Kundalini yoga and meditation to achieve a higher level of integration to body, mind, and soul and hence more awareness, control, and choice to the individual. Gurucharan Khalsa explains that Humanology treats and refines the psyche of the soul (Bhajan and Khalsa, 1998).

Humanology is the study of how to achieve a mind that naturally thinks and acts from a balanced, conscious perspective. As a therapeutic orientation, the system can be used to create an internal state that is dynamic, attractive, peaceful, and creative.

The thoughts of our mind give way to our feelings and actions. Our thoughts connect with our beliefs and nourish our lives, just as much as the food we eat. The ability to be aware of and consciously choose our foundational beliefs and daily thoughts is central to Humanology.

Some of the major goals of this orientation are to create a stable, internal emotional self, and then *choose* how one wants to behave with others based on intuition and compassion. These objectives are achieved through therapeutic interventions and through the practice of Kundalini yoga and meditation.

Personality disorders are a perfect match for Humanology because it can affect the underlying mental and physiological patterns of these maladaptive traits. In the next two sections, we will look at the use of Humanology with borderline and narcissistic personality disorders.

USING HUMANOLOGY WITH BORDERLINE PERSONALITY DISORDER PATIENTS

Description

Interest in an understanding of and treatment for borderline personality disorder has grown tremendously over the past decade. The current DSM estimates that in America, about 2 percent of the population at large, 10 percent of all outpatients, and as many as 20 percent of psychiatric inpatients have borderline personality disorder.

The DSM defines the general diagnostic criteria for a borderline personality disorder (BPD) in this way: "The essential feature of a Borderline Personality Disorder is a pervasive pattern of instability in interpersonal relationships, self-image, and affects, and marked impulsivity that begins in early adulthood and is present in a variety of contexts" (American Psychiatric Association, 2000, p. 706).*

Symptoms can range from mild to severe, and you may find a little bit of yourself (or your teenager!) in the description that follows. In an interesting book titled *I Hate You—Don't Leave Me!* Jerold Kriesman and Hal Straus (1991) explain that people who truly have borderline personality disorder lack the ability to moderate the waves of their emotions or control their external behaviors.

Individuals with borderline personality disorder have unstable moods. Although they often express a bitter sadness, they can also exhibit bursts of inappropriate anger or anxiety that can last for hours or days, sometimes followed by guilt or shame. They may feel empty or bored, or pursue new, thrill-seeking activities, such as gambling or unsafe driving. In addition, they are unstable in the way they view other people. For example, in the beginning of relationships they at first idealize friends and lovers as marvelous caregivers, but when the day of inevitable disappointment arrives, there is no measured response. Instead, an extreme reversal of opinion is dictated. One day, a friend is seen as "wonderful"; the next day that same friend is seen as "totally uncaring" or "cruelly punishing."

At the same time, individuals with this syndrome are absolutely frantic to avoid real (or imagined) rejection or abandonment (Linehan, 1995). Just the thought of possible rejection or separation can lead to an extremely intense emotional reaction, which can be accompanied by a wild emotional outburst with little or no thought of its effects on another person (Druck, 1989).

This pattern of instability holds true for self-image as well. Individuals with borderline personality disorder often shift their goals, values, careers, and opinions without rational reference. In the most

*Reprinted with permission from the *Diagnostic and Statistical Manual of Mental Disorders,* Fourth Edition, Text Revision, Copyright 2000, American Psychiatric Association.

extreme cases, individuals with borderline personality disorder make recurrent suicidal threats and/or attempts.

Treatment

In this section, we will look at the evolving applications of Humanology for the treatment of mild to moderate borderline personality disorders. As described, borderline personality disorder is marked by both unstable emotional states and erratic behavior. Humanology is particularly effective in treating the primary problems for people with BPD, because two of the major outcomes of this therapy are (1) the creation of a stable, internal emotional self and self-image and (2) increased emotional and behavioral control.

Creating an Internally Stable State (Key Principle: Beneath the Neuroses Is a "True Self")

Several key principles and methods are used in Humanology to help clients create internally stable emotional states. In this section, we examine the concept of the "true self" and how to activate it.

Individuals with BPD have unstable self-images. At the core of this spiritual approach is the belief that underneath all our neuroses, hidden agendas, and personality disorders is a true, stable self, which we can choose to empower. People with BPD can be taught to access these "true selves" to achieve a new, more secure identity.

A typical approach to the deeper identity in Humanology has three parts:

1. The first technique is an elaboration of the different parts of the self. (I recommend various psychotherapies, such as neuro-linguistic programming [NLP], which are very effective tools.)
2. The second technique is a consistent morning practice of yoga and meditation. Specific Kundalini yoga sets and meditations reset a person's physiology, relax and balance the body and mind, and give a consistent experience of spirit, which connects the individual to a larger spiritual reality. Numerous studies have researched the ability of yoga and meditation to reduce depression and anxiety (Stein, 2003).

3. The third technique is to model for patients the process of transforming negative thoughts with positive thoughts. This practice
in essence is a mental form of martial arts. For example, a
thought comes up: "Oh, he will leave me. I know it!" Then, with
equal emotion, you answer, *"No!* I am a wonderful woman! I
forgive me my faults, and I am protected!" This new thought re-
directs the mind away from the negative, to the true reality
within, where you and your soul are one.

Increasing Emotional and Behavioral Control (Key Principle: Thoughts Initiate Emotions)

People with borderline personality disorders need help understanding how their internal cognitive processes interact with the other
people in their lives. Humanology uses two techniques: a therapeutic
dialogue and a yoga and meditation strategy. Using any of the highly
effective cognitive therapies over the course of the therapy, the goal is
to help the client become aware of the *details* of the interactions
between

- the client's thoughts,
- how these thoughts manifest in communication and behavior, and
- the responses that these communications then elicit from others.

In essence, then, a relationship can be described as an interpersonal
cycle in which a person's construal processes lead to a characteristic
set of communications and behaviors, which in turn elicit a set of
predictable responses. Therapy, from the Humanology perspective,
helps the client to become aware of this entire process in order to create a new organization of his or her choosing. The object of this work
is to allow the client to *choose* how he or she feels and reacts.

Kundalini yoga and meditation are also used to directly influence
the physical patterns and internal psychological structure. For example, the client might be asked with proper framing, strength of therapeutic alliance, and absence of any values conflict to do a series of exercises in a specific synergetic combination, called a "kriya," for
twenty to thirty minutes followed by a meditation such as the following that builds the ability to perceive yourself and others clearly past
emotional surges of thoughts and feelings (KRI, 2003).

Meditation for a Calm Heart*

Sit with spine straight and chin slightly in. Look straight with the eyes 1/10th open. Place the left hand on the center of the chest at the heart center (see Figure 8.1). Keep the palm flat against the chest, fingers parallel to the ground, pointing right. Raise the right hand up to the right side as if giving a pledge. Touch the tip of the index finger to the tip of the thumb.

The palm faces forward and the elbow is relaxed near the side with the forearm perpendicular to the ground (see Figure 8.2). Concentrate on the breath. Regulate each bit of the breath consciously. Inhale slowly and deeply through both nostrils. Suspend the breath in and raise the chest. Retain it as long as possible. Then exhale smoothly, gradually, and completely. When the breath is totally out, lock the breath out for as long as possible without strain or gasping. Continue this pattern for three to thirty-one minutes. At then end, inhale and exhale strongly three times. "The posture and breath meditation induces a deep feeling of calmness and a still point in the psyche from which conscious choice over thoughts and reactions to them is facilitated" (G. Khalsa, interview, October 2003).

Case Example: Stephen, Revisited

Although borderline personality disorder is more common in women, this case is of a man that I'll call Stephen. Some years ago, Stephen came to me for therapy just after his therapist had died. He was a good man in his forties, independently wealthy, and able to donate some of his time to noble works. His challenge was that he was very, very lonely. All of his relationships with women were tumultuous and short-lived. No woman had withstood what I termed "his test for constant approval." If a woman showed any doubt in him, even for a short period of time, he would reject her and banish her from his life. Upon further discussion, I found that in addition to the test for constant approval, Stephen thought that most women were not really pretty enough for him anyway.

In fact, when Stephen actually did meet a woman he thought was pretty enough, he became terrified that she would reject him. In response to this perceived possible rejection, Stephen quite often found that he became extremely sullen. At other times he would fly into wild accusatory and seemingly irrational rages at the woman he was interested in. This erratic behavior would cause the woman to leave him.

FIGURE 8.1. Body Position for the Meditation for a Calm Heart

Stephen's own self-image was also quite unstable: he wavered between thinking he was a good, caring human being and thinking that he was a person with an empty life, devoid of any meaning. He entered therapy, a willing student, looking forward to making a change.

Using an approach similar to Humanology as just described, we reviewed in detail, how Stephen thought, felt, and reacted during specific stressful situations. We also developed internal strategies to calm his mind and reduce his fears. Over the course of a year, Stephen came to understand that he *wanted* to be able to control his emotional states. He began to see that "loving someone," for example, is a state of mind. I explained to him that actually, contrary to common cultural beliefs, people cannot "make you love them" or

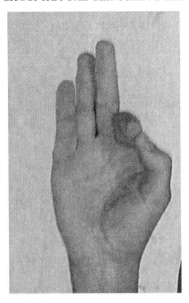

FIGURE 8.2. Position of Right Hand for the Meditation for a Calm Heart

conversely "make you hate them." "Loving someone" is a choice. The individual chooses this mind state based on specific criteria, consistent with the "true self" just described in the Humanology section. The more Stephen chose to live in specific emotional states, the more liberated and happy he became.

Everyone has heard the phrase, "He really pushes my buttons!" Translated, this phrase means that someone else "makes you" have an emotional reaction. In our talks together, I explained to Stephen that one of the psychological goals of life is to "have control over your buttons." In this way, no one but you can determine your state of well-being. Another not-so-old saying many are familiar with is, "He who dies with the most toys wins." I revised this phrase for Stephen to state, "He who lives with the least number of pushable buttons wins."

Stephen sincerely wanted to win. He developed the ability to observe his internal reactions and control them to some extent. He also developed a more "stable sense of self"—a personality he wanted to strive to become. In addition, Stephen practiced specific yoga and meditations, which were designed to increase his internal stability and his control over his behaviors. This practice helped to make him become, generally, more calm. He developed a long-term friendship with a woman for the first time in many years.

And then one day, it happened. He came into the office with a big smile on his face and said, "I think I met a woman I can marry!" After another year of intense back and forth, love and hate reactions, he also relaxed his "exam for constant approval" and finally chose to marry. He promised her "everlasting, though somewhat conflicted, adoration" and they were married. We will meet Stephen's partner in the case study related to narcissism.

USING HUMANOLOGY WITH NARCISSISTIC PERSONALITY DISORDER PATIENTS

Description

The DSM-IV-TR defines the general diagnostic criteria for a narcissistic personality disorder (NPD) in this way: "The essential feature of Narcissistic Personality Disorder is a pervasive pattern of grandiosity, need for admiration, and lack of empathy that begins by early adulthood and is present is a variety of contexts" (American Psychiatric Association, 2000, p. 714).*

Narcissistic traits can be quite common in teenagers. Although many generations of parents have spent sleepless nights worrying about their teens, most teens will outgrow, or at least significantly dampen, these characteristics. For the person who develops narcissistic personality disorder, the symptoms range from mild to severe.

The current DSM (APA, 2000) estimates that about 1 percent of the population at large and 2 to 16 percent of all people seeking psychological treatment are diagnosed with narcissistic personality disorder. The term *narcissistic* has entered conversational dialogue to mean an ego-driven, selfish person.

Individuals with narcissistic personality disorder present themselves to others in a grandiose, entitled way. They can be arrogant, haughty, jealous, and condescending. They commonly overestimate their abilities and appear boastful and pretentious. They expect to receive whatever they want, no matter what the implications are for the other person.

People who are in relationship with someone with narcissistic personality disorder describe an emotionally cold person who lacks sensitivity and empathy. Individuals with narcissistic personality disorder tend to form relationships only with those who might advance

---

*Reprinted with permission from the *Diagnostic and Statistical Manual of Mental Disorders,* Fourth Edition, Text Revision, Copyright 2000, American Psychiatric Association.

their goals or in some way enhance their self-esteem. Often, they will undervalue the accomplishments of others. They may talk excessively about themselves, with little interest in the other person. If they do recognize that someone they know has a vulnerability, they may view it with contempt and as a weakness.

On the other hand, individuals who have narcissistic personality disorder can also be very charming. Their driving ambitions may make them remarkably successful. Their internal experiences vacillate between an empty coldness to grandiose fantasies. They are extremely sensitive to criticism. If they feel blamed or criticized, they may withdraw or attack, or create an appearance of humility that masks and, in a sense, protects their underlying feeling of superiority (Johnson, 1987).

Treatment

Similar to the previous DSM description, Dimaggio et al. (2002) explain that NPD can arise because of a deficit in two metacognitive skills: the inability to access one's own internal feelings, as well as a separate skill that would allow a person to activate his or her understandings of the emotions of others. "Narcissists are not able to link an inner state with relationship variables" (p. 425). Simply put, their intuition is not functioning as it should.

Stephen Johnson (1987) tried to humanize the narcissistic personality. His book begins this way:

> Some of my best friends are narcissists. . . . In the main these people contribute a good deal to their fellow human beings, but they pay dearly in pain and aliveness for their driven achievements. They are too busy proving their worth—or more properly, disapproving their worthlessness—to *feel* the love, appreciation, and joy of human connectedness. (p. 3)

Therapy, then, involves reaching behind the grandiose manifestations to the person's heart. Humanology can be very effective in treating problems associated with NPD because among its assets are its abilities to teach intuition and compassion.

Increase the Ability to Be Intuitive (Key Principle:
Intuition Is the Guide to a Good Life)

People with narcissistic personality disorder lack an intuitive sense of themselves and of their place in the context of the people around them. Humanology approaches this issue from two directions: a therapeutic intervention and a yoga/meditation strategy.

The therapeutic intervention involves creating an "intuitive signature"—an easily recognized visceral/mental pattern that tells the client what is true. These patterns are often called "gut feelings" (a feeling at the heart or stomach) or "light bulbs." In Humanology, it is believed that everyone has the potential to have a beautifully honed intuition. Some intuitive signatures are more complex, but once known, these patterns are very reliable and the client will understand how he or she and others feel.

Many meditations are said to increase your intuitive ability. Kundalini yoga and meditation are known to foster consciousness. In fact, the system is known as the "Yoga of Awareness." In this case, the client might be asked to do a simple eleven-minute meditation such as the following to achieve this goal (KRI, 2000).

To Develop the Signature of Intuition*

Sit with a straight spine. Place the hands in front of the chest at the heart center with the fingers interlaced and the index fingers pointing up (see Figures 8.3 and 8.4). The eyes are closed for each of the three parts:

A. Chant the mantra sounds: ong, namo, guroo, dev namo, continuously for three to eleven minutes. Stay mindful at the end for a minute.
B. Keep the same posture and breathe slowly as you watch the breath. Let every thought go after noticing it. Enter into a thoughtless state for three to eleven minutes.
C. Stay in the same position and begin a rapid, steady diaphragmatic breath through the nostrils at 120 strokes a minute that is equal in and out. The technique is called Breath of Fire. Continue for three to eleven minutes. To end, inhale deeply, hold the

---

*Copyright Yogi Bhajan 2004. All rights reserved.

breath as you compress the muscles of the ribcage and spine. Exhale powerfully through the mouth. Repeat three times and relax.

This meditation is a good example of a powerful combination of rhythm, relaxation, and stimulation that anchors a new state of awareness and perception in the practitioner. It is useful for cracking an insular ego and developing enhanced recognition of subtle emotional and social cues in others, especially when used along with therapeutic humanological dialogue. (G. Khalsa, interview, October 2003)

Increase Tolerance and Compassion (Key Principle: Live from the Heart)

Love is a state that you can choose. In our modern society, we think that others "make us angry" (or sad or loving), but the truth is that we can choose our reactions. People with narcissistic personality disorder believe they have no control over their emotions; they simply feel empty or cold at times.

As Stephen Johnson (1987) points out in a previous quote, therapy involves getting to the person's heart, behind the grandiosity to his or her vulnerability. People with NPD have an exquisite vulnerability, and if the therapist can stay very tuned to that innocence, a therapeutic and healing relationship can be built. Yoga and meditation are also known to open the door to compassionate feelings. Kundalini meditations often use beautiful, enchanting mantras—this technique brings a full heart, even when it has been empty for a long time.

Case Example: Jackie

The DSM estimates that about 50 to 75 percent of the cases of NPD are men. The case I introduce today is a woman, who I will call Jackie. Stephen, the man we met earlier, introduced her to me. Stephen was right: she was a very beautiful and very intelligent woman, the kind that most people are drawn to. Like Stephen, she had had her share of difficult relationships. She had had a couple of serious boyfriends; each seemed to be the best man on the planet when she first started dating him. But with each man, she realized that she had been wrong—they just were not as caring and smart as she had thought they were; in fact, they were boring and irritating. Stephen

FIGURE 8.3.

seemed different. He was very attentive, and he was already successful, so that was not a worry for her. "I like Stephen," she said. "I can feel that he adores me and wants to take care of me. I like that. I was always looking for a man of his caliber."

When they first married, they did well together, and I did not see Stephen as a client for quite a while. Then one day, Jackie called and asked to see me. After checking with Stephen and making sure that Jackie understood that I had been Stephen's therapist and that they were both comfortable with this arrangement, we agreed to meet.

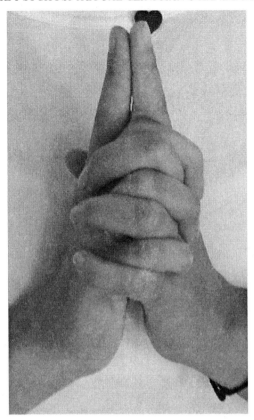

FIGURE 8.4.

Jackie spoke quite softy. "I'm afraid I married the wrong man. He is so quick to yell. I feel like he can't control himself. I don't think I love him anymore, and I just feel empty."

Jackie was withdrawing quickly. In her mind, Stephen was making her feel empty and distressed. "Stephen doesn't pay enough attention to me. He doesn't want to spend time with me, just talking and connecting. I've repeatedly asked him to stop yelling, but he does not care enough to stop. Sometimes, I try to stop a fight by walking away from his yelling, but amazingly, he follows me and continues yelling!"

I asked her why Stephen was acting this way and she said she had no idea. Jackie was vulnerable in this first session, and I stayed with her until she could feel her sadness. The empty, cold feeling went away, but now her sadness needed to be addressed.

I knew that Stephen was a willing student and that he would try to learn—if they could talk with each other and openly acknowledge their needs. I sent her home to talk with him to ask why he yelled and seemed so distant.

It turned out that Stephen was terrified that she would leave him. Over time, they each learned to take responsibility for their own feelings, instead of accusing each other, and they learned more tolerance and acceptance of each other's flaws. I recommended a meditation to do together. It helped Stephen to feel less afraid, and it helped Jackie to become more intuitive and to feel more connected.

CONCLUSION

Psychospiritual systems contain valuable techniques to add to a therapists' toolkit. In this chapter I have introduced a system, Humanology, which is gaining practitioners and inspiring new applications and training. This psychospiritual system can be effectively used to create an internal mental state that is dynamic, attractive, peaceful, and creative. The techniques of Humanology teach you how to achieve and maintain this state of mind.

Marsha Linehan's work with dialectic behavioral therapy provides a good model for the development of a new psychological framework. She created a model with procedures that could be replicated and studied. Although certain aspects of yoga and meditation have been researched, if Humanology is to go forward and gain the wide acceptance and use it warrants, more scientific research documenting clinical effects and mechanisms should be done. This rich area is ready for exploration and application in the expanding psychospiritual therapeutic field.

REFERENCES

American Psychiatric Association (2000). *Diagnostic and Statistical Manual of Mental Disorders,* Fourth Edition, Text Revision. Washington, DC: American Psychiatric Association.

Bhajan, Y. and Khalsa, G. (1998). *The Mind: Its Projections and Multiple Facets.* Espanola, NM: Kundalini Research Institute.

Di Maggio, G., Semerari, A., Falcone, M., Nicolò, G., Carcione, A., and Procacci, M. (2002). Metacognition, states of mind, cognitive biases, and interpersonal cycles: Proposal for an integrated narcissism model. *Journal of Psychotherapy Integration,* 12(4), 421-451.

Druck, A. (1989). *Four Therapeutic Approaches to the Borderline Patient.* Northvale, NJ: Jason Aronson Inc.

Goldstein, E. (1990). *Borderline Disorders: Clinical Models and Techniques.* New York: The Guilford Press.

Johnson, S. (1987). *Humanizing Narcissistic Style.* New York: W.W. Norton and Co.

Kernberg, O. (1984*). Severe Personality Disorders.* New Haven: Yale University Press.

Kriesman, J. and Straus, H. (1991). *I Hate You—Don't Leave Me!* New York: Avon Books.

Kundalini Research Institute (KRI) (2000). Kundalini Research Institute Archives, Yogi Bhajan. November 28, 2000.

Kundalini Research Institute (KRI) (2003). *The Aquarian Teacher: International Kundalini Yoga Teacher Training Manual, Level 1.* Espanola, NM: Kundalini Research Institute.

Linehan, M. M. (1993a). *Cognitive-Behavioral Treatment of Borderline Personality Disorder.* New York: The Guilford Press.

Linehan, M. M. (1993b). *Skills Training Manual for Treating Borderline Personality Disorder.* New York: The Guilford Press.

Linehan, M. M. (1995). *Understanding Borderline Personality Disorder: The Dialectical Approach Program Manual.* New York: The Guilford Press.

Linehan, M. M., Armstrong, H., Suarez, A., Allmon, D., and Heard, H. (1991). Cognitive-behavioral treatment of chronically parasuicidal borderline patients. *Archives of General Psychiatry,* 48, 1060-1064.

Linehan, M. M., Tutek, D., Heard, H., and Armstrong, H. (1992). Interpersonal outcome of cognitive behavioral treatment for chronically suicidal borderline patients. *American Journal of Psychiatry,* 151(12), 1771-1775.

Ronningstam, E. (1998). *Disorders of Narcissism.* Washington, DC: American Psychiatric Press.

Stein, J. (2003). Just say om. *Time Magazine,* August 4, Vol. 162, #5, pp. 48-56.

Chapter 9

Assessment and Treatment of Conduct Disorders: A Moral Reasoning Model and Psychospiritual Approach

Celia A. Drake
Deborah J. Lewis

INTRODUCTION

To know, to love and to serve is the trinomial of all religions, but the child is the true maker of our spirituality. He teaches us the plan of nature for giving form to our conduct and character, a plan fully traced out in all its details of age and work, with its need for freedom and intense activity in accordance with the laws of life. What matters is not physics, botany, or work of the hand, but the will, and the components of the human spirit which construct themselves by work.

Maria Montessori
The Absorbent Mind, p. 201

Childhood behavioral disorders such as conduct disorder and oppositional defiant disorder which are referred to in the aggregate as disorders of conduct or disruptive behavior disorders, are increasing (Fonagy et al., 2002). According to the *Diagnostic and Statistical Manual of Mental Disorders* (DSM-IV-TR) (American Psychiatric Association, 2000), the prevalence of conduct disorder alone among the general child population is estimated to be from 1 percent to more than 10 percent. Children diagnosed with disorders of conduct account for many of the referrals to mental health practitioners. Symptoms and behaviors associated with disorders of conduct are on a continuum from mild intensity to those with significant consequences including aggression and serious crime. Recent research at the National Institute of Mental Health (2003) cites increased incidents of violent acting out in children and adolescents. Researchers such as Hare and Forth (2001) are also concerned with the relationship of childhood disorders of conduct as precursors to adult psychopathology, specifically antisocial personality disorder and psychopathy.

Etiology

Understanding the etiology of disorders of conduct is complex and requires integration from many disciplines such as neurophysiology, psychiatry, psychology, systems theory, and theology. For the evaluating clinician, careful consideration of the physiological, environmental, academic, behavioral, social, and spiritual contributions to the problem produces the most complete picture and allows for multiple paths of intervention. Psychospiritual approaches are well suited to add as assessment and treatment tools for these disorders. Available techniques can provide guides for the child to develop the resources, values, capabilities and will that is both the glue and the character of the developing child. Psychospiritual techniques such as meditation can enhance the prime skills needed of self-awareness, self-assessment, and self-control as well as to enhance learning.

Defining Conduct Disorder

The DSM-IV-TR (American Psychiatric Association, 2000, p. 93) defines conduct disorder as a "repetitive and persistent pattern in which the basic rights of others or major age-appropriate societal norms or rules are violated."* Behavioral manifestations include lack of guilt or remorse, inflated or low self-esteem, lack of frustration tolerance, poor modulation of anger, and recklessness. Associated behavioral disturbances are substance abuse, sexual acting out, academic difficulties, and social problems. A high incidence of comorbid disorders exists including learning disabilities, substance abuse, and attention and mood disorders (Fonagy et al., 2002). According to the DSM-IV-TR (APA, 2000), onset ranges from preschool years to middle childhood or adolescence. Prior to exhibiting the symptoms of conduct disorder, children may begin to manifest behaviors of oppositional defiant disorder such as defiance, temper outbursts, lack of responsibility, and violation of rules. Children who exhibit severe behavioral disturbances and symptoms have an increased risk for developing antisocial personality disorder and substance abuse disorders as adults (APA, 2000).

In the DSM-IV-TR (APA, 2000) children with conduct disorder are noted to demonstrate patterns of behavior related to violations of rules and basic rights including the presence of three or more of the following: (1) aggression to people and animals; (2) destruction of property; (3) deceitfulness or theft; and (4) serious violations of rules. Impairment in social, academic, or occupational functioning must be present and, if over age eighteen, the diagnostic criteria for antisocial personality disorder must not be present. Conduct disorder is further specified as aggressive versus nonaggressive. This disorder is diagnosed more frequently in males than females. Careful evaluation of behaviors is indicated to delineate the etiology of behaviors and delineation of comorbid treatable disorders.

Assessment

Traditional diagnostic assessment includes identifying symptoms and behaviors that are generally accepted in diagnostic categories. Some childhood diagnostic categories that identify behavioral disturbances include oppositional defiant disorder, conduct disorder, and attention disorders, i.e., attention deficit hyperactivity disorder and

---

*Reprinted with permission from the *Diagnostic and Statistical Manual of Mental Disorders,* Fourth Edition, Text Revision, Copyright 2000, American Psychiatric Association.

attention deficit disorder. Behavioral disturbance may also be associated with mood disorders such as anxiety, depression, and bipolar disorder.

Mental health professionals' traditional assessment of behavioral disorders in childhood is typically comprised of a structured psychiatric and/or psychological interview and a history from parents. Formal psychoeducational or neuropsychological assessment is sometimes utilized. Rating scales of behavioral disorders completed by parents and teachers are utilized with greater prevalence if the children are suspected of having attention difficulties.

Assessment should be a multifaceted approach with examination of the child's functioning across all domains, i.e., physiological, environmental, academic, behavioral, social, and spiritual. Assessment of the child's environment and identification of risk and protective factors should also be included (Bloomquist and Schnell, 2002; Connor, 2002). Risk factors include genetic predisposition for mental illness and/or alcohol or substance abuse, poor physical health or nutrition, developmental delays, attention deficits, learning disabilities, familial criminal history, active alcohol or substance abuse, parents with personality disorders, poor environment, lack of role models for social and academic achievement, lack of social success, and difficulty navigating complex ethical and moral decisions. Protective factors include social support, intelligence, academic success and learning ability, social skills, positive peer relationships, leisure interests and talents, physical health and abilities, mental well-being, environmental support, family resources (time, money, interest, stability), religious affiliation or spiritual connection, capacity for emotional maturity and empathy, and positive role models. Because of the complex etiology of conduct disorder, comprehensive assessment that identifies risk and protective factors is critical to developing appropriate treatment strategies and recommendations.

The behavior exhibited by children with conduct disorder has a disturbing impact on self-esteem and overall psychosocial functioning. Although various approaches for the treatment of conduct disorder are used, the prognosis for successful treatment is often guarded and dependent upon availability of those interventions found to be most successful. There is vocal societal concern for the demonstration of aggressiveness and disregard for societal norms, especially when it is exhibited by children and adolescents. Treatment interventions have been extensively reviewed and efficacy documented (Fonagy et al., 2002; Bloomquist and Schnell, 2002; Henggeler et al., 1998), but availability of these therapeutic interventions may be limited in many communities. Although children with conduct disorder frequently have behavior problems in school, the lack of availability of successful interventions may leave school personnel with little intervention other than punitive measures, e.g., detentions and/or suspensions. Families are often directed to find some means to cope with these children with little direction as to what or where meaningful interventions are available. Multisystemic therapy (MST), which intervenes at many system levels (family, school, community), has been found to be most promising (Fonagy et al., 2002) as a therapeutic intervention; however ready access to the extensive training required for practitioners may not be available.

The Rationale for a Psychospiritual Model

Although some behavioral disorders may readily respond to traditional mental health interventions, such as medication and psychotherapy, others do not.

Central to behavioral disturbances in conduct disorder is violation of others' rights and/or violation of societal norms or rules. Inherent in every culture are value systems. Values evolve in a complex interplay with the rules, laws, religion, and social concerns of the community. Education of children in every culture, either formally or informally, includes training in moral conduct. Optimally, exposure to moral development and education begins the day of birth. As with any ability, some children have a natural talent to develop moral behavior in spite of environmental limitations. All children need to be taught, but some require specific remediation of conduct skills. Families are the first exposure to ethical and/or moral training. Additional exposure in community settings, through schools, peers, religious practices, and other settings will either reinforce or conflict with the child's initial family exposure. Religious beliefs, although diverse, have provided the basic moral tenets in the development of most cultures. Religion has greatly influenced, if not founded, the values, ethics, and morals in most modern cultures. Although aspects of religion and spirituality are present in the fabric of cultures, the ethical threads are, at times, difficult to tease out, and therefore can be difficult to expressly teach. It is possible to teach moral reasoning and principles of ethical conduct that will complement, not conflict, with someone's religious faith.

If a child is raised without a context that models values, ethical actions, and "good people," moral development may not occur in the way that benefits the greater culture. Particular capacities such as empathy, remorse, and joy are useful in the ability to understand the consequences of our actions on others, to conform our behavior, and to learn from our mistakes. "We have no means of discriminating between right and wrong if we do not take into account others' feelings, others' suffering" (Dalai Lama, 1999, p. 28).

The capacity of empathy requires an individual to experience the point of view of another and to experience, in part, what another experiences. Ethical behavior also requires individuals to conform their actions in accordance with a greater moral understanding and to delay acting on impulses. A child with conduct disorder may have limited or no empathic capacity. Some may be able to develop empathy while others may not. Even with the absence of empathy, however, ethical decision making can be taught; but it would be limited to conforming behavior to rules.

Some treatment interventions of conduct disorders do emphasize techniques of moral reasoning, however, specific emphasis on teaching ethical decision making and empathy skills is a primary focus in psychospiritual interventions. In utilizing the interventions that specifically address this issue of ethics, consideration is given to spiritual models that teach morality and ethics in the absence of or in conjunction with religious beliefs.

Religion has been the source of codes of conduct that permeate Western (and other) cultures and serve as sources of moral inspiration, e.g., the Golden Rule, Ten Commandments. Numerous religious and spiritual traditions can serve as models for good human behavior. A particular religion is not required in order to develop "basic human values, that is a sense of caring, a sense of responsibility, and a sense of forgiveness" (Dalai Lama, 2003, p. 149). "Besides, religious belief is no guarantee of moral integrity. . . . But here let me say that no one should suppose it could ever be possible to devise a set of rules or laws to provide us with the answer to every ethical dilemma, even if we were to accept religion as the basis of morality. Such a formulaic approach could never hope to capture the richness and diversity of human experience. It would also give grounds for arguing that we are responsible only to the letter of those laws, rather than for our actions" (Dalai Lama, 1999, p. 27).

Children with conduct disorder are not always acting like good human beings. Intervention may require either development or reenforcement of values that are consistent with the basic tenets of "goodness" in human behavior. The precise definition of "goodness" can and has been debated. We propose looking to philosophers and theologians who have searched for universal moral principles. For example, the Baha'i have looked for commonalities among the major religions to help discover universal moral principles. According to the Baha'i, fundamental in each major religion is some variation of the Golden Rule, demonstrating a cross-cultural and historical concern regarding the treatment of others. Furthermore, questions of moral philosophy have been pondered since ancient times. Ancient philosophers such as Socrates believed ethics were the single most important ingredient in a good life (Kreeft, 2004).

Interest in utilizing spiritual interventions in mental health has increased in recent decades (Benson and Stark, 1996; Murphy and Donovan, 1997). The use of meditation techniques for the treatment of, or as a treatment adjunct for, medical and psychiatric conditions has become more commonplace. The context of a spiritual teaching is important to understand if that context is to become a resource for teaching moral development. Spiritual practice may offer specific techniques that may impact the psychological development and well-being of the participant. Because of the neurobiological basis for the development of the self (Schore, 1994) and the identification of brain structure associated with the development of moral functioning and empathy, techniques in spiritual practices that are found to impact brain function (Austin, 1998) may provide a basis for utilizing specific meditation techniques and/or other spiritual practices. Basic relaxation techniques, e.g., focusing on the breath, in Western society, have for its roots ancient spiritual practice and meditation techniques.

Brain-Behavior Research and Implications for Conduct Disorder Conceptualization and Treatment

Deficits in frontal lobe functioning, specifically right orbital frontal functioning, have been found to be associated with behavioral dyscontrol. Identification of the brain/behavior model of biophysical functioning for disorders of conduct would indicate the need to develop interventions that specifically and positively impact different parts of the brain. Identification of particular structures of the brain related to specific behavioral constructs, e.g., empathy, impulse control, and aggression, provide a beginning scientific basis for treatment interventions beyond those traditionally used. Disorders of conduct can be conceptualized in many ways including as disorders of specific brain functioning.

While a specific part of the brain may be impacted in any intervention, because of the unitary functioning of the brain, other parts may also be positively or negatively impacted. Specific delineation of brain functions and related behavioral manifestations may lead to the potential of meditation or other spiritual practices to treat conduct disorders and/or comorbid disorders often diagnosed with conduct disorder.

Brain-behavior relationships are complex. Abilities such as self-regulation and emotional modulation have multiple interacting components. Psychobiological systems such as the immune system, once thought to be independent of any emotional or mental factors, are now presumed to be affected by a person's stress level and environmental condition. Individuals have been successfully trained to regulate physical and mental conditions such as stress and anxiety.

Disorders of conduct can be conceptualized, in part, as a brain disorder resulting in the inability to behave morally and follow an ethical decision-making process.

THE CASE FOR SPIRITUAL INTERVENTION

Spiritual modalities did not develop as a means to treat behavioral or psychiatric disorders, but rather to enhance the well-being, develop consciousness, and ultimately lead to enlightenment. Because of the psychophysiological impact of different spiritual techniques, the potential exists to utilize such techniques in conjunction with established interventions for physical and mental disorders. Limitations of current mental health interventions coupled with the treatment resistance of serious psychiatric conditions, calls for consideration of techniques that are not traditionally utilized. Ancient spiritual and meditative techniques may powerfully impact psychosocial development and therefore have utility as a therapeutic modality. Research on a variety of techniques, e.g., yoga and meditation, shows promise for their use in psychiatric treatment and in the treatment of disorders of conduct (Murphy and Donovan, 1997). Interest in integrating scientific and spiritual meditative practices is evidenced by the recent conference at Massachusetts Institute of Technology sponsored by the Mind and Life Institute of Investigating the Mind: Exchanges Between Buddhism and the Biobehavioral Sciences on How the Mind Works (Kalb, 2003).

The advent of research that offers the identification of the neurobiological basis for behavior, and the increasing interest in spiritual practices and specific techniques for treatment, provides a multidimensional context for the development and enhancement of functioning.

Meditation techniques may provide development and training of the mind (Bhajan and Khalsa, 1998). Through meditation and spiritual practice the potential to transform the mind and attitudes is present (Dalai Lama, 2003). Although there are many definitions of meditation, the Dalai Lama (2003) suggests that it is a spiritual discipline that allows some control of one's thoughts and emotions. With regular practice and intervention, multiple levels may be positively impacted, e.g., physical, mental, and spiritual.

The development of consciousness and awareness of self and action through spiritual practice offers the opportunity to optimize functioning. Increase in focus and attention, decrease in aggressiveness and impulsivity, and the development of thoughtfulness are found to be benefits from meditative practice. The objective viewer, as trained through spiritual practice, e.g., meditation, offers a relationship with the mind to achieve mastery (Bhajan, 1997). Actions are then not out of thoughtless habits, impulses, emotions, or patterns but consciousness, choice, and awareness. Neutrality and the capacity for responsiveness versus reactivity develop. The development of self may be enhanced or constrained by genetic and/or environmental factors. With the opportunity to teach children a context and tools to control problematic and impulsive behaviors and alter brain development, meditation as a behavioral intervention holds promise.

Reference to the context of spiritual practice is the framework inherent in any spiritual practice. Imparting the tenets of ethical conduct is not always a straightforward, easy task. As noted by Fischer (2003), "ethical conduct requires the sensitivity and readiness to discern what's right in the circumstances that are arising just now." Although it may be difficult to achieve unanimous agreement about morality and ethics, it is important to reach a basic agreement about what constitutes ethical conduct. The major religious traditions all have developed moral systems that have helped people discern ethical conduct, although religious faith does not ensure moral behavior. Secular people can act ethically. So, how can we help develop "good" human beings?

The need for moral training is essential if the individual is to develop responsibility for self and others. The context for moral development extends beyond parents to other caretakers and members of the community. At the point therapeutic intervention is called for, a failure in development and/or across systems in which the child is developing is identified.

Because conduct disorder is often characterized by a basic lack of consciousness and forethought, spiritual practice may provide the means for the development of ethical thinking as well as mastery over the mind. Meditation as a training tool is not just a means to achieve an altered state of consciousness but can also help develop awareness beyond the automatic baseline awareness that informs our ordinary human states. With developing levels of awareness, maturity, and consciousness, children are able to develop capacities of self-regulation (to calm themselves), consider options, and recognize needs in others, i.e., empathy. Acting beyond immediate basic states affords broader opportunities to be responsive and to behave responsibly to self and others.

The development of attention and focus inherent in meditation offers the opportunity to act out of consciousness and consideration. In disorders of conduct, the absence of connectedness to self and others beyond basic needs creates disruptions in functioning. With the development of protective factors, the capacity to respond meaningfully and ethically is possible even in the presence of multiple risk factors.

Austin (1998, p. 69) quotes William James, the father of psychology, "The faculty of voluntarily bringing back a wandering attention, over and over again, is the very root of judgment, character, and will."

The Use of Spiritual Techniques with Children

Through religion, children have exposure to spiritual modalities to teach beliefs and values. However, techniques and practices are increasingly available within a variety of contexts. The use of specific spiritual techniques will be dependent upon developmental status and maturity. The introduction of techniques is possible for even young children. Treatment of children requires intervention with caregivers, whether parents or others. If models of spiritual practice are to be reinforced and changes in behavior supported, education of primary caregivers is essential.

A variety of spiritual and meditation techniques are available including focus on the breath, mindfulness, chanting, prayer, and yoga. Because of well-established traditions, meditative practices that are prescriptive for specific problems are available. Specific to meditative and spiritual practices in Kundalini yoga (Bhajan and Khlasa, 1998) are practices that develop meditative insight and specific development of skills. Breathwalk (Khalsa and Bhajan, 2000) is an example of a meditation walking technique that is an integrating exercise, mindfulness, breathwork, and redirection of internal dialogues. Meditative and spiritual interventions are also available in formats that have appeal to children and adolescents (De Brunhoff, 2002; Buckley, 2003).

Some of the most effective meditation-based tools are not widely known yet. Meditation is sometimes defined narrowly as only directed attention. The richness and effectiveness of the meditative traditions is much broader (Bhajan and Khalsa, 1998). The following is an example of a meditative technique that is part of the Humanology system of psychology and Kundalini yoga founded by Yogi Bhajan (Khalsa, personal communication, 2003). The meditation includes a posture, focus, and the use of rhythmical sound, e.g., chanting. It requires a physical effort as well as attention. It is used to develop the integration of the frontal cortex with the areas of attention control (like the anterior cingulate) and impulse (like the amygdala). Children as young as five may practice this meditation. They start with a few minutes and build very gradually to a steady practice of eleven minutes. Older adolescents and adults can practice as well and extend the time to thirty-one minutes. If the practice begins at an early age, it is said to affect self-control, judgment, and attention in profoundly positive ways.

Kundalini Meditation
to Balance Impulse and Intelligence*

Sit with a straight spine either cross-legged on the floor or in a chair with both feet on the ground (see Figure 9.1). Extend the arms forward and up with the palms facing down, fingers straight. Interlock the thumbs. The bases of the hands are held at the level of the top of the head (see Figure 9.2). Close the eyes. Raise the eyes gently and focus at the brow. Now chant these sounds. Inhale and repeat these sounds four times on one breath. You can begin with fewer repetitions and build up. The sounds are *sat nam, sat nam, sat nam, sat nam, sat nam, sat nam, whahe guroo.* They are done in a steady monotone, four cycles taking about fifteen seconds.

When working with a client, the time immediately after doing this meditation is a rich therapeutic moment. Reexamining behaviors, changing internal dialogues, and getting beyond stress reactions are all strongly facilitated with this practice and progress naturally along with the internal nervous system changes to enhance a sense of self and self-control. It has the universal effects of meditation (relaxation response, presence, mood control) with specific effects emphasized as well (frontal lobe development, impulse control, stress resilience). Dozens of meditative techniques are well suited to a full spectrum of treatments to optimize the impact for individualized profiles.

A THERAPEUTIC MODEL
OF ETHICAL DECISION MAKING

Any technique, whether meditation, yoga, psychotherapy, or even detention, can develop an individual. Techniques may be harmful, beneficial, or neutral. We propose that techniques, however powerful they are, require a context. We propose that a context for life creates a purpose, a meaning, a container for techniques and then experience.

FIGURE 9.1. Body Position for the Kundalini Meditation to Balance Impulse and Intelligence

FIGURE 9.2. Position of Hands for the Kundalini Meditation to Balance Impulse and Intelligence

The context, techniques, and experiences can further the aim in a positive direction. Any aspect of life has the potential to be a powerful teacher. An ethical context lends meaning to each individual action and each experience.

SPIRITUAL TECHNIQUES IN THE TREATMENT OF CONDUCT DISORDER

As suggested, models of ethical decision making provide a context to assist the individual to develop appropriate moral decision making and reasoning. Models provide identification of values that are consistent with responsible and respectful treatment toward self and others. Benefits of appropriate responses as well as consequences for problematic actions are delineated. Training in ethical models is one aspect of treatment. The other is the development of the mind and the capacity for control. Cognitive interventions include referencing ethical models. Meditative techniques train the mind so that the individual may act in a thoughtful and respectful manner. As most spiritual traditions have meditation as a practice, a broad spectrum of techniques may be accessed in those traditions. As noted, however, religious belief is not necessary to utilize spiritual practices that are beneficial to the development of overall well-being.

There has been prior work in developing ethical decision-making models in psychology, for example the work of Bass et al. (1996) and Bersoff (2003).The following is our model ethical decision-making process that is the foundation for the process of assessment and development.

Ethical Decision-Making Process

1. Recognize a context for morality.
2. Identify ethical and moral problems as such.
3. Stop, focus, breathe, relax (even if momentary), or pray.
4. Use objective observer/neutral stance.
5. Consult trusted sources (role models, texts).
6. Generate alternatives (others can help).
7. Determine consequences for each alternative (follow through all possible consequences for self and others).

8. Choose a path and act.
9. Evaluate the outcome and self-critique.
10. Return to Step 3 if necessary.
11. Make repairs if necessary.

The child's ability is initially assessed for each step of the process. For example, in Step 2, can children identify ethical and moral problems as such? Can they recognize when one exists and under what circumstances? If not, intervention and development of this becomes part of the treatment plan. Sample assessment inquiries and interventions/development ideas are given for each of the ethical decision-making steps in Table 9.1.

THE THERAPIST AS SPIRITUAL TEACHER AND MORAL EDUCATOR

Psychospiritual interventions are not devoid of the values of those imparting them. Inherent in mental health intervention is the aspect of education. The same awareness and development based in spiritual techniques may well be part of the value system or ethical context in which a therapist acts. Whatever worldview, beliefs, religion, or spiritual training that the therapist has in his or her repertoire should be utilized in treatment. Whatever spiritual or religious context present in the family or the community of the patient may be a link to the ethical context that is proposed. The therapist should understand the tenets and basis of techniques, be well trained in specific techniques, and be aware of potential risks or benefits. Education of parents or caregivers who provide consent for treatment is essential if treatment modalities are to be provided.

Therapists may embrace their own religious or spiritual backgrounds if indicated. The utilization of techniques of a religion or spirituality requires one to act ethically and in congruence with one's values and larger community values. If therapists have an "eclectic" spiritual background and pull from many sources for techniques and values, then teaching and counseling from this broader context is appropriate for them and will be conveyed in their work. If therapists are devout and well versed in a particular religious background, they may

TABLE 9.1. Model of Ethical Decision Making/Moral Reasoning Summary Table

Decision-making step	Assessment methods	Interventions and development methods
Context and practices	Query about religious background and training, values, beliefs, spiritual practices, rituals, and their usefulness to the child. Does the child have a context for morality and at what depth?	Help renew or establish institutionalized or uninstitutionalized religious interest or religious inquiry, spiritual inquiry, philosophical, psychological, or scientific inquiry. What will help establish a moral foundation?
Identifying ethical/moral problems	Does the child have a capacity to identify moral problems as moral problems? Has he or she learned from prior instances? Give sample moral issues and dilemmas and evaluate the quality of the reasoning.	Practice with teaching stories from sacred texts, fables, moral issues. Begin with simple stories (e.g., The Boy Who Cried Wolf) and advance the complexity until the child can identify the moral issues.
Stopping, focusing, relaxing, centering, praying	Does the child already have a practice of deep breathing, relaxation, or imagination (formal or informal) generally, and when faced with a moral problem or does the child react impulsively?	Establish or advance a practice of deep breathing, meditation, yoga, or other practice. Begin building consciousness and awareness.
Adopting objective observer/neutral stance	Can the child adopt a neutral stance or objective observer? If so, for how long and under what circumstances? Can the child do it (1) in hindsight, (2) at the time of the incident, (3) before the incident, or (4) not at all? Where is the child on the continuum of responsiveness to reactivity?	Dialogue using real instances for the child's life. Begin with developing hindsight about how to remain neutral and view the situation non-judgmentally. As the child advances with relaxation and centering practices, he or she will begin to observe in the present, and then in preparation of moral instances.
Consulting trusted sources	Does the child have trusted adults and peers, texts, or other sources? What is the quality and availability of those sources, and are they utilized?	Help the child develop a personal "library" of sources. Begin community outreach (e.g., mentoring programs, school and community activities) and family treatment.

Generating alternatives	Can the child generate alternatives? Has he or she found a creative form of expression?	Plausibility is not crucial here: quantity and creativity are the focus. Practice problem solving with multiple solutions (no "right" answers). Help the child find a creative outlet (arts, music, journaling).
Recognizing consequences and outcomes for each alternative	Can the child follow each generated possibility (generated by self and trusted sources) through to a logical conclusion? Can he or she see the consequences to self and to others?	Practice with stories with moral issues that do not have an ending. Have the child generate solutions and evaluate each solution generated by the child and trusted sources to a conclusion. Evaluate the outcomes with regard to empathy and consequences.
Choosing and acting	Can the child articulate priorities? Can the child reason, choose, and follow through? Can the child trust himself or herself to act?	Learn to weigh and prioritize outcomes that may all each have pros and cons. Practice with situations from the child's life, weighing the consequences.
Evaluating the outcome and self-critique/self-reflection	Can the child maintain resolve or flexibility when appropriate? Does the child have the capacity to self-reflect and learn? Does he or she have the ability for self-compassion and a concept of lifelong moral development? Can the child evaluate the entire process?	This is developed through dialogue (therapy, group work, houses of worship) and role models demonstrating an ability to learn from past mistakes, holding one to high moral standards, and having compassion for oneself and others. If the child has the capacity to learn this, it is learned through models and dialogue in multiple contexts.
Return to step three if necessary	If the child decides the solution was a mistake, return to the practice and begin again.	Help the child relax in the face of error, and move ahead.
Make repairs if necessary	How does the child deal with making mistakes (blames, takes responsibility, hides)? Can he or she make repairs?	Help the child recognize that mistakes are a natural part of life and that the earlier one can make repairs, the better. Demonstrate methods of repair.

work from that perspective. There is no need to "whitewash" any approach to make it more palatable. However, therapists need to be open to bridging approaches to the variety of ethnic, cultural, and religious diversity we may encounter with clients. Assessment of the client's own source of moral values is indicated to provide a link and basis for needed training.

The therapist needs to be open to a parallel moral developmental process: development occurring within himself or herself simultaneous with and as part of the process of development in the client. Self-awareness and support networks are important for the therapist to work with this type of ambiguous developmental process. Therapeutic work with conduct-disordered children requires a level of ethical clarity. However, overconfidence or moral "righteousness" will not impart the reasoning ability, the tolerance for ambiguity, and the complexity inherent in the ethical decision-making process delineated previously.

The following case was chosen as an example of a child at risk who was beginning to exhibit problematic behaviors including those associated with conduct disorder.

Case Example: Jose

Jose was seen on a weekly basis over a nine-month period. The therapist, Susan, had contact with the child and both parents. Susan utilized traditional assessment and therapeutic interventions including those from psychotherapeutic models. Susan identified risk and protective factors to determine where she needed to intervene and what the existing strengths of Jose and his family were. Susan included techniques in her work with Jose that were spiritually based, including meditation techniques such as walking meditation and breathing techniques.

Jose was a fourteen-year-old, second-generation Mexican-American who was living in a metropolitan area in Arizona. His parents were married and he had one older sister who also lived in the home. His extended family lived nearby and they were involved in his life on an almost daily basis. The family was devoutly Catholic and his mother attended church regularly. He had two paternal uncles who were in prison. Both of his parents worked and his father had consistent employment in a janitorial company for more than twenty years. His mother had her own small housecleaning business. According to the family, the neighborhood where they owned a two-bedroom home had experienced an increase in violence and gang activity over the previous five years. Although Jose was repeating the eighth grade and was functionally illiterate, he was not receiving special services. He was referred to mental health treatment by a school guidance counselor and a community program for youth at risk because of truancy, petty theft, and suspected gang activity. He had been held in detention once the year before, for several hours, for truancy. His mother's primary language was Spanish and she spoke very little English. Although she suspected that her son needed reading assistance, she had difficulty advocating for him in the school system because of these language differences. Susan noted several risk and protective factors, including learning differences, law violations and impulsivity, lack of interest in his family's rich cultural and spiritual heritage, the parents' previous lack of ability to advocate for Jose in the school system, peer relationships that were suspected of being gang related, and the deteriorating neighborhood.

The strengths Susan noted were Jose's family support and positive role models, the family's strong religious and cultural traditions, the parents' stability and willingness to participate in treatment, and Jose's willingness to participate in treatment. Other protective factors were Jose's desire to please his parents and teacher, his desire to "succeed," and his ability to experience empathy.

Susan's assessment included identification of a spiritual and religious context for Jose (Step 1) that provided a moral basis for behavior. Jose identified the "Golden Rule" as part of his value system, and this was used as the foundation for inquiry regarding moral decision making. Susan's intervention included helping him identify and draw from his existing spiritual and religious beliefs through discussions. He was able to identify moral and ethical issues (Step 2); however, in the context of his life, this did always equate to conforming to lawful behavior. Jose was not able to focus and inhibit problematic behaviors because of his impulsiveness. Therefore, Susan began to intervene at this stage. Her interventions included strategies to begin to develop the capacity to center and focus through a practice of walking meditation and visual imagery. Jose began to become more nonjudgmental by examining past actions and reflecting without reactivity. Jose began to redefine some of the events in his past as moral decisions that he believed were positive and those that were mistakes (truancy) that had unwanted outcomes for him (detention) and others (mother was upset). This gave him the opportunity to begin to develop objectivity regarding his actions. Susan helped to find a mentoring program for Jose. The mentoring program provided resources to reinforce moral teachings outside of his religious background. This program also gave Jose a chance to meet new friends, develop social skills, and practice his ethical decision making. The mentoring program included work in diversity training. This diversity training with peers and mentors offered Jose exposure to other cultures and different ways of approaching moral problems. These guided group experiences with individuals from different cultural backgrounds also offered training in compassion and empathy for others. He also had the opportunity to experience others' compassion and support for him.

Susan had identified Jose's learning differences (functional illiteracy) as a risk factor. Susan assisted Jose's parents in advocating for their son's learning needs. Jose began to receive reading assistance and eventually recognized that he had an academic problem that could be remediated, and was not due to lack of motivation or intelligence. Reading better positively impacted his self-esteem. He began to appreciate his parents' efforts in advocating for him in the school system. Jose's trust of adults and authority figures was enhanced. His school attendance improved and he began to be able to articulate life events in terms of consequences for himself and others. He began to have some sense of empowerment regarding his own destiny. Incidents of oppositional behavior declined as did other acting-out behaviors. Jose was able to learn basic meditation techniques, which he reported assisted him in many ways including relaxation, mental clarity, decreasing impulsivity, and in general decision making.

CONCLUSION: DEVELOPMENT AND UTILIZATION OF SPIRITUAL TECHNIQUES AS THERAPEUTIC INTERVENTION

Therapists can draw upon ancient techniques that are recognized and utilized outside Western culture. Spiritual practices have become much more commonplace as treatment methods for both medical and psychological disorders. Interest has increased in identifying research models and techniques to measure the utility of spiritual practices well-known to have benefits in Eastern culture and now Western culture. Without specific research information, people may be reluctant to accept such spiritual practices as recognized modalities for psychiatric disorders. With increasing anecdotal information of the benefits of spiritual practices such as meditation or yoga, the demand for these interventions for enhanced general well-being and treatment of psychiatric disorders is increasing. A research base of the benefits of spiritual techniques in medical and psychiatric conditions is developing. If techniques such as meditation or yoga are to be utilized, professionals will require education from legitimate teachers to learn of the benefits and gain access to those techniques. Professional acceptance within medicine, psychiatry, and psychology requires an openness to consider alternative interventions that are spiritually based and to research the efficacy of these interventions. Mental health practitioners can develop their own spiritual practices and access information and provide resources for the veracity of psychospiritual practice. As practitioners become educated in spiritual practices, research continues, and education of professional boards and associations is undertaken, increased support and acceptance of psycho-spiritual interventions will likely occur.

REFERENCES

American Psychiatric Association (2000). *Diagnostic and Statistical Manual of Mental Disorders* (Fourth Edition, Text Revision). Washington, DC: American Psychiatric Association.

Austin, H. (1998). *Zen and the Brain*. Cambridge, MA: The MIT Press.

Bass, L., DeMers, S., Ogloff, J., Peterson, C., Pettifor, J., Reaves, R., Retfalvi, T., Simon, N., Sinclair, C., and Tipton, R. (1996). *Professional Conduct and Discipline in Psychology*. Washington, DC: American Psychological Association and the Association of State and Provincial Psychology Boards.

Benson, H. and Stark, M. (1996). *Timeless Healing*. New York: Scribner.

Bersoff, D. (2003). *Ethical Conflicts in Psychology*, Third Edition, Washington, DC: American Psychological Association.

Bhajan, Y. (1997). *The Master's Touch*. Los Angeles, CA: The Kundalini Research Institute.

Bhajan, Y. and Khalsa, G. (1998). *The Mind*. Espanola, NM: The Kundalini Research Institute.

Bloomquist, M.L. and Schnell, S.V. (2002*). Helping Children with Aggression and Conduct Problems*. New York: The Guilford Press, Inc.

Buckley, A. (2003). *The Kids' Yoga Deck*. San Francisco, CA: Chronicle Books.

Connor, D.F. (2002). *Aggression and Antisocial Behavior in Children and Adolescents*. New York: The Guilford Press, Inc.

The Dalai Lama (1999). *Ethics for the New Millennium*. New York: Riverhead Books.

The Dalai Lama (2003). *Transforming the Mind*. Hammersmith, London: Thorsons.

De Brunhoff, L. (2002). *Babar's Yoga for Elephants*. New York: Harry N. Abrams.

Fischer, N. (2003). Sometimes Full, Sometimes Half Full. *Shambhala Sun,* 12(1), 42-47.

Fonagy, P., Target, M., Cottrell, D., Phillips, J., and Kurtz, Z. (2002). *What Works for Whom? A Critical Review of Treatments for Children and Adolescents*. New York: The Guilford Press, Inc.

Hare, R. and Forth, A. (2001). *(Conference) Assessing Psychopathy: Clinical and Forensic Applications of the PCL-R*. Phoenix, AZ.

Henggeler, S.W., Schoenwald, S.K., Borduin, C.M., Rowland, M.D., and Cunningham, P.B. (1998). *Multisystemic Treatment of Antisocial Behavior in Children and Adolescents*. New York: The Guilford Press, Inc.

Kalb, C. (2003). Dalai Lama. Moment for Meditation. *Newsweek,* September 22, p. 10.

Khalsa, G. and Bhajan, Y. (2000). *Breathwalk*. New York: Broadway Books.

Kreeft, P. (2004). What Would Socrates Do? The History of Moral Thought and Ethics. Barnes and Noble Publishing: New York.

Montessori, M. (1994). *The Absorbent Mind.* Oxford, England: ABC-Clio, Ltd.

Murphy, M. and Donovan, S. (1997). *The Physical and Psychological Effects of Meditation.* Sausalito, CA: Institute of Noetic Sciences.

National Institute of Mental Health (NIMH) <www.nimh.nih.gov>.

Schore, A.N. (1994). *Affect Regulation and the Origin of the Self.* Hillsdale, NJ: Lawrence Erlbaum Associates.

Chapter 10

Bipolar Disorder
and Western Anosognosia

Jeffrey Rediger

INTRODUCTION

Mood disorders—principally forms of depression and bipolar disorder—constitute some of the most ravaging illnesses of the modern world. The morbidity and mortality is comparable to such diseases as hypertension, coronary artery disease, and diabetes mellitus. The suffering that results in diminished work productivity, familial stress or loss, and, frequently, suicide, wreaks a tremendous toll not only on individuals but also on families and society.

Research by Gerald Klerman and colleagues (1985) suggests that the incidence of mood disorders may be increasing, especially in the younger age groups, and that this may be associated with the rising rates of alcohol and substance abuse. In addition, both depression and bipolar disorder are now being seen and diagnosed more frequently in children as well.

Major depression has a lifetime prevalence of about 10 to 25 percent for women, and 5 to 12 percent for men (Blazer et al., 1994). Bipolar disorder, in contrast, has a lifetime prevalence of about 2 percent and manifests relatively evenly in both men and women, but typically has a more devastating course. This means that about 5 million people in the United States alone suffer from bipolar disorder. Fifteen to 20 percent of these people will commit suicide eventually, and many more than that will make repeated, unsuccessful attempts to end their lives. Even without suicide, a woman who is diagnosed with the illness at age twenty-five will lose, on average, about fourteen years of effective lifetime functioning (Sadock and Sadock, 2000).

In this chapter, I outline our peculiarly Western anosognosia as it bears on traditional conceptions and treatments of psychiatric illness—in this case, bipolar disorder—and point in a direction that I find theoretically useful. I will describe some of the relatively unexamined assumptions that have influenced current approaches and then illustrate how these approaches, though important, do not always account for the whole picture or what people actually experience. A narrow Western ontology often introduces unnecessary resistance into the relationship between the doctor and his or her patient and leaves many patients feeling lost or unfairly pathologized. As a result, patients feel bereft, without a path that reconciles their deep inner longings with the need for a concrete and well-grounded life.

BIPOLAR DISORDER
AND THE HISTORICAL STRENGTHS
AND LIMITS OF WESTERN THOUGHT

Ancient writings clearly indicate that disorders of mood have existed for thousands of years and that few illnesses plague human life and culture with such regularity. Hippocrates (460-377 B.C.) distinguished melancholia from mania and argued that melancholia was a biochemical abnormality related to the overproduction of one of the dark humors (black bile). Under the influence of the planet Saturn, the melancholic temperament made the spleen secrete black bile, and this resulted in a darkened mood.

Mania, or a state of raving madness with exalted mood, was also described by the ancient Greeks. Although a few others commented briefly on it, Aretaeus of Cappadocia (ca. A.D. 150) is generally credited with making the clearest connection between melancholia and mania. His description shows how little has changed:

There are infinite forms of mania but the disease is one. If mania is associated with joy, the patient may laugh, play, dance night and day, and go to the market crowned as if victor in some contest of skill. The ideas the patients have are infinite. They believe they are experts in astronomy, philosophy, or poetry. . . . The patient may become excitable, suspicious, and irritable; hearing may become sharp . . . [he may hear] noises and buzzing [in] the ears; or may have visual hallucinations; bad dreams and his sexual desires may get uncontrollable; aroused to anger, he may become wholly mad and run unrestrainedly, roar aloud; kill his keepers, and lay violent hands upon himself. . . . They are prone to change their mind readily; to become base, mean-spirited, illiberal, and in a little time extravagant, munificent, not from any virtue of the soul, but from the changeableness of the disease. (cited in Sadock and Sadock, 2000, p. 1286)

The Greeks based their concepts of health and illness on the harmony and balance of the four humors (Sadock and Sadock, 2000, p. 1287). The sanguine humor (blood), which was thought to promote amiability and activity, could in excess lead to mania, as could a mixture of black and yellow bile (yellow bile was thought to make people choleric; e.g., irritable and hostile).

Over the course of the following centuries, discussions about mania and depression, and of illness in general, occurred in the context of the developing intellectual categories that over time have come to characterize Western culture. The Cartesian crystallization of this approach that took root during the Enlightenment in seventeenth-century Europe posited, in its quest for clear, indubitable knowledge and freedom from ecclesiastical heteronomy, that truth about the natural world could be obtained only from the evidence of the five senses. This not only liberated scientists to explore the natural world, but also sharply separated different spheres of knowledge from one another.

This shift occurred over the course of several centuries and was captured in some of its most dramatic moments by such men as Copernicus or Galileo, when they argued for theories of the natural world to be based on physical evidence rather than theological decree. This bid was important because of the way in which, over a period of many centuries, truth about the natural and spiritual worlds had devolved to decisions made by ecclesiastical authorities that were then externally imposed on people's lives. The essential correlation between the inner longings of the heart to know God and an institutional structure that supports and nourishes those longings was lost, at least to some degree, and truth about either oneself or the natural world was no longer rooted in personal experience as much as in papal bulls. So, as the following will show, the integration of matters psychiatric and spiritual should not just be about the correlation of psychiatric and theological knowledge. One must also ask how these disciplines and their institutional commitments, particularly in regard to their conceptions about the locus of power and authority, bear on the individual human person.

The bid for a new medicine that was devoted to both the evidence of the five senses and to human rights found one of its clearest expressions in Philippe Pinel's (1745-1826) advocacy for humane treatment of the mentally ill. This advance paved the way for a medicine and psychiatry based on observation and descriptive nosology rather than on externally imposed moral and theological categories. The modern approach to bipolar disorder was then firmly established on clinical grounds by the painstaking methodology and longitudinal observations of Emil Kraepelin (1856-1926). In 1899, he described manic depression in a form that matches most of the criteria used to diagnose bipolar I disorder today. Since then, the biological basis of bipolar disorder and its susceptibility to medical treatment have received considerable attention. Given the deeply human tendency to place moral judgments on what is not adequately understood, there has fortunately been relatively less emphasis on etiologies that root bipolar disorder simply in debauchery, drunkenness, or immoderate lifestyles.

TRADITIONAL DIAGNOSIS

Mood disorders are diagnosed more frequently than they used to be, not only because they seem to be more prevalent but also because symptoms that used to be subscribed under the rubric of schizophrenia or character disorders are now considered to have an underlying basis in mood. This conceptual shift is due to several factors. First, a comparison of diagnostic practices and patterns in the United States and Britain yielded the surprising result that patients in the United States had a higher likelihood of being diagnosed with schizophrenia than their British counterparts, even though the symptoms were similar. This awareness helped shift the diagnostic landscape. In addition, the discovery that many patients thought to have relatively intractable character disorders respond positively to the newer antidepressants also has led psychiatrists to believe that what were formerly considered problems of character are actually disorders of mood (Akiskal and McKinney, 1973).

Mood disorders are usually distinguished, most broadly, by their polarity: unipolar (depressive episodes only) and bipolar (depressive episodes alternating with manic, hypomanic, or mixed episodes).[1] It is not unusual for a person who was originally diagnosed with unipolar depression to eventually have, usually during a time of severe personal stress, a first episode of mania, and to subsequently suffer from bipolar disorder. Thereafter, the bipolar highs and lows typically become more extreme and more frequent, with greater devastation not only in the patient's life but also in the lives of loved ones. It used to be thought that manic or hypomanic symptoms were found, by definition, only in the context of preceding depressive episodes. In fact a small minority of patients do experience manic or hypomanic symptoms without clear episodes of depression. Most patients with periods of elevated mood, however, do have an identifiable history of experiencing symptoms at the depressive "pole."

Although depression and mixed states are more common in women than men (about 2:1), frank mania occurs more often in men. In addition, although depression is more common during the dark months of winter, during the spring hospital wards swell with people experiencing manic exacerbations ("springtime madness"). Bipolar disorder also occurs more frequently and at an earlier age of onset in those who have suffered sexual, physical, or mental abuse during childhood.

The DSM-IV-TR discusses four different bipolar disorders: bipolar I disorder, bipolar II disorder, cyclothymic disorder, and bipolar disorder NOS (or "not otherwise specified"). They are diagnosed when at least one episode of mania, hypomania, or mixed symptoms has occurred. Bipolar I disorder is the classic form of bipolar disorder that is sufficiently severe to markedly impair occupational and social functioning, often requires hospitalization to prevent harm to oneself or others, and may include psychotic features (see Exhibit 10.1). The mania often escalates over a period of one or two weeks and may include grandiosity or inflated self-esteem, as well as a diminished need for sleep. The person may talk, seemingly without end, and often with pressured speech. The person's thoughts may seem to race wildly from one topic to another, and he or she may run from activity

EXHIBIT 10.1. Criteria for Manic Episode

A. A distinct period of abnormally and persistently elevated, expansive, or irritable mood, lasting at least 1 week (or any duration if hospitalization is necessary).
B. During the period of mood disturbance, three (or more) of the following symptoms have persisted (four if the mood is only irritable) and have been present to a significant degree:
    (1) inflated self-esteem or grandiosity
    (2) decreased need for sleep (e.g., feels rested after only 3 hours of sleep)
    (3) more talkative than usual or pressure to keep talking
    (4) flight of ideas or subjective experience that thoughts are racing
    (5) distractibility (i.e., attention too easily drawn to unimportant or irrelevant external stimuli)
    (6) increase in goal-directed activity (either socially, at work or school, or sexually) or psychomotor agitation
    (7) excessive involvement in pleasurable activities that have a high potential for painful consequences (e.g., engaging in unrestrained buying sprees, sexual indiscretions, or foolish business investments)
C. The symptoms do not meet criteria for a Mixed Episode.
D. The mood disturbance is sufficiently severe to cause marked impairment in occupational functioning or in usual social activities or relationships with others, or to necessitate hospitalization to prevent harm to self or others, or there are psychotic features.
E. The symptoms are not due to the direct physiological effects of a substance (e.g., a drug of abuse, a medication, or other treatment) or a general medical condition (e.g., hyperthyroidism).

Note: Manic-like episodes that are clearly caused by somatic antidepressant treatment (e.g., medication, electroconvulsive therapy, light therapy) should not count toward a diagnosis of Bipolar I Disorder.

Reprinted with permission from the *Diagnostic and Statistical Manual of Mental Disorders,* Copyright 2000, American Psychiatric Association.

to activity with either euphoria or agitation and hostility. Often an increase in risky behaviors occurs that has a high likelihood of bringing about painful consequences to the person, such as excessive spending, poor business decisions, or sexual indiscretions. A person may become frankly psychotic, for example, believing that he or she can fly or that the FBI is tracking every move. Suicidal actions are often precipitated, either as accidents that result from the person's poor decision making or because of the sheer suffering associated with being unable to sleep for days on end.

The other forms of bipolar disorder vary from type I only in that the symptoms are less extreme (type II), less severe but more chronic (cyclothymia), or either less classic in their presentation or during a situation when the exact etiology is still being determined (NOS). To make a diagnosis of bipolar disorder, one must first rule out medical or substance abuse-related causes as well as the influence of other medicines, and adequately differentiate the bipolar symptoms from other mood or thought disorders.

Before moving on, a few comments should be made about the genetic and neurobiological correlates of bipolar disorder. The evidence for a genetic basis for bipolar disorder is stronger than that for major depression. A more robust connection exists between the incidence of the disorder in individuals and its occurrence in their biological parents. Also, when monozygotic and dizygotic twins are considered, a higher concordance rate for bipolar disorder is found among monozygotic twins.

Recent advances indicate the presence of multiple areas of neurobiological vulnerability in bipolar disorder, not only in the arena of mood but also in cognition, motor skills, and reward mechanisms. PET scans and functional MRIs reveal changes in blood flow and glucose utilization. Also, alterations occur in the thalamic output of corticotropin-releasing hormones involved in the release of stress hormones.

TRADITIONAL TREATMENT

Although the research and clinical literature is abundant with both psychotherapeutic and psychopharmacological strategies for the treatment of major depression, the literature for bipolar disorder deals almost exclusively with pharmacological solutions. This is most likely due not only to the fact that modern bipolar treatment began with the discovery of lithium's dramatic efficacy in the treatment of mania, but also because it is rarely easy nor possible to have a productive discussion with someone who is manic. Psychotherapeutic approaches are critical to the care and management of bipolar disorder but in many cases cannot become a central part of treatment until the person can tolerate useful discussions.

Treatment has evolved in recent years from a model that emphasizes the degree to which bipolar disorder is related to matters of consciousness and will to a model more akin to that of modern cancer treatment. In the latter model, early diagnosis and aggressive techniques are considered the mainstays of treatment. Patients typically do not recognize that their poor judgment and sexual or financial risk-taking behaviors are actually symptoms of a medical illness that requires rapid and aggressive treatment. Many patients, particularly during the early stages of mania, feel smarter and love how they feel, and they often prefer to stay as far away as possible from the terrible hopelessness of depression. They feel adamant that, with a little less sleep or a little "extra energy," they can join just one more committee or perform just a little better at work. Unfortunately, in many cases, sustained hypomania is the goal but frank mania is the inevitable result.

Because the personal and familial costs associated with bipolar disorder are so high, good treatment is critically related to early detection and rapid intervention. Because it is a chronic illness that often worsens over time, especially without intervention, treatments frequently are long term and prophylactic in nature. Some of the research suggests that a person with a first bipolar episode who has a positive family history should be started on long-term prophylactic treatment, and that doing so actually has a neuroprotective effect against the brain changes that occur with subsequent episodes.

The modern era of bipolar disorder treatment began when lithium, a natural element found in the periodic table of elements, was found to be dramatically helpful in the treatment of bipolar symptoms. This discovery revolutionized treatment during the second half of the twentieth century, though the past twenty years have seen its use relativized by growing concerns about its safety and the discovery of other effective medicines. The long-term effects on the kidney and the need for patients to undergo blood draws as often as every month to ensure that the lithium remains within a narrow therapeutic window renders its use difficult in many situations. In addition, in recent years, lithium use has been offset by several other medicines. Depakote or Tegretol, for example, seem to do a better job at stabilizing rapid cycling, dysphoric, or paranoid mania as well as recurrent episodes. A variety of medicines are used when combination pharmacotherapy is indicated. Benzodiazepines and antipsychotics are frequently prescribed, especially for the acute stabilization of mood. The newer serotonin-dopamine antagonists, such as Zyprexa, Seroquel, Clozapine, Risperdal, and occasionally Abilify are also proving to be quite helpful.

Treatment is often divided into the three general phases of acute care, continuation treatment, and long-term prophylaxis. Somewhat well-established standards exist for the kinds of treatment that research and clinical lore suggest are most helpful during each of these phases. The patient and his or her family need to be thoroughly educated about each of these stages in an ongoing manner, and the clinician should expect that patients will, for a longer or shorter period of time, experiment with the need for medicines, particularly when they feel euthymic (the medications no longer seem necessary) or manic (they like how they feel). Patients and families require a great deal of assistance in understanding how morbid or lethal the consequences can be of not taking the medications and sometimes are helped by knowing that approximately 50 percent of patients relapse within the first five months after discontinuing their medications, and 80 to 90 percent within the first 1.5 years (Sadock and Sadock, 2000). They also should know that going off and on medicines repeatedly seems to breed medication-resistant symptoms.

Both the patient and his or her family need to become as clear as possible about the early warning signs and predictors of relapse. For some people, this will be two nights in a row with less than four hours of sleep. For others, the patient's concentration will become poor or he or she will begin joining extra committees at work. Whatever it is for that particular individual, the signs must be recognized as soon as possible so that a full relapse can be averted.

Assistance in developing self-care skills is also critical, since the normalization of sleep, diet, and exercise as well as the reestablishment of healthy relationships go a long way toward stabilizing the mood. After the person has begun to stabilize, it is important to help him or her gain insight into the illness and take appropriate responsibility for the actions that have already occurred, as well as for what can be done to develop problem-solving and communication skills that will avert damage when symptoms recur in the future.

One approach that is particularly helpful involves the use of mood charts that record the relative highs and lows of mood as well as the frequency of fluctuations over the individual's lifetime. These charts can contain a great quantity of information and their pictorial nature often facilitates patients' understanding of how the illness affects them, as well as how mood symptoms have fluctuated with major life events, stressors, holidays, or different seasons. One of the most difficult aspects of treating bipolar disorder is the split that often occurs between subjective perception and the relatively objective observations by others. These charts help reintegrate the subjective and objective aspects of the illness because the patients are often surprised to recognize—often on their own as they construct the chart—that things were not quite as they thought, that a medicine that did not feel helpful at the time actually was associated with one of their better periods of functioning, in spite of significant stress, etc. Also, as the completion of the chart requires consultation on the part of the patient with other family members or friends, past events become clarified and agreement is more easily reached on the relationship of the person's mood to these events.

AN INTEGRATIVE APPROACH

When I was a medical student and on the neurology rotation, I took care of a woman who had suffered a stroke in her right hemisphere. She had what is called anosognosia, which means that she was not aware that she had a neurological deficit. In her case, because of the particular location of her stroke, she was unaware that the left half of the world existed. When I asked her to draw a clock, she drew only its right half. When I lifted her left arm and held it in front of her eyes so that she could see it, she thought that the arm was mine. When I tried to show her that the arm was hers, she repeatedly insisted that that was impossible. She kept her head turned to the right side of the room and at that time had no mental construct for comprehending or even learning that a left half of the world or a left half of her body existed.

This, I believe, is not too far from the situation in which the Western mind currently finds itself in regard to understanding some of the capacities that for the most part remain latent within the human psyche. Modern science has had a profound influence on the Western mind, to such an extent that many people find it nearly impossible to come to grips with any aspects of reality that do not conform to a strictly materialist vision. This, in spite of the fact that a careful reading of the great minds who established the intellectual basis for Western culture (e.g., Plato's Socrates, the teachers in the Greek mystery schools, and even Aristotle) reveals quite clearly that, for them, the epistemological quest, even in regard to knowledge of the physical world, contains an irreducible contribution from the knowing subject that transcends the evidence of the five senses. Modern physics and the autobiographies of great scientists also demonstrate how limited objectivist epistemologies have been. They cannot find a central place for a human person in flourishing and complex interaction with a real world.

One of the main theses of this chapter is that many things are going on in the world outside of the narrow band of reality so well defined by the Western intellectual tradition and that was, for example, such a central part of my medical school, residency, and even seminary trainings. My clinical experience indicates that many individuals live double lives, with experiences that they dare not tell psychiatrists or other clinicians, and even their families, for fear of being regarded as crazy. As I have listened to them, I have come to believe that some of them do not suffer from a mental illness, and that numinous or spiritual experiences, with adequate integration, can be overwhelmingly positive in their effects. These experiences often hold tremendous authority in individual lives because of the compelling beauty and luminosity with which they are associated or the way in which the experience is felt to have been uniquely crafted for them. They can facilitate surprising and dramatic shifts in the individual toward health and wholeness and sharply increase a person's capacity to give and receive love from others and work productively. The phenomenology of these experiences appear to transcend particular religious or cultural commitments. In other words, the external details of belief for a Jew, Muslim, or Christian may vary, but persons in any of these traditions or others may have experiences that follow surprisingly comparable patterns.

William James (1842-1910) was one of the earlier and more prominent Western thinkers to systematically explore states of healthy and higher consciousness. Since then, as Eastern philosophy has slowly devolved into the West, what is now called a transpersonal approach to psychiatry has developed. This approach accepts that more dimensions to human consciousness are present than have been readily acknowledged by the Western mind. James Fadiman described this approach to the human mind as follows:

> Transpersonal psychotherapy includes the full range of behavioral, emotional, and intellectual disorders as in traditional psychotherapies, as well as uncovering and supporting strivings for full self-actualization. The end state of psychotherapy is not seen as successful adjustment to the prevailing culture but rather the daily experience of that state called liberation, enlightenment, individuation, certainty or gnosis according to various [spiritual] traditions. (As cited by Boorstein, 1996, p. 3)

The orientation and scope of this type of spiritual psychology is different. The point is not to become "normal" but to seek the conditions that promote self-liberation so that one can become the self that one truly is within the context of a much larger ontology.

How does all of this relate to bipolar disorder? First, by this brief review of the history of the relationship between science and religion I hope to draw out some of the strengths and limits of current conceptual schemas for bipolar disorder. I am also trying to expose the vulnerability of all epistemological maps when inflexibly applied: They reduce the richness and mystery of human experience to something less than it actually is.

Current conceptions of bipolar disorder, helpful as they may be, are rooted in a Cartesian conceptual framework that falsely dichotomizes body from mind and analyzes various aspects of the person to the neglect of adequate attention to the whole person. This type of problem plagues every aspect of modern medicine and especially in hospitals where, for example, the daily retinue of renal, neurological, and cardiac specialists contribute their sophisticated recommendations, but no one attends to the fact that the person is not eating or misunderstands the diagnosis and what he or she can be doing to help himself or herself.

From the perspective of ordinary medical science, bipolar disorder represents a cluster of symptoms that should be expunged. From the transpersonal or spiritual perspective discussed here, two issues place treatment in a larger context: first, the person is a person first and this, rather than any particular diagnosis or disease process, is the primary reality; second, even when the diagnostic criteria have been satisfied, higher levels of being and functioning occasionally reconfigure how bipolar symptoms are best understood.

The primacy of personhood is not merely a theoretical abstraction. Patients sense immediately—almost as soon as they walk in the door—whether they are seen primarily as individuals or as a "disease process," and if they sense the former, some sort of natural healing resources are galvanized within them. The patient is so much more than his or her symptoms. Understanding this generates a healthy ambivalence about current diagnostic classifications, not because of any particular problem with the diagnostic nomenclature, but because of the overwhelming tendency of modern medicine to focus on parts to the exclusion of the whole.

We have become accustomed to relegating apparent physical problems to the physician, psychological difficulties to the psychologist, and spiritual problems to the priest or minister. Though such distinctions are useful and have been critical to the development of Western capacities for specialization, what is generally not accounted for is the overarching reciprocity and interconnection that supercedes and overcomes all such distinctions. For it is the human person who stands behind all aspects of his or her personage and integrates them into a complex whole.

A person is not just his or her disease. He or she is also a spouse or an employee, a grandparent or a PTA parent, a person much like ourselves with aspirations, longings, and fears. The illness is more than a disease process; it is also an existential crisis in that person's life, and in a way goes far beyond being simply an emotional response to the fact that they have been struck with an illness. Our illnesses often are more related to the consciousness with which we live our lives, with how we live and what we fear or are trying to learn than is easily understood within our current conceptual schemas. For example, the heart is more than a pump; it is also the vital epistemological organ with which we establish some sort of feeling connection with the world. Is it just coincidence that an overly analytical culture, which is relatively "cut off below the neck," also tops the list for incidence of heart disease? What we think, believe, feel, and commit ourselves to has a dramatic impact on what eventuates in our bodies.[2]

For complex historical reasons, the Western mind developed in such a way that emphasizes the persona that one reveals to the world over a more deeply ontological understanding of personhood. In other words, we tend to ascribe a relatively high ontological rank to appearances and rank-order them on a sort of hierarchy rather than paying primary attention to the reality that, from a spiritual perspective, all human beings are God's children, or children of the Divine Life. What tends to take relative primacy, then, is whether one is young or old, attractive or plain, successful or less so, sick or healthy—i.e., where one falls on the hierarchy. In such a setting, what matters is that one be "normal" and have as many attributes as possible that are regarded as desirable according to the hierarchy. What everyone privately knows at some level, however, is that the hierarchy is untrue and in fact rooted in fear. From a larger spiritual perspective, all persons are just that—persons—and the hierarchy of fear has no ontological reality.

In my experience, even Western theological systems have difficulty seeing the person from a larger perspective.[3] In the more mystical traditions, the human spirit (e.g., the "spiritual life") is not another aspect of the person as much as it is that which vitalizes the whole. The influence of Eastern spiritual writings (in this case, Eastern orthodox writings) helped me begin to see that the spiritual life of the human being has to do with that which surrounds and permeates both body and mind. In other words, spirit animates all other aspects of the person and is the life and meaning that the person brings to the world. This category is more human than theological, as theological is typically understood, in juxtaposition to the psychological and medical.

In a certain sense, it is the Life behind life. It is the unrepeatable, flourishing vitality that makes the person who he or she is.[4]

An approach to the world that emphasizes the wholeness of the human person has effects that radiate through all levels of theory and practice. In Eastern traditions, for example, insight and experience often weigh in over rational analysis and extended periods of psychotherapy. Unlike Western thought in which the psychological, ethical, and spiritual spheres are kept relatively separate, the Eastern traditions are full of stories in which these dimensions exist in a natural integration, which more easily promotes reflection and insight. For example:

> A Sufi sage once asked his disciples to tell him what their vanities had been before they began to study with him.
>
> The first said, "I imagined that I was the most handsome man in the world."
>
> The second said, "I believed that, since I was religious, I was one of the elect."
>
> The third said, "I believed I could teach."
>
> And the fourth said, "My vanity was greater than all these; for I believed that I could learn."
>
> The sage remarked: "And the fourth disciple's vanity remains the greatest, for his vanity is to show that he once had the greatest vanity." (Shah, 1972, p. 47)

Because the classical spiritual writings, particularly in the East, place relatively more emphasis on the common humanity shared by all, rather than ascribing much importance to the persona that one wears, overly sharp distinctions between the physician and the one who is ill lose their meaning. The first step of the fourfold path of Buddhist spirituality is to recognize that all is despair. In other words, although it may be less obvious in some rather than others, the existential situation is the same for all; only the details vary.[5]

A medicine rooted in this kind of ontology would look dramatically different. For such a medicine of the person to become a reality, physicians and clinicians would themselves need to undergo a particular type of inner development so that they could better understand both themselves and their patients. Many situations of mutual resistance between doctor and patient would be eliminated with the simple understanding that their common humanity trumps the roles that they are each playing, in this case, of doctor and patient. The roles have their place in the same way that actors need to play their parts for the play to move forward; however, the astute clinician always senses when to lay aside the white coat and speak not as a doctor but as a human person.

The previous discussion mentioned that this type of spiritual psychology, or transpersonal approaches in general, accept that consciousness contains dimensions that are not readily accepted by traditional worldviews, and that such experiences are not necessarily pathological or symptoms that should simply be eliminated with medication. To begin seeing this is to have one's world begin to open.

For example, one of my first conscious encounters with a situation that went beyond the way I was used to thinking at that time was as follows. Approximately three years ago, when I was still a resident in psychiatry, a young man diagnosed with bipolar disorder began to see me shortly after becoming clean and sober for the first time. As I began to get to know him, I was surprised by how dedicated he was to sobriety and to obtaining a college degree. He had one of the most violent histories that I had seen. He was repeatedly beaten bloody by his alcoholic ex-Marine father until the day came when his father left the family forever. During the next few years he crouched in a corner while his mother repeatedly gave herself to different men in exchange for heroin—sometimes several times during the same evening. He left home after his mother approached him sexually. While living at his father's, his stepmother leveled a shotgun on him at one point and reportedly cheered his father on during the fistfights that occurred between them. At fifteen, he ran away from his father as well and spent the next ten years dealing drugs and fighting in gangs.

He was known on the service as a "difficult patient." I knew that he had had years of involvement with the mental health system—sometimes court-ordered—and that he also had a history of difficult relationships with the psychiatrists and clinicians who had been assigned to his care. I asked him why things were different now and what had helped him attain sobriety and begin such clear efforts for a new life. What he said surprised me.

He told me that he gave up the drugs and alcohol after his dead Native American grandmother, who herself had been alcoholic, appeared to him one night in a dream, sat down on the edge of his bed, and told him to give up the alcohol. He had been particularly struck by what he took to be her surprise at his tattoos, which he had not had during the years when she had been alive.

Shortly after that, he became clean and sober for the first time and began making plans for college. That dream did more for him in five minutes than ten years of regular contact with psychiatrists and other clinicians. With a few setbacks, the progress persisted, in spite of the fact that he continued to live in a slum with his mother and four angry and depressed, occasionally hard-drinking, veterans. He continued to see me for both low-dose medication and psychotherapy, but something essential had shifted and I was not so much treating an illness as I was helping him get to where he wanted to go. Accepting his experience as somehow important seemed to melt the resistances that had characterized many of his prior clinical relationships and allowed us to really get to work.

To understand his experience as being simply the reflection of psychotic or dissociative processes and of a reality that does not exist implies a pathologization of his experience and symptoms that was deeply aversive to him. What traditional psychiatry tends to view as symptoms to be removed, he viewed as the clarion call to a new life.

Since then, I have listened to other patients or people involved in our research at the institute report experiences that I am not sure can be adequately accounted for within the framework of traditional psychiatric or medical assumptions. Stories in the classic spiritual writings also raise difficult questions for the Western maps of reality and consciousness that have been too quickly adopted in psychiatry, even by some of its finest minds. Jean-Martin Charcot (1825-1893), for example, director of the famous Salpetriere mental hospital for women in Paris, photographed the women he was treating for hysteria in poses labeled "Ecstatic State" and "Beatitude" and argued that such women were across the board suffering from delusions. And Sigmund Freud's colleague, Josef Breuer, dubbed Saint Teresa of Avila the "patron saint of hysteria," though he did admit that she was "a woman of genius with great practical capacity" (Medwick, 1999, p. xv). The reader can decide whether Saint Teresa's experiences added or detracted from her immensely fruitful and busy life, and whether psychiatry has understood her well. Following is an excerpt of Saint Teresa's writing:

> It pleased our Lord that I should sometimes see this vision. Very close to me, on my left, an angel appeared in human form, which is not how I usually perceive them—though I do once in a while. Even though angels often appear to me, I don't actually see them, except in the way I mentioned earlier. But our Lord willed that I should see this vision in the following way: he was not tall but short, and very beautiful, and his face was so aflame that he seemed to be one of those superior angels who look like they are completely on fire. They must be the ones called cherubim—they don't tell me their names—but I am very aware that in heaven there is such a difference between some angels and others, and between these and still others, that I would not know how to explain it. In his hands I saw a large golden spear, and at its iron tip there seemed to be a point of fire. I felt as if he plunged this into my heart several times, so that it penetrated all the way to my entrails. When he drew it out, he seemed to draw them out with it, and left me totally inflamed with a great love for God. The pain was so severe, it made me moan several times. The sweetness of this intense pain is so extreme, there is no wanting it to end, and the soul isn't satisfied with anything less than God. This pain is not physical, but spiritual, even though the body has a share in it—in fact, a large share. So delicate is this exchange between God and the soul that I pray God, in his goodness, to give a taste of it to anyone who thinks I am lying. (as quoted in Medwick, 1999, pp. 56-57)

Of course one could argue that she was a master of illusion and an unparalleled, charismatic manipulator of power. One would need to explain a number of things, not least of which is the perilous and life-risking position such experiences placed one in during the years of the Inquisition, especially since she was a woman. In spite of these dangers, she wove a path that preserved her complex inner life in the context of perilous circumstances, and also founded an order, was an outstanding administrator, and wrote with such beauty that she continues to find a large readership, even today, 800 years later. To this day, only two women have been honored as "doctors" of the Catholic Church, and she is one of them. Delusional or not, her autobiographical *Vida,* filled as it is with passages like this, has inspired a wide variety of responses, from George Eliot, who made her the *genius loci* of her novel *Middlemarch,* to Gian Lorenzo Bernini, who immortalized her in his famous sculpture *The Ecstasy of Saint Teresa* in the Cornaro Chapel of Santa Maria della Vittoria, Rome.

On the basis of accounts like this and my repeated clinical experience, I believe that it is worth examining whether some mystical experiences actually have a beneficial impact on the recipient and increase his or her capacities for healthy love and work. Some individuals seem to function better than others and do so in part *because* of their untraditional experiences.

Because people suffering from acute mania often are hyperreligious, therapists need to distinguish a genuine religious impulse from manifestations of illness. In mania, the religiosity is driven, and close examination reveals that it is a flight not toward oneself (which is the sign of a true spirituality) but away from the self that one truly is. Soren Kierkegaard's *Sickness unto Death* provides, in my opinion, one of the best descriptions of the self that I have seen—important both for its phenomenological relevance and theoretical power:

> The self is the conscious synthesis of infinitude and finitude which relates itself to itself, whose task is to become itself, a task which can be performed only by means of a relationship to God. But to become oneself is to become concrete. But to become concrete means neither to become finite nor infinite, for that which is to become concrete is a synthesis. Accordingly, the development consists in moving away from oneself infinitely by the process of infinitizing oneself, and in returning to oneself infinitely by the process of finitizing. (Kierkegaard, 1941, pp. 162-163)

He then describes how any human existence that wills to become infinite is in despair, for the self is a synthesis of both the infinite and the finite. The finite is the limiting factor and the infinite is the expanding factor. Infinitude's despair is the fantastical, the limitless; finitude's despair, on the other hand, is to lose one's self, not by evaporation into the infinite, but by becoming entirely finitized, by having become, instead of a self, a number, "just one man more, one more repetition of this ever-lasting *Einerlei*" (Kierkegaard, 1941, p. 166).

According to Kierkegaard, one's capacity for the infinite is a gift from God and an attribute of the divine. Imagination is one of the self's most sublime gifts:

> The fantastical is doubtless most closely related to fantasy, imagination, but imagination in turn is related to feeling, knowledge, and will, so that a person may have a fantastic feeling, or knowledge, or will. Generally speaking, imagination is the medium of the process of infinitizing; it is not one faculty on a par with others, but, if one would so speak, it is the faculty *instar omnium* [for all faculties]. What feeling, knowledge, or will a man has, depends in the last resort upon what imagination he has, that is to say, upon how these things are reflected, i.e., it depends upon imagination. . . . Imagination is the origin of the categories. The self is reflection, and imagination is reflection . . . which is the possibility of the self. (Kierkegaard, 1941, pp. 163-164)

Kierkegaard is saying, in part, that the intensity of the capacity for imagination is a reflection of the capacity for becoming a self. But the fantastical, lacking that dialectical concreteness that brings the self back to itself, so carries the self into the infinite that it cannot return to itself. In this way, the self is volatized more and more and at last the impulses in the self become such that one may love, but only with a sort of inhumane abstraction, as in the way that one may expound on his or her embracing love for all humanity, yet experience great difficulty in individual relationships. Too much undialectical infinity results in a form of inebriation.

The difficulty with typical conceptualizations of bipolar disorder is that patients know at some level—and very clearly feel—that their mania has at its core something that is important, even critical, for their lives. The mania is an untethered longing for ecstasy, for the infinite. To explain it as simply an illness that must be medicated away feels like a denial of the deepest longings in the soul. A mutual resistance is soon formed between doctor and patient, with the doctor trying to remove the mania and the patient feeling like the doctor is trying to excise something vital.

Client Stories

Here is what one of my patients, Mary, said:

> I am definitely a more spiritual person since becoming bipolar, although I have been a "Christian" most of my life. Although I experience a far greater depth of emotions since becoming bipolar, I feel it also goes beyond emotions and I experience a deeper relationship with the Person of God. For this reason I would not trade bipolar even with all of its misery for "good" mental health.

Another patient, Tom, described his experience as follows. Note his tendency toward abstraction (infinitizing) and the absence of a similarly robust movement toward the concrete:

> From an early age, I have thought and felt about deeply abstract things. I'm sure that anybody with this disorder has to be deeply connected with his or her spiritual self. To me it almost seems like a rule. Haven't we all had thoughts when we feel totally detached from our bodies and are trying to grasp the meaning of life itself, or the significance of things outside us—whether it is other humans, or nature's little wonders? As I think about this, I can see that there is a silver lining to how this terrible disease affects us. Sometimes, I think that the really great spiritual leaders such as Buddha probably had bipolar disorder. I'm not trying to glorify this disease. But it does tell us one thing—so what if we can't be successful in the conventional sense. But we can do our utmost to make this world a better place. I really mean this. At the end of the day, often when my brain switches back to normal mode, I can see my actions and emotions as a third person—the way I sometimes hurt others and myself, or the needless thoughts I felt [*sic*]. At those rare and prized moments, I tell myself I will try to do my best to have some meaning to my life. I want to love myself and others around me. I even have a secret plan—one day when I make lots of money, I'm going to make a

big anonymous donation. I know this all sounds like I'm blowing my own horn, but this is seriously how I have felt at times and I'm certain other people whom this disease affects, have felt something similar.

People feel great conviction when they say that they feel closer to God during periods of mania. They are so convinced of this that it is not an easily discussible issue, even after the mania is resolved, and it should not be easily dismissed or pathologized. Unfortunately, neither the church nor most clinicians are able to articulate a conceptual pathway that adequately accounts for the patient's experience and points the direction forward in a way that fits for both the patient and the clinician. Here is Mary again:

> I have had several hypomanic episodes where I am elevated just to the point that life is exceedingly easy and joyful. I become consumed with reading my Bible, prayer, church, Bible studies, everything is about God and I am full of such hope. When in this state I inevitably believe I have turned some corner. I then view the whole diagnosis as possibly wrong. My problem seems only to be one of sin and lack of trust in God until it begins again with depression. I feel it coming on but am trying to hang on to my faith, but the ease of it is gone. After a couple weeks or so of crying out to God and trying to repent and asking a lot of forgiveness I seem to give up a bit, get lethargic and just unable to pray, not able to embrace His Word the same way. And I feel so guilty. And I start thinking "Maybe I really am bipolar" alternating with thoughts that I am using bipolar as an excuse somehow. I am so tired of this. It causes me to doubt the sincerity of my faith.

Mary's account shows how much individuals can feel torn between two different views of the world, neither of which provides an adequate understanding of their experiences. Such confusion can contribute to years of wasted energy and developmental moratorium. Unfortunately, science (and therefore psychiatry) and Western theology have developed in reaction to and in isolation from each other; this has led to a partial falsification of both.

I have had a number of clinical experiences in which a person clearly met the criteria for bipolar disorder type II but was also having positive transcendent experiences of the type just described. These individuals have often been persons with well-developed ego strength and a clear ability to think clearly and rationally about their experiences. They are individuals who are able to live with an expanded consciousness without drowning in its deeper seas. The clinical task for these individuals is to get their feet back under them and to find a place where they talk about their experiences without being regarded *ipso facto* as crazy. In some situations medicine is helpful; in others, it is contraindicated and the person can do well without it. Although criteria for bipolar disorder may apply at one level, a different, higher order operates in these situations. In the same way, a child operating within the stage of concrete operations believes that the moon is actually moving along with the car, whereas an adult recontextualizes the same experience with the knowledge added by a capacity for formal operations.

The individuals who present with frank bipolar I disorder are often those with less ego strength or greater biological vulnerability. They become radically infinitized, to use Kierkegaard's language. These individuals are less likely to be able to manage their symptoms and cannot manage an expanded consciousness without distortion or loss of self. They need help not only getting grounded in a healthy and balanced lifestyle, but also require traditional psychopharmacology and associated therapies. Still, however, resistance can be significantly defused and development promoted by the type of understanding outlined previously.

Other forms of language and experience have a great deal to add to Western psychiatric conceptions. Eastern teachings about the Kundalini tradition, for example, seem to have great explanatory relevance for the kinds of symptoms that are occasionally misread as symptoms of mania. These symptoms can occur when meditation is too activating, as well as in other situations. Again, what the unpracticed eye may read as mania is occasionally about something else entirely (Sannella, 1987).

CONCLUSION

The incidence of bipolar disorder may well be increasing. It certainly is diagnosed much more frequently than in the past. This could be related to several factors, as discussed previously, but it may also be connected with the revival of spirituality that is circling the world. A casual perusal of the top sellers in bookstores and at airport kiosks clearly indicates, in contrast to Nietzsche's statement, "God is dead," that interest in God and related matters is alive and well. In fact, it may be more appropriate to say instead that "Nietzsche is dead." As the longing for the spiritual life continues to grow, the incidence of bipolar disorder may also continue to increase, and it will therefore become increasingly important to understand the infinitizing fire that fuels it.

In the foregoing, I have made frequent reference to the perceptual difficulties—the anosognosia—that the Western mind faces in its efforts to understand phenomena that exist outside the narrow band of consciousness that it apprehends. The Western mind is brilliant and unparalleled in its elucidation of the area illuminated by Descartes' streetlamp. However, its further development and, in my opinion, survival depend on being willing to explore the larger world outside that sphere. The following story of conversations that occurred during three different epochs is a good example of where we have come from and where we are at the current time:

Conversation in the Fifth Century

"It is said that silk is spun by insects, and does not grow on trees."

"And diamonds are hatched from eggs, I suppose? Pay no attention to such an obvious lie."

"But there are surely many wonders in remote islands?"

"It is this very craving for the abnormal which produces fantastic invention."

"Yes, I suppose it is obvious—when you think about it—that such things are all very well for the East, but could never take root in our logical and civilized society."

Conversation in the Sixth Century

"A man has come from the East, bringing some small live grubs."

"Undoubtedly a charlatan of some kind. I suppose he says that they can cure toothache?"

"No, rather more amusing. He says that they can 'spin silk.' He has brought them with terrible sufferings, from one Court to another, having obtained them at the risk of his very life."

"This fellow has merely decided to exploit a superstition which was old in my great-grandfather's time."

"What shall we do with him, my Lord?"

"Throw his infernal grubs into the fire, and beat him for his pains until he recants. These fellows are wondrously bold. They need showing that we're not all ignorant peasants here, willing to listen to any wanderer from the East."

Conversation in the Twentieth Century

You say that there is something in the East which we have not yet discovered here in the West? Everyone has been saying that for thousands of years. But in this century we'll try anything: our minds are not closed. Now give me a demonstration. You have fifteen minutes before my next appointment. If you prefer to write it down, here's a half-sheet of paper. (Shah, 1972, p. 25)

Although Western psychological understanding also has much to offer the East, I believe that Western psychology has a great deal to learn from these traditions, and that we would do well to pay particularly close attention to the esoteric teachings of these traditions and seek to correlate them with the findings of modern science. Their relevance may not be immediately obvious to a consciousness affixed to an overvaluation of material existence. But perseverance will bear a heavy fruit, well worth waiting for.

NOTES

1. Hypomania refers to manic symptoms that fall along the same trajectory of manic symptoms but are less severe. The usual dividing line is that hypomanic symptoms do not adversely disrupt one's work or social life. Mixed symptoms refer to a condition in which symptoms of both depression and mania coexist.

2. This kind of statement can be misunderstood in many ways because it makes sense only in the context of a different kind of cultural milieu. When I say that con-

sciousness impacts our bodily existence, I am referring to more than what our conscious selves know and accept. We carry many different types of knowing within us, much of which we live but at best with limited awareness. Particularly because of the current Western cultural milieu, we often know more than we can tell. We live between a dialectic of knowing and not knowing, and often do not allow ourselves to know what we really know or believe to be true. One part of this is that we do not know how to talk about or even allow ourselves to be aware of ways of knowing not legitimated by Western culture. We have conscious selves; however, we also have subconscious and superconscious selves and participate in a sort of "collective unconscious." These different "selves" can be in direct conflict with each other and the person may not be aware of what he or she really knows or believes. For example, a common clinical experience is to hear a person wax eloquent about what he or she believes—e.g., that God is love—when clearly, at a more primal and subconscious level, the person has organized his or her life around a deep fear that God is a judge out to get him or her.

3. I would like to make clear that this difficulty derives not from a failure within Christianity but from the way in which Christianity has changed as Western thought took hold. Christianity was originally a mystical faith.

4. This sort of approach to the human person presupposes that the "spiritual life" cannot be separated from any aspect of the person or his or her life. The route to "godliness" cannot be reached without attaining that which is universally human. That which may not be consciously spiritual often is, and intensely so. Paul Tillich (1957), for example, defined religion as "one's ultimate concern," whatever that may be for that particular person. One's ultimate concern is often different from what the person consciously believes his or her ultimate concern to be.

5. The Buddhist statement that "all is despair" is not the negative or despairing beginning that it may seem to be. It is a recognition, in part, that one cannot recover one's soul without recognizing that something is missing.

REFERENCES

Akiskal, H. and McKinney, W. (1973). Depressive disorders: Toward a unified hypothesis. *Science,* 182:20.

American Psychiatric Association (2000). *Diagnostic and Statistical Manual of Mental Disorders* (Fourth Edition, Text Revision). Washington, DC: American Psychiatric Association.

Blazer, D.G., Kessler, R.C., McGonagle, K.A., and Swartz, M.S. (1994). The prevalence and distribution of major depression in a national community sample: The National Comorbidity Survey. *American Journal of Psychiatry,* 151:979.

Boorstein, S. (1996). *Transpersonal Psychotherapy* (Second Edition). New York: State University of New York Press.

Kierkegaard, S. (1941). *The Concept of Dread and the Sickness unto Death.* Walter Lowrie (ed.). Princeton, NJ: Princeton University Press.

Klerman, G., Lavori, P., Rice, J., Reich, T., Endicott J., Andreasen, N., Keller, M., and Hirschfield, R. (1985). Birth-cohort trends in rates of major depressive disorder among relatives of patients with affective disorder. *Archives of General Psychiatry,* 42:689.

Medwick, C. (1999). *Teresa of Avila: The Progress of a Soul.* New York: Alfred A. Knopf.

Sadock, B.J. and Sadock, V.A. (2000). *Kaplan and Sadock's Comprehensive Text-book of Psychiatry* (Seventh Edition). New York: Lippincott Williams and Wilkins.

Sannella, L. (1987). *The Kundalini Experience: Psychosis or Transcendence?* Lower Lake, CA: Integral Publishing.

Shah, I. (1972). *The Magic Monastery.* New York: E. P. Dutton.

Tillich, P. (1957). *Dynamics of Faith.* New York: Harper & Row.

Chapter 11

Spiritual and Transpersonal Approaches to Psychotic Disorders

David Lukoff

TRADITIONAL VIEWS OF PSYCHOSIS

Western Society

Psychotic and religious experiences have been associated since the earliest recorded history. The Old Testament uses the same term in reference to madness sent by God as a punishment for the disobedient and to describe the behavior of prophets (Rosen, 1968). Socrates declared, "Our greatest blessings come to us by way of madness, provided the madness is given us by divine gift" (Dodds, 1951, p. 61). Historically in the West and in many other cultures, such experiences have been considered signs of possession by spirits who were sometimes beneficent and sometimes not. Buddhist medicine also considers spirit possession the cause of unusual states including both transformative experiences and mental illnesses (Epstein and Topgay, 1982).

In contemporary Western society, anomalous experiences such as seeing visions and hearing voices, although they occur during intense spiritual experiences, are often viewed as symptoms of a psychotic disorder. (I use the term *disorder* instead of *illness* to avoid labeling it as solely a biological disorder.) People in the midst of such experiences have difficulty obtaining support from either the health care system or religion: "Both western religion and science lack the cognitive models and language to describe such states in a nuanced way, just as western culture fails to support those experiencing these states with a viable cultural language" (Douglas-Klotz, 2001, p. 71). Many religions such as organized Christianity eliminate elements of experiential spirituality. Consequentially, "If a member of a typical congregation were to have a profound religious experience, its minister would very likely send him or her to a psychiatrist for medical treatment" (Grof, 1986, p. 332).

Mainstream Mental Health Perspective

At the turn of the twentieth century, Jaspers, one of the founders of the diagnostic nomenclature, concepts, and methods used in psychiatry and psychology, referred to an "abyss of difference" between the distorted psychic life of the schizophrenic and others (Jaspers, 1963, p. 219). Laing (1982) has criticized the placing of all emphasis on the presumed patients' responsibility for making their realities understandable to others: "Both what you say and how I listen contribute to how close or far apart we are" (p. 38).

Standard psychiatric treatment for psychotic disorders involves hospitalization, medication, little or no psychotherapy, and immediate return to the community. However, this approach can freeze the process, leaving the person unable to complete it, and therefore returning to the same type of experiences (Perry, 1974). In an interview study, "The most subjectively frightening aspect of their experience was psychiatric hospitalization itself" (Jackson, 2001, p. 189). The pathologizing and stigmatizing medical approach may account for the surprising finding that the cure rate and level of dysfunction of persons with psychotic disorders is considerably lower in nonindustrial societies (Kirkness, 1997).

PSYCHOSPIRITUAL PERSPECTIVES ON PSYCHOSIS

Similarities Between Psychotic Disorders and Spiritual Experiences

Based on a cross-cultural survey, Prince (1992) concluded that

> Highly similar mental and behavioral states may be designated psychiatric disorders in some cultural settings and religious experiences in others. . . . Within cultures that invest these unusual states with meaning and provide the individual experiencing them with institutional support, at least a proportion of them may be contained and channeled into socially valuable roles. (p. 289)

People who had such experiences may have, in ancient Western as well as traditional cultures, been esteemed for their mystical experiences and enjoyed privileged status as shamans, prophets, visionaries, or saints.

The similarity between psychotic symptoms and mystical experiences has received acknowledgment and discussion in the mental health field (Arieti, 1976; Boisen, 1962; Buckley, 1981; James, 1958). Both involve escaping the limiting boundaries of the self, which leads to an immense elation and freedom, as the outlines of the confining selfhood melt down. The need to transcend the limiting boundaries of the self has been postulated to be a basic neurobiological need of all living things (Newberg, D'Aquili, and Rause, 2001). However, in persons with psychotic disorder, "the sense of embodied self is transcended before it has been firmly established. . . . Disintegration and further fragmentation are the likely results" (Mills, 2001, p. 214). Some psychotic experiences are better understood as crises related to the person's efforts to break out the standard ego-bounded identity: "trials of the soul on its spiritual journey" (House, 2001, pp. 124-125). Such revitalizing experiences sometimes lead to changes in the entire culture (Wallace, 1956).

Research has confirmed the overlap between psychotic and spiritual experiences. Peters, Joseph, and Garety (1999) assessed the incidence of delusions using a standard interview and rating criteria among members of new religious movements (NRMs, such as Moonies), nonreligious people, Christians, and patients hospitalized for psychotic disorders. They found that those in the NRM group could not be distinguished from the inpatients by the presence of delusions, but could by their higher level of distress.

Detailed cases showing that psychotic symptoms can occur in the context of spiritual experiences rather than mental illness have been published by Jackson and Fulford (1997) and Lukoff (1991, 1996,

1985). Greenberg, Witzum, and Buchbinder (1992) describe four young men who explored Jewish mysticism and became psychotic. Their hallucinations, grandiose and paranoid delusions, and social withdrawal were indistinguishable from those of many mystics. Pathological and spiritual phenomena cannot be distinguished by form and content, but need to be assessed in the light of the values and beliefs of the individual.

Differences Between Psychotic Disorders and Spiritual Experiences

In his classic study on mystical experiences, Leuba (1929) found that mystical experiences "are not characteristic of religious life alone" (p. 217). Campbell (1972) maintained that the psychotic individual, the mystic, the yogi, and the LSD user are all plunged into the same deep inward sea. However,

> The mystic, endowed with native talents for this sort of thing and following stage by stage, the instruction of a master, enters the waters and finds he can swim: whereas the schizophrenic, unprepared, unguided, and ungifted, has fallen or has intentionally plunged, and is drowning. (p. 216)

Wapnick (1969) makes a similar distinction: psychosis is an incomplete withdrawal from the spirit state, a failure to return to this reality. Clarke (2001) suggests that psychosis and profound spiritual experiences initially follow a common process, which can encompass euphoria, bewilderment, and horror. However, in high states of arousal, the cognitions of ordinary consciousness become less accessible.

In Ken Wilber's (1980) spectrum model of consciousness, psychosis is neither *prepersonal* (infantile and regressive) nor *transpersonal* (transcendent and absolute), but is *depersonal*—an admixture of higher and lower elements. Wilber (1980) writes: "[Psychosis] carries with it cascading fragments of higher structures that have ruinously disintegrated" (p. 64). Thus, he continues, psychotic persons "often channel profound spiritual insights" (p. 108). Similarly, Jung acknowledges that fragments of archetypal spiritual themes and symbols occur frequently in the experiences of psychotic persons but points out that "the associations are unsystematic, abrupt, grotesque, absurd and correspondingly difficult if not impossible to understand" (Jung, 1960, pp. 262-263). However, Perry (1974), who founded an innovative treatment facility for persons having first psychotic episodes, views psychosis more positively as a renewal process in which the psyche is seeking to fundamentally reorganize itself.

Spiritual Validity of Psychotic Experiences

Transpersonal psychology takes seriously and investigates beliefs such as the survival of the soul after bodily death.

> If we start to believe in reincarnation and the preexistence of souls . . . is it possible that some so-called psychotics may be slipping into a non-physical dimension and picking up material and confusing it with common consensus reality? (Tobert, 2001, p. 39)

Therefore, delusions might actually result from sensitivity to dimensions of experience not part of consensual reality but which might still be valid. Jerome Stack (1997), a Catholic Chaplain at Metropolitan State Hospital in Norwalk, California, for twenty-five years, observed that many people with mental disorders do have genuine religious experiences:

> Many patients over the years have spoken to me of their religious experience and I have found their stories to be quite genuine, quite believable. Their experience of the divine, the spiritual, is healthy and life giving. Of course, discernment is important, but it is important not to presume that certain kinds of religious experience or behavior are simply "part of the illness." (p. 24)

Crises of Spiritual Development: The Spiritual Emergency

The connection between spiritual development and psychological problems was first noted by Roberto Assagioli (1989) who described how a person's behavior may become inflated and grandiose as a result of intense experiences associated with spiritual practices: "Instances of such confusion are not uncommon among people who become dazzled by contact with truths too great or energies too powerful for their mental capacities to grasp and their personality to assimilate (Assagioli, 1989, p. 36).

Beginning in the 1960s, interest in Asian spiritual practices such as meditation, yoga, and tai chi, as well as experimentation with psychedelic drugs, triggered many nonordinary experiences, some of which were problematic for their practitioners.

> The contemporary spiritual scene is like a candy store where any casual spiritual "tourist" can sample the "goodies" that promise a variety of mystical highs. When novices who don't have the proper education or guidance begin to naively and carelessly engage mystical experiences, they are playing with fire. (Caplan, 1999, p. 74)

Stanislav and Christina Grof founded the Spiritual Emergency Network in 1988 (Grof and Grof, 1989) to help people experiencing crises related to their spiritual practices and experiences. They described spiritual emergencies as

> critical and experientially difficult stages of a profound psychological transformation that involves one's entire being. They take the form of nonordinary states of consciousness and involve intense emotions, visions and other sensory changes, and unusual thoughts, as well as various physical manifestations. These episodes often revolve around spiritual themes; they include sequences of psychological death and rebirth, experiences that seem to be memories from previous life times, feelings of oneness with the universe, encounters with various mythological beings, and other similar motifs. (p. 31)

The diagnostic concept of a spiritual emergency helps delineate a healthy process that sometimes occurs in the course of spiritual development, in which a person presents with psychotic features. But the symptoms will resolve spontaneously with appropriate support and can lead to improvements in well-being, enhanced emotional and psychosomatic health, and an increased awareness of the spiritual dimension in one's life.

DIFFERENTIAL DIAGNOSIS

From Spiritual Emergency to Spiritual Problem: The Transpersonal Roots of the DSM Category

The inclusion in the DSM-IV of a new diagnostic category called Religious or Spiritual Problem in 1994 marked a breakthrough. For the first time, distressing religious and spiritual experiences were acknowledged as nonpathological problems. The proposal for this diagnostic category had its roots in the concerns of transpersonal psychologists about the misdiagnosis and treatment of spiritual emergencies. Lukoff, Lu, and Turner (1992) expanded the proposal to include religious problems in order to gain support from the task force on DSM-IV for adding the new diagnostic category.

> Religious or Spiritual Problem (V62.89): This category can be used when the focus of clinical attention is a religious or spiritual problem. Examples include distressing experiences that involve loss or questioning of faith, problems associated with conversion to a new faith, or questioning of other spiritual values which may not necessarily be related to an organized church or religious institution. (American Psychiatric Association, 2000, p. 741)*

Spiritual emergencies warrant the DSM-IV diagnosis of religious or spiritual problem, even when psychotic symptoms may be present, including hallucinations and delusions. In this way, the religious or spiritual problem is comparable to the bereavement category for which the DSM-IV notes that even when a person's reaction to a death meets the diagnostic criteria for major depressive episode, the diagnosis of a mental disorder is not given because the symptoms result from a normal reaction to the death of a loved one. Similarly, in spiritual emergencies, hallucinations, delusions, disorientation, and interpersonal difficulties occur so frequently that they should be considered normal and expectable reactions.

---

*Reprinted with permission from the *Diagnostic and Statistical Manual of Mental Disorders,* Fourth Edition, Text Revision, Copyright 2000, American Psychiatric Association.

Misdiagnosis of Spiritual Emergencies

Iatrogenic problems may occur if spiritual emergencies are misdiagnosed and mistreated, possibly leading to some of the poor outcomes associated with psychosis. The clinician's initial assessment can significantly influence whether the experience is integrated and used as a stimulus for personal growth or repressed as a sign of mental disorder, thereby intensifying an individual's sense of isolation and blocking his or her efforts to understand and assimilate the experience. Instead of unusual subjective experiences being embraced in our culture as an *opportunity* and invitation to enlarge a person's circle of being, they are routinely psychopathologized and chemically suppressed. Wilber (1984) suggests this is a relatively easy discrimination: "Anybody familiar with *philosophia perennis* can almost instantly spot whether any of the elements of the particular psychotic-like episode have any universal-spiritual components" (p. 147). Agosin (1992), however, emphasizes the difficulty of distinguishing spiritual emergencies from episodes of mental disorder since, "Both are an attempt at renewal, transformation, and healing" (p. 52). Other mental health professionals working in the transpersonal field stress the importance of careful diagnostic assessments when questions of psychosis are concerned (Hastings, 1983; Lukoff, 1985).

Differential Diagnosis of Spiritual Emergency and Psychotic Disorders

Some confusion in distinguishing intense spiritual experiences from psychosis has been created by failing to make the critical distinction between prerational states and authentic transpersonal states. Wilber maintains that the "pre/trans fallacy" has been perpetuated, "Since both prepersonal and transpersonal are, in their own ways, nonpersonal, they tend to appear similar, even identical, to the untutored eye" (Wilber, 1993, p. 125).

Diagnostic Criteria for Spiritual Emergency

Considerable overlap is found among the criteria proposed for making the differential diagnosis between psychopathology and authentic spiritual experiences (Agosin, 1992; Grof and Grof, 1989;

Lukoff, 1985). I have proposed the following three criteria based on both research on factors that predict positive outcomes from psychosis as well as the extensive case study literature on spiritual emergencies:

1. Phenomenological overlap occurs with one of the types of spiritual emergency
2. Prognostic signs are indicative of a positive outcome
3. The person is not a significant risk for homicidal or suicidal behavior

Phenomenological overlap with spiritual emergency. The clinician needs to be able to recognize phenomenological characteristics of spiritual emergencies. As an example, five criteria for phenomenological overlap with a mystical experience are presented.

a. Ecstatic mood. The most consistent feature of the mystical experience is elevation of mood. Laski (1968) describes it as a state with "feelings of a new life, another world, joy, salvation, perfection, satisfaction, glory" (p. 84).
b. Sense of newly gained knowledge. Feelings of enhanced intellectual understanding and the belief that the mysteries of life have been revealed are commonly reported in mystical experiences (James, 1958; Leuba, 1929).
c. Perceptual alterations. Mystical experiences often involve perceptual alterations ranging from heightened sensations to auditory and visual hallucinations.
d. Delusions with spiritual themes. In contrast, the following statements from schizophrenic patients illustrate different themes.
   My brain has been removed.
   A transmitter has been implanted into my brain and broadcasts all my thoughts to others.
   The Mafia is poisoning my food and trying to kill me.
Familarity with the range and variation of content in spiritual experiences and psychosis is essential for determining which delusions have genuine spiritual themes.

e. Absence of conceptual disorganization. Systematic compari-
sons of first-person accounts of mystical experiences and
schizophrenia have found that "Thought blocking and other
disturbances in language and speech do not appear to accompany the mystical experience" (Buckley, 1981, p. 521). Therefore, the presence of conceptual disorganization, as evidenced
by disruption in thought, incoherence, and blocking, would
indicate the person is experiencing a mental disorder.

Prognostic signs are indicative of a positive outcome. Good prognostic indicators, validated by outcome studies, can help predict positive long-term outcome (Lukoff, 1985).

a. good pre-episode functioning
b. acute onset of symptoms during a period of three months or
less
c. stressful precipitant to the psychotic episode
d. a positive exploratory attitude toward the experience

*The person is not a significant risk for homicidal or suicidal be-
havior.* Psychotic disorders can be the basis for homicidal and suicidal behaviors. Both John Lennon and President Reagan were shot
by persons with previously diagnosed psychotic disorders. Arieti and
Schreiber (1981) have described the case of a multiple murderer
whose auditory hallucinations from God and delusions of being on a
religious mission fueled his bizarre and bloody killings.

Based on their experience working with an ultraorthodox Jewish
sect in Israel, Greenberg and Witzum (1991) have proposed criteria
that distinguish normative religious beliefs and experiences from
psychotic symptoms: Psychotic experiences involve special messages from religious figures, exceed accepted beliefs, may be terrifying, or be associated with deterioration of social skills and personal
hygiene. These criteria should be viewed as guidelines and applied in
a culturally and contextually sensitive manner. Greenberg and Witzum (1991) also point out that "Differentiating religious beliefs and
rituals from delusions and compulsions is difficult for therapists
ignorant of the basic tenants of that religion" (p. 563).

The DSM-IV-TR (APA, 2000) also highlights the need for cultural
sensitivity when clinicians assess for schizophrenia in cultural situa-

tions different from their own: "Ideas that may appear to be delusional in one culture (e.g., sorcery and witchcraft) may be commonly held in another" (p. 306).*

Co-Occurance of religious and spiritual problems with psychotic disorders. In the DSM-IV, the diagnosis of a religious or spiritual problem is an Axis I condition and can be assigned along with a co-existing Axis I disorder. Co-occurrence of a religious and spiritual problem with psychotic disorder occurs frequently. Among hospitalized patients, religious delusions were present in 25 percent, and over half of patients' hallucinations were religious. Goodwin and Jamison (1990) suggest that there "have been many mystics who may well have suffered from manic-depressive illness—for example, St. Teresa [of Avila], St. Francis, St. John [the Divine]" (p. 362). Religious or spiritual problems can be coded along with an Axis I disorder whenever the spiritual dimensions are addressed in treatment.

Psychospiritual Treatment of Spiritual Emergencies and Recovery from Psychosis Spiritual Emergencies

There is already a body of clinical literature, particularly detailed case studies (Cortright, 1997; Lukoff, 1988, 1991; Lukoff and Everest, 1985), that illustrates effective approaches for working with spiritual emergency patients in crisis. The following nine interventions are culled from this literature.

- Normalize.
- Create a therapeutic container.
- Help patient to reduce environmental and interpersonal stimulation.
- Have patient temporarily discontinue spiritual practices.
- Use the therapy session to help ground the patient.
- Suggest the patient eat a diet of "heavy" foods and avoid fasting.
- Encourage the patient to become involved in simple, grounding, calming activities.

---

*Reprinted with permission from the *Diagnostic and Statistical Manual of Mental Disorders,* Fourth Edition, Text Revision, Copyright 2000, American Psychiatric Association.

- Encourage the patient to draw, mold clay, make music, journal, write poetry, dance.
- Evaluate for medication.

Normalize

People in the midst of intense spiritual crises need a framework of understanding. Mental health theory has provided little guidance in this area and has often pathologized religious and spiritual experiences. Often the lack of understanding, guidance, and support allows such experiences to go out of control. The term *spiritual emergency* provides a nonpathological understanding and is a gateway for patients, family, and friends to the rapidly developing literature on these types of problems.

> First, it gives the person a cognitive grasp of the situation, a map of the territory he or she is traversing. Having a sense of the terrain and knowing others have traveled these regions provides considerable relief in itself. Second, it changes the person's relationship to the experience. When the person (and those around him or her) shifts into seeing what is occurring as positive and helpful rather than bad and sick, this changes the person's way of relating to the experience. (Cortright, 1997, p. 173)

Clarke (2001) recommends cognitive therapy that normalizes psychotic experience by emphasizing to the patient the overlap with spiritual experiences.

Jung (1964) described how providing a normalizing framework helped in the following case:

> I vividly recall the case of a professor who had a sudden vision and thought he was insane. He came to see me in a state of complete panic. I simply took a 400-year-old book from the shelf and showed him an old woodcut depicting his very vision. "There's no reason for you to believe that you're insane," I said to him. "They knew about your vision 400 years ago." Whereupon he sat down entirely deflated, but once more normal. (p. 58)

Create a Therapeutic Container

When a person's psyche in energized and activated, he or she needs contact with a person who empathizes, provides a loving appreciation of the qualities emerging through the process, and who facilities the process rather than attempts to halt or interfere with it. Brant Cortright highlights the qualities required of the therapist:

> In spiritual emergency, the personal presence of the therapist is key. Although some people are able to sail these waters successfully by themselves, for many people the presence of one or more wise compassionate guides on this journey can be of enormous help. . . . Warmth and compassion combined with a degree of softness and gentleness are essential. Additionally, a certain calmness and quiet confidence serves to energetically reassure and soothe the apprehension and alarm that are frequently present. (Cortright, 1997, p. 174)

Help Patient to Reduce Environmental and Interpersonal Stimulation

The person undergoing a spiritual emergency needs to be shielded from the psychic stimulation of the everyday world, which is usually experienced as painful and interfering with the inner process. The therapist needs to work with the patient to determine the specific people and situations that exacerbate the dysfunctional aspects of the spiritual emergency.

Have Patient Temporarily Discontinue Spiritual Practices

Meditation teachers who hold intensive retreats are familiar with this risk from intensive practice and have developed strategies for managing such occurrences (see case example). Yoga, Qigong, and other spiritual practices can also be triggers. Usually teachers advise ceasing the practice temporarily. It can be reintroduced as the person becomes more stable.

Use the Therapy Session to Help Ground the Patient

Therapy sessions can be used in various ways depending on the phase of spiritual emergency and its specific features. Sovatsky (1998), clinical director of the Kundalini Clinic, uses psychotherapy to enable a client to connect with the here and now by focusing on the relationship with the therapist instead of getting lost in the mind-chatter of despair.

Suggest the Patient Eat a Diet of "Heavy" Foods and Avoid Fasting

Grains (especially whole grains), beans, dairy products, and meat are considered grounding ("heavy") foods as opposed to fruit, fruit juices, and salads. Sugar and stimulants such as caffeine are also not advised.

Encourage the Patient to Become Involved in Simple, Grounding, Calming Activities

Gardening and other simple tasks, such as knitting, housecleaning, shoveling, and sorting, help people bring their consciousnesses back into their bodies. Walks in nature have the added benefit of enhancing tranquility and a calm mind. However, competitive sports would be contraindicated as too stimulating.

Encourage the Patient to Use Creative Expression

Creative arts, such as drawing, painting, making music, journaling, writing poetry, and dancing, can help people express and work through their inner experiences. The language of symbol and metaphor can help integrate what can never be fully verbalized.

Evaluate for Medication

Some practitioners, such as Perry (1974), have argued that medication only inhibits a person's ability to concentrate on the inner work and mutes the psychic energy needed to sustain the effort to move the process forward. Medication can freeze the process in an unfinished state. However, sometimes the process is so intense that the person is overwhelmed and becomes very anxious. That person could benefit from slowing down the process. Victor, a psychiatrist and psychopharmacologist, combines a transpersonal approach with low doses of tranquilizing or antipsychotic medication to alleviate some of the most distressing feelings while still allowing the person to assimilate the experience.

> It becomes a challenge to determine whether the person can actively work with the pain therapeutically toward further psychological growth. . . . One important role of pharmacotherapy is to titrate the level of symptoms, whether they be pain, depression, anxiety, or psychotic states, so that they can be integrated by the person in the service of growth. (Victor, 1995, p. 332)

The major criterion I use in deciding whether to make a referral for medication evaluation is whether the person is in a situation that can support his or her involvement in intensive inner process. A person living in a communal setting, such as a spiritual retreat center, can go much deeper while being cared for physically and supported in working through the crisis. I observed this at the Ojai Foundation, a retreat center, when a person went into a spiritual emergency that required round-the-clock attention. The community provided full-time support for two weeks until the person could maintain on her own.

However, people living in less supportive environments often do need to maintain themselves at a higher level of functioning. Otherwise, they risk hospitalization, loss of their livelihoods, living situations, and other essentials. I would always refer for a medication evaluation if I thought a patient might be a risk to others, but this is rare in a spiritual emergency. However, spiritual emergency patients can engage in risky behaviors such as driving recklessly, which does endanger others. Therefore, a risk assessment is part of an assessment for medication and must take into account the spiritual emergency patient's support system. Of course, any use of medication should be with the full understanding and consent of the person, who should be an active participant in the decision making.

Case Example: Jack's Patient

Jack Kornfield, a psychologist and experienced meditation teacher, described what he termed a spiritual emergency that took place at an intensive meditation retreat he was leading.

An "overzealous young karate student" decided to meditate and not move for a full day and night. When he got up, he was filled with explosive energy. He strode into the middle of the dining hall filled with 100 silent retreatants and began to yell and practice his karate maneuvers at triple speed. Then he screamed, "When I look at each of you, I see behind you a whole trail of bodies showing your past lives." As an experienced meditation teacher, Kornfield recognized that the symptoms were related to the meditation practice rather than signs of a manic episode (for which they also meet all the diagnostic criteria except duration). The meditation community handled the situation by stopping his meditation practice and starting him jogging, ten miles in the morning and afternoon. His diet was changed to include red meat, which is thought to have a grounding effect. They got him to take frequent hot baths and showers, and to dig in the garden. One person was with him all the time. After three days, he was able to sleep again and was allowed to start meditating again, slowly and carefully. (Adapted from Kornfield, 1993)

RECOVERY AS A SPIRITUAL JOURNEY

Mental health systems in this country are undergoing a quiet revolution as former patients and other advocates are working with mental health providers and government agencies to incorporate spirituality into mental health care. Although the significance of spirituality in substance abuse treatment has been acknowledged for many years in twelve-step programs, this is a new development in the treatment of psychotic mental disorders. Recovery incorporates spirituality to create an orientation of hope rather than the "kiss of death" that diagnoses such as schizophrenia once held.

During the postpsychotic phase, a major part of the work of recovery involves helping clients construct a new narrative, a fresh story of their lives (White and Epston, 1990). Or as Hillman (1983) describes it, the client comes to therapy to be "restoryed." People recovering from psychotic disorders have rich opportunities for spiritual growth, along with challenges to its expression and development. Based on what I learned from my own psychotic episode (Lukoff, 1991), and through my work with other individuals who had similar episodes over the past thirty years, integrating such experiences into a personal spiritual journey involves three phases:

Phase 1: Telling one's story
Phase 2: Tracing its symbolic/spiritual heritage
Phase 3: Creating a new personal mythology

Telling One's Story

In my work with patients at Camarillo State Hospital, UCLA, and the San Francisco VA, having them tell their stories has been the important first step in integrating a psychotic episode. It often helps to talk about and write out a full account of all one has experienced. Constructing a simple time line marked with ages and key events serves a therapeutic ordering function.

Tracing Its Symbolic/Spiritual Heritage

During psychosis, the mind is driven to reveal its deepest, most intimate workings, images, and structures.

> Minimally, the experience of psychotic illness is a call to the Symbolic Quest. Psychotic illness introduces the individual to themes, conflicts, and resolutions that may be pursued through the entire religious, spiritual, philosophical and artistic history of humanity. This is perhaps enough for an event to achieve. (Bebe, 1982, p. 252)

Exploration of the many spiritual and mythic symbols encountered in psychosis can be an important part of the recovery process.

In a study of thirty successful recovery narratives, Jacobson (2001) found a recurrent theme that emphasized "what happened" as a spiritual or philosophical crisis during which the self is destroyed and then re-created in the light of a newly realized truth. Many found a community of practicing Buddhists, the Bible, or philosophy helped them re-create a new sense of an enlightened self with enhanced wisdom and compassion. Many people experience recovery from a psychotic disorder as part of their spiritual journey. This was eloquently expressed by consumer advocate Jay Mahler.

> My being aware that I'm on a spiritual journey empowers me to deal with the big, human "spiritual" questions, like: "Why is this

happening to me? Will I ever be the same again? Is there a place for me in this world? Can my experience of life be made liveable? If I can't be cured can I be recovering . . . even somewhat? Has my God abandoned me. . . . That's my spiritual journey, that wondering. That's my search. (Mahler, in Weisburd, 1996, p. 2)

Creating a New Personal Mythology

Weaving a psychotic episode into a life-affirming personal mythology is essential for recovery. Unfortunately, many beliefs that people develop regarding an episode of mental disorder are dysfunctional and emphasize pathological qualities. Because these are not attuned to the person's actual needs, capacities, or circumstances, such myths do not serve as constructive guides during recovery (Feinstein and Krippner, 1988).

Some clinicians have expressed the concern that having patients discuss their delusional experiences could exacerbate their symptoms by reinforcing them. I led a study of a holistic health program conducted at a state psychiatric hospital in which participants actively explored their psychotic symptoms. They participated in groups such as "Schizophrenia and Growth," which encouraged them to compare their experiences to those of mystics, Native American vision quests, and shamanic initiatory crises, and this work did not result in exacerbation of symptoms (Lukoff et al., 1986).

Mind-Body Practices

Mindfulness techniques such as meditation have great potential that has not been well explored in clinical outcome studies even though one survey of patients with serious mental disorders in the community found that 43 percent practice meditation to support their recovery (Russinova, Wewiorski, and Cash, 2002). In addition to the well-established stress- and anxiety-reduction benefits, the meditative state reduces brain activity that can fuel psychotic symptoms and thus heals the sense of fragmentation that accompanies psychosis (Mills, 2001).

Conditions and situations occur when meditation is contraindicated. One study found that intensive meditation can trigger acute psychotic episodes in individuals with a history of schizophrenia (Walsh and Roche, 1979). However, a therapist who has developed skills with meditation can incorporate meditation, given appropriate attention to preparation of the patient. For example, my holistic health program for schizophrenic patients (Lukoff et al., 1986) incorporated meditation without any adverse effects. I began meditation training by playing music by Steven Halpern, who has researched and recorded nonrhythmic music that induces a relaxed state. This music enabled patients to achieve a meditative sense of calm amid voices and paranoid delusions that many were experiencing. I have also conducted walking meditation sessions with patients at the San Francisco VA day treatment program. The patients, a majority of whom had diagnoses of psychotic disorders, found walking in silence calming and mood elevating.

Spiritual Support

The mental health professions have a long history of ignoring and pathologizing religion (Lukoff, Lu, and Turner, 1992). For instance, Freud described religion as a type of "hallucinatory bliss." Albert Ellis asserted, "The less religious [patients] are, the more emotionally healthy they will tend to be" (Ellis, 1980, p. 637). However, the cumulative data from over 1,600 studies show otherwise: religion is overwhelmingly associated with positive mental health and recovery from psychotic mental disorders (Koenig, McCullough, and Larson, 2001). As the APA Task Force on Religion and Psychiatry (American Psychiatric Association, 1990) reported: "The religious convictions of patients can be used effectively in therapy. Religion can be a usable support system for the patient even when the therapist believes the patient's religious system has no objective value" (p. 542).

Spiritual support involves the degree to which a person experiences a connection to a higher power (e.g., God or other transcendent force) that is actively supporting, protecting, guiding, teaching, helping, and healing. Some researchers have suggested that the subjective experience of spiritual support may form the core of the spirituality-health connection (Mackenzie et al., 2000). Persons with mental disorders utilize spiritual support to improve functioning, reduce isolation, and facilitate healing. Religious practices (such as worship and prayer) appear to protect against severity of psychiatric symptoms and hospitalization, enhance life satisfaction, and speed recovery in mental disorders (Koenig, McCullough, and Larson, 2001; Randal, Simpson, and Laidlaw, 2003).

In studies of recovery narratives, Fallot (1998) found that although at times organized religion had been experienced as stigmatizing and rejecting, on the whole personal spiritual experience of relationship with God was helpful in building identity, self-responsibility, hope, a sense of divine support and love, the courage to change and an acceptance of what cannot be changed, and connection with faith communities. Another study (Sullivan, 1993) found that spiritual beliefs and practices were identified as essential to their success in recovery by 48 percent of informants.

Spiritual support can include the following:

Educating the client about recovery as a spiritual journey with a potentially positive outcome

Encouraging the client's involvement with a spiritual path or religious community that is consistent with his or her experiences and values

Encouraging the client to seek support and guidance from credible and appropriate religious or spiritual leaders

Encouraging the client to engage in religious and spiritual practices consistent with his or her beliefs (At times, this might include engaging in a practice together with the client such as meditation, silence, prayer, or singing.)

Modeling one's own spirituality (when appropriate), including a sense of spiritual purpose and meaning, along with hope and faith in something transcendent

Another form of spiritual support is to address dysfunctional beliefs about their disorders that many patients hold. One study of fifty-two psychiatric inpatients found that 23 percent believed that sin-related factors, such as sinful thoughts or acts, are related to the development of their illness (Sheehan and Kroll, 1990).

Case Example: Sally

Sally Clay (1987), an advocate and consultant for the Portland Coalition for the Psychiatrically Labeled, has written about the important role that religious experiences played in her recovery following two years of hospitalization while diagnosed with schizophrenia. While hospitalized, she had a powerful religious experience that led her to attend religious services.

> My recovery had nothing to do with the talk therapy, the drugs, or the electroshock treatments I had received; more likely, it happened in spite of these things. My recovery did have something to do with the devotional services I had been attending. At the Hartford Institute of Living (IOL), I attended both Protestant and Catholic services, and if Jewish or Buddhist services had been available, I would have gone to them, too. I was cured instantly—healed if you will—as a direct result of a spiritual experience. (Clay, 1987, p. 89)

Many years later Clay went back to the IOL to review her case records, and found herself described as having "decompensated with grandiose delusions with spiritual preoccupations." She complains that "Not a single aspect of my spiritual experience at the IOL was recognized as legitimate; neither the spiritual difficulties nor the healing that occurred at the end" (p. 90).

Clay is not denying that she had a psychotic disorder at the time, but makes the case that, in addition to the disabling effects she experienced as part of her illness, a profound spiritual component was ignored. The lack of sensitivity to the spiritual dimensions of her experience on the part of mental health and religious professionals was detrimental to her recovery. Nevertheless she has persevered in her belief that

> For me, becoming "mentally ill" was always a spiritual crisis, and finding a spiritual model of recovery was a question of life or death. Finally I could admit openly that my experiences were, and always had been, a spiritual journey—not sick, shameful, or evil. (Clay, 1995, p. 27)

REFERENCES

Agosin, T. (1992). Psychosis, dreams and mysticism in the clinical domain. In F. Halligan and J. Shea (Eds.), *The fires of desire* (pp. 41-65). New York: Crossroad.

American Psychiatric Association (1990). Guidelines regarding possible conflict between psychiatrists' religious commitments and psychiatric practice. *American Journal of Psychiatry*, 147, 542.

American Psychiatric Association (2000). *Diagnostic and statistical manual*, Fourth edition, Text revision. Washington, DC: American Psychiatric Association.

Arieti, S. (1976). *Creativity: The magic synthesis*. New York: Basic Books.

Arieti, S. and Schreiber, F. (1981). Multiple murders of a schizophrenic patient. *Journal of the American Academy of Psychoanalysis*, 36, 1325-1330.

Assagioli, R. (1989). Self-realization and psychological disturbances. In S. Grof and C. Grof (Eds.), *Spiritual emergency: When personal transformation becomes a crisis* (pp. 27-48). Los Angeles: Tarcher.

Bebe, D. (1982). Notes on psychosis. *Spring*, 9, 233-252.

Boisen, A. T. (1962). *The exploration of the inner world.* New York: Harper and Row.

Buckley, P. (1981). Mystical experience and schizophrenia. *Schizophrenia Bulletin*, 7, 516-521.

Campbell, J. (1972). *Myths to live by.* New York: Viking Press.

Caplan, M. (1999). *Halfway up the mountain: The error of premature claims to enlightenment.* Prescott, AZ: Hohm Press.

Clarke, I. (2001). Cognitive behavior therapy for psychosis. In I. Clarke (Ed.), *Psychosis and spirituality: Exploring the new frontier* (pp. 15-26). London: Whurr.

Clay, S. (1987). Stigma and spirituality. *Journal of Contemplative Psychotherapy*, 4, 87-94.

Clay, S. (1995). The Tao of madness. *International Association of Spiritual Psychiatry Journal*, 3, 19-27.

Cortright, B. (1997). *Psychotherapy and spirit: Theory and practice in transpersonal psychotherapy.* Albany: State University of New York Press.

Dodds, E. (1951). *The Greeks and the irrational.* Berkeley: University of California Press.

Douglas-Klotz, N. (2001). Missing stories: Psychosis, spirituality, and the development of Western religions hermeneutics. In I. Clarke (Ed.), *Psychosis and spirituality: Exploring the new frontier* (pp. 53-72). London: Whurr Publishers.

Ellis, A. (1980). Psychotherapy and atheistic values: A response to A. E. Bergin's "Psychotherapy and Religious Issues." *Journal of Consulting and Clinical Psychology*, 48, 635-639.

Epstein, M. and Topgay, S. (1982). Mind and mental disorders in Tibetan medicine. *Revision*, 5(1), 67-79.

Fallot, R. (1998). Spiritual and religious dimensions of mental illness recovery narratives. In R. Fallot (Ed.), *Spirituality and religion in recovery from mental illness* (pp. 35-44). Washington, DC: New Directions for Mental Health Services.

Feinstien, D. and Krippner, S. (1988). *Personal mythology: The psychology of your evolving self.* Los Angeles: Jeremy P. Tarcher.

Goodwin, F. and Jamison, K. (1990). *Manic-depressive illness.* New York: Oxford University.

Greenberg, D. and Witzum, E. (1991). Problems in the treatment of religious patients. *American Journal of Psychotherapy*, 65(4), 554-565.

Greenberg, D., Witzum, E., and Buchbinder, J. (1992). Mysticism and psychosis: The fate of Ben Zoma. *British Journal of Medical Psychology*, 65, 223-235.

Grof, S. (1986). *Beyond the brain: Birth, death, and transcendence in psychotherapy.* Albany: State University of New York Press.

Grof, S. and Grof, C. (Eds.) (1989). *Spiritual emergency: When personal transformation becomes a crisis.* Los Angeles: Tarcher.

Hastings, A. (1983). A counseling approach to parapsychological experience. *Journal of Transpersonal Psychology*, 15(2), 143-167.

Hillman, J. (1983). *Healing fiction*. New York: Station Hill Press.

House, R. (2001). Spiritual experience: Healthy psychoticism? In I. Clarke (Ed.), *Psychosis and spirituality: Exploring the new frontier* (pp. 107-126). London: Whurr Publishers.

Jackson, M. (2001). Psychotic and spiritual experience: A case study comparison. In I. Clarke (Ed.), *Psychosis and spirituality: Exploring the new frontier* (pp. 165-190). London: Whurr Publishers.

Jackson, M. C. and Fulford, K. W. (1997). Spiritual experience and psychopathology. *Philosophy, Psychiatry and Psychology*, 1, 41-65.

Jacobson, N. (2001). Experiencing recovery: A dimensional analysis of recovery narratives. *Psychiatric Rehabilitation Journal*, 24, 248-256.

James, W. (1958). *The varieties of religious experience*. New York: New American Library of World Literature.

Jaspers, K. (1963). *General psychopathology*. Manchester: Manchester University Press.

Jung, C. G. (1960). *The psychogenesis of mental disease*. Princeton, NJ: Princeton University Press.

Jung, C. G. (1964). *Man and his symbols*. London: Aldus.

Kirkness, B. (Ed.) (1997). *Target schizophrenia*. London: National Schizophrenia Fellowship.

Koenig, H., McCullough, M., and Larson, D. (Eds.) (2001). *Handbook of religion and health*. New York: Oxford University Press.

Kornfield, J. (1993). *A path with heart: A guide through the perils and promises of spiritual life*. New York: Bantam Books.

Laing, R. (1982). *The voice of experience*. New York: Pantheon.

Laski, M. (1968). *Ecstasy*. New York: Greenwood Press.

Leuba, J. H. (1929). *Psychology of religious mysticism*. New York: Harcourt Brace.

Lukoff, D. (1985). The diagnosis of mystical experiences with psychotic features. *Journal of Transpersonal Psychology*, 17(2), 155-181.

Lukoff, D. (1988). Transpersonal therapy with a manic-depressive artist. *Journal of Transpersonal Psychology*, 20(1), 10-20.

Lukoff, D. (1991). Divine madness: Shamanistic initiatory crisis and psychosis. *Shaman's Drum*, 22, 24-29.

Lukoff, D. (1996). Transpersonal psychotherapy with psychotic disorders and spiritual emergencies with psychotic features. In B. Scotton, A. Chinen, and J. Battista (Eds.), *Textbook of transpersonal psychiatry and psychology* (pp. 271-281). New York: Basic Books.

Lukoff, D. and Everest, H. C. (1985). The myths in mental illness. *Journal of Transpersonal Psychology*, 17(2), 123-153.

Lukoff, D., Lu, F., and Turner, R. (1992). Toward a more culturally sensitive DSM-IV: Psycho-religious and psycho-spiritual problems. *Journal of Nervous and Mental Disease*, 180(11), 673-682.

Lukoff, D., Wallace, C. J., Liberman, R. P., and Burke, K. (1986). A holistic health program for chronic schizophrenic patients. *Schizophrenia Bulletin*, 12(2), 274-282.

Mackenzie, E. R., Rajagopal, D. E., Meibohm, M., and Lavizzo-Mourey, R. (2000). Spiritual support and psychological well-being: Older adults' perceptions of the religion and health con. *Alternative Therapies in Health and Medicine,* 6(6), 37-45.

Mills, N. (2001). The experience of fragmentation in psychosis: Can mindfulness help? In I. Clarke (Ed.), *Psychosis and spirituality: Exploring the new frontier* (pp. 211-222). London: Whurr Publishers.

Newberg, A., D'Aquili, E., and Rause, R. (2001). *Why God won't go away: Brain science and the biology of belief.* New York: Ballantine Books.

Perry, J. (1974). *The far side of madness.* Englewood Cliffs, NJ: Prentice-Hall.

Peters, E. R., Joseph, S., and Garety, P. A. (1999). The assessment of delusions in normal and psychotic populations. *Schizophrenia Bulletin,* 25, 553-576.

Prince, R. H. (1992). Religious experience and psychopathology: Cross-cultural perspectives. In J. F. Schumacher (Ed.), *Religion and mental health* (pp. 281-290). New York: Oxford University Press.

Randal, P., Simpson, A., and Laidlaw, T. (2003). Can recovery-focused multimodal psychotherapy facilitate symptom improvement in people with treatment resistant psychotic illness? *Australian and New Zealand Journal of Psychiatry,* 37, 720-727.

Rosen, G. (1968). *Madness in society.* New York: Harper and Row.

Russinova, Z., Wewiorski, N., and Cash, D. (2002). The integration of psychiatric rehabilitation services in behavioral health care structures: A state example. *Journal of Behavioral Health Services Research,* 29(4), 381-393.

Sheehan, W. and Kroll, J. (1990). Psychiatric patients' belief in general health factors and sin as causes of illness. *American Journal of Psychiatry,* 147(1), 112-113.

Sovatsky, S. (1998). *Word from the soul: Time, East/West spirituality, and psychotherapeutic narrative.* Albany: State University of New York Press.

Stack, J. (1997). Organized religion is but one of the many paths toward spiritual growth. *The Journal,* 8(4), 23-26.

Sullivan, W. (1993). "It helps me be a whole person": The role of spirituality among the mentally challenged. *Psychosocial Rehabilitation Journal,* 16(3), 125-134.

Tobert, N. (2001). The polarities of consciousness. In *Psychosis and spirituality: Exploring the new frontier* (pp. 29-52). London: Whurr.

Victor, B. (1995). Psychopharmacology and transpersonal psychology. In B. Scotton, A. Chinen, and J. Battista (Eds.), *Textbook of transpersonal psychiatry and psychology* (pp. 327-334). New York: Basic Books.

Wallace, A. (1956). Stress and rapid personality changes. *International Record of Medicine,* 169(12), 761-774.

Walsh, R. and Roche, L. (1979). Precipitation of acute psychotic episodes by intensive meditation in individuals with a history of schizophrenia. *American Journal of Psychiatry,* 136, 1085-1086.

Wapnick, K. (1969). Mysticism and schizophrenia. *Journal of Transpersonal Psychology,* 1, 49-67.

Weisburd, D. (1996). Spirituality: Publisher's note. *The Journal,* 8(4), 2-3.

White, M. and Epston, D. (1990). *Narrative means to therapeutic ends.* New York: W.W. Norton and Company.

Wilber, K. (1980). *The spectrum of consciousness.* Wheaton, IL: Quest.

Wilber, K. (1984). The developmental spectrum and psychopathology: Treatment modalities. *Journal of Transpersonal Psychology,* 16(2), 137-166.

Wilber, K. (1993). The pre/trans fallacy. In R. Walsh and F. Vaughan (Eds.), *Paths beyond ego* (pp. 124-130). Los Angeles: Tarcher.

Chapter 12

Journey into the Heart:
Sufi Ways for Healing Depression

Arife Ellen Hammerle

Depression is a deep psychological and spiritual ailment afflicting many people today who live lonely, empty, and isolated lives. In this era we desperately need to revitalize humanity through the application of psychospiritual treatment. This chapter explores the inner dimension of healing and treatment methods for depression through balancing the psychological and spiritual paradigms. An integrative, psychospiritual treatment paradigm creates a dimension of transformation that uses the natural healing potential in each of us to treat and heal depression for many people. As a Sufi psychotherapist I actively apply the paradigms of healing in the sacred wisdom teachings to create a new vision that brings clarity and strength to the awareness of the unity within the individual so the self is no longer lost and empty within the depressive illness.

This chapter focuses on an approach to therapy that taps what Houston Smith (1958) calls humankind's "fundamental thrust at unification." The healing dimension in all religions is an effort to increase the capacity to see our selves as belonging to the whole existence as a form of unity explored in this chapter. The case examples and approaches in this chapter demonstrate how this insight is applied clinically to the treatment of depression.

259

INTRODUCTION

Depressive disorders affect approximately 19 million American adults. The suffering from depression endured by many people burdens our society, families, and the world. More than 10 percent of the U.S. population has experienced clinical depression. Furthermore, the relapse rate for depression is staggering. Once depression affects an individual it generally remains a chronic lifelong illness, unless we work from an integrative stance informed by psychospiritual wisdom.

In the nineteenth century depression was viewed as a weakness in temperament. In the twentieth century the pathogenesis was derived from a Freudian theoretical construct that related it to guilt and shame. By the 1960s scientific and psychological research indicated the existence of two different types of depression, endogenous and neurotic. Endogenous disorders originate from within the body with a possible genetic basis. Neurotic disorders are a reactive type directly correlated with environmental factors such as loss, death, abandonment, or major traumas that function as precipitating factors. During the 1980s research shifted from the cause to the effect on people's lives. Impaired functions and symptoms then became the mode of diagnosing and treating depression.

Depressive symptoms include negative thoughts, moods, behaviors, and functional changes identified as neurovegetative signs, such as fatigue, lack of interest in life, and insomnia. Depression is a public health problem because it afflicts the general population and results in high treatment costs and lost productivity. It can cause greater problems in functioning than general health conditions and increase the risk of morbidity and mortality from co-occurring health conditions, such as heart attack, cancer, and other life-threatening illnesses. Depression remains frequently underdiagnosed and undertreated.

Evidence based on genetics, neuroscience, psychology, spirituality, and clinical research indicates that depression is a disorder that directly affects the body, mind, and spirit. Indeed, modern brain imaging techniques reveal that in depressed patients neural circuits regulating mood, thought, sleep, appetite, and behavior function improperly and the neurotransmitters used by nerve cells to communicate are imbalanced. Spirituality facilitates the healing process for many who use prayer and meditation to consolidate their energy and guide inner transformational healing. This healing process facilitates the sacred opening to an expanded understanding of self in a state of inner stability and balance. In addition, research indicates that understanding spirituality and genetics in conjunction with environmental factors, brain chemistry, shifting negative thought patterns, and somatic awareness, together with antidepressant medications, can work for coordinated treatment in order to improve the vital quality of care, for healing, and the prevention of relapse.

A great gap exists in research and validation of psychospiritual approaches to effective treatment for depression compared to the more traditional treatments. Some work has begun with studies using mindfulness, exercise, and prayer. This area is open for new research and exploration to complement the clinical approaches being used by many practitioners.

DEPRESSION: TRADITIONAL VIEW OF ETIOLOGY, SYMPTOMS, AND TREATMENT

The *Diagnostic and Statistical Manual of Mental Disorders,* Fourth Edition, Text Revision (DSM-IV-TR) describes the primary criteria for depression (APA, 2000). The primary features of depression recognize the significance of the extensive diminishment of engagement on the physical, mental, and emotional levels. Individuals differ in response to their depression and recovery processes.

Major depressive episode symptoms include depressed mood most of the day, nearly every day; markedly diminished interest or pleasure in all, or almost all, activities, most of the day, nearly every day; significant weight loss when not dieting or weight gain or decreases in appetite nearly every day; insomnia or hypersomnia nearly every day; psychomotor agitation or retardation nearly every day; fatigue or loss of energy nearly every day; feelings of worthlessness or excessive or inappropriate guilt; diminished ability to think or concentrate, or indecisiveness, nearly every day; recurrent thoughts of death, recurrent suicidal ideation without a specific plan, or suicide attempt or a specific plan for committing suicide (American Psychiatric Association, 2000, p. 162).*

---

*Reprinted with permission from the *Diagnostic and Statistical Manual of Mental Disorders,* Fourth Edition, Text Revision, Copyright 2000, American Psychiatric Association.

Current research indicates that genes play a significant role in creating a predisposition toward depression. Apparently, multiple gene variants act in conjunction with environmental risk factors, developmental events, and learned behaviors to create a constellation of factors that account for the development and expression of depressive disorders.

Environmental and psychosocial issues are well-established markers for increased risk factors in depression. Stressful life events may trigger recurrent episodes of depression in some people while in others recurrence may develop without identifiable triggers.

Hormonal abonormalities also play a significant role in the development of depression. The hypothalamic-pituitary-adrenal (HPA) axis regulates much of the body's response to stress. When this is stimulated by a physical or psychological stressor, the production of corticotrophin-releasing factor (CRF) increases. In depression the HPA hormonal system is frequently overactive and the level of CRF increases. Our understanding of the complex relationships between the glands, stress, and depression is increasing rapidly.

Depression research is on the cutting edge of advancing the clinical understanding and application to treatment. It brings together in a collaborative manner scientific disciplines to effectively use the tools of biology, genetics, psychology, genetics, epidemiology, and behavioral science to develop a comprehensive understanding of the factors that influence depression. Translating these discoveries into clinically relevant information holds great promise for disentangling the complex causes of depression and for advancing effective treatment modalities. When we bring these studies together with psychospiritual research we can develop a new treatment modality that encompasses the entire human system as a unit of balance—body, mind, and spirit.

Depression is a complex disorder for which we have created many distinct categories or diagnoses. The degree and variation among those who suffer from depression in terms of symptoms, course of illness, and response to treatment is quite high, which suggests that depression has a complex interaction of causes. The variability of depression increases the level of difficulty in terms of research and treatment. Recent psychospiritual research has been able to develop an understanding of the different forms of depression and the identification of effective treatments for individuals based on symptom presentation.

One of the challenges facing scientists, researchers, and clinical professionals today is treatment refractory, which is the hard to treat depression. Approximately 20 percent of cases remain treatment refractory with minimal long-term improvement, negative side effects, and relapse. Traditional treatment modalities that have been recommended for the treatment of depression include the following:

- *Psychotherapy*—The two primary areas of psychotherapy that are traditionally used to treat depression are cognitive-behavioral therapy (CBT) and interpersonal therapy (IPT). CBT works to change negative thinking and behavior, and IPT works to change the disturbed style of interpersonal relationships that contribute to depression. Many research studies conducted by the National Institute of Mental Health indicate that when psychotherapy is combined with conjunctive treatment a positive outcome is often increased.
- *Electroconvulsive therapy* (ECT)—ECT is a traditional technique for treatment of depression, although it is stigmatizing, has a high relapse rate, and may cause negative long-term side effects. Current research studies indicate that the dose of electricity and placement of the electrodes either unilaterally or bilaterally influence the treatment effectiveness and level of side effects.
- *Pharmacologic treatment*—SSRIs (selective serotonin reuptake inhibitors), MAOI (monoamine oxidase inhibitors), and tricyclic antidepressants are widely prescribed in conjunction with psychotherapy. Medications are generally used to stabilize the severity of symptoms, although they are insufficient as a treatment modality.

Women and Depression

Depression has been identified as the most significant mental health risk for women. Research indicates that women are afflicted with depression at a rate of two times that of men each year in the United States. Risk factors for depression include socioeconomic factors, economic problems, racial/ethnic discrimination, lower educational and income levels, segregation into low-status and high-stress jobs, unemployment, poor health, large family size, marital dissolution and single parenthood, and high rate of physical and sexual abuse (McGrath et al., 1990, cited in apa.org issues). The traditional view of etiology includes genetics, environmental stress, and hormonal abnormalities.

PSYCHOSPIRITUAL VIEW OF ETIOLOGY, SYMPTOMS, AND TREATMENT

Mindfulness-Based Cognitive Therapy for Depression (MBCT)

The power of mindful attention techniques lies in the increased capacity to use an "empty self" to create a profound receptivity to the spiritual domain, thereby allowing the person to access transcendent awareness (see Suzuki et al., 1960, pp. 94-95). Generally, cognitive therapy has been shown both quantitatively and qualitatively to reduce the risk of relapse for depression. This research has been expanded by Buddhist researchers to include spirituality as an integral aspect of the treatment for depression. Depression involves both biological changes in the brain and psychological changes in the way we feel. MBCT is designed to combine treatment modalities that teach new ways to work with thoughts and feelings. "The core skill that the MCBT program aims to teach is the ability, at times of potential relapse, to recognize and disengage from mind states characterized by self-perpetuating patterns of ruminative, negative thought" (Segal, Williams, and Teasdale, 2002, p. 77). MCBT works by shifting the focus from content to process and from doing to being. Through eight intensive sessions the client progressively learns to shift to an intentional use of awareness and attention. Clients learn to integrate new skills so that they may make choices to take care of themselves differently when their moods shift toward sadness. Mindfulness is the core skill.

Mindfulness has been described as paying attention in a particular way: on purpose, in the present moment, and nonjudgmentally. . . . Awareness of the pattern of thought, feelings, and bodily sensations that characterize relapse-related mind states (and the doing mode of mind more generally) is an essential first step in recognizing the need for corrective action. Intentionally (on purpose) changing the focus and style of attention is the mental gear lever by which processing can be switched from one cognitive mode to another. And the nonjudgmental, present moment, focus of mindfulness indicates that it is indeed very closely related to the being mode of mind. (Segal, Williams, and Teasdale, 2002, p. 77)

This treatment approach provides clients with a positive resource for coping with the pain of depression. By altering negative thinking through cultivating access to inner courage and wisdom gained through the practice of mindful awareness the individual accesses psychospiritual awareness. Finally, the skills taught are integrated around the ultimate aim of the program: staying well and preventing future relapse (Segal, Williams, and Teasdale, 2002). Clients can begin to attend to their fragility with self-respect and care. Overall, MBCT provides clients with skills for responding positively to the automatic thought patterns that trigger depression and relapse.

This psychospiritual method of understanding and healing depression is based on rebalancing the entire system, primarily through intention, awareness, concentration within the heart, and positive thought processes. Rebalancing necessitates an internal energetic shift toward healing and stability. The constancy of breath is utilized to create positive activation of health within the moment.

Psychospiritual Paradigm of Sufi Psychology

Sufi psychology presents us with a psychospiritual approach to healing that bridges scientific knowledge with the wisdom of the ineffable spiritual experience. Sufism is an ancient wisdom tradition that has existed for over 1,400 years. Sufism contributes a theoretical foundation from which we can understand the etiology, symptoms, and treatment of depression.

In her book *Psychology in Sufism*, Amineh Pryor explains concisely that

[S]ufism is the erphan (understanding) of Islam and is also known as the mystical branch of Islam. Islam means peace. The meaning of the word mystical, as it refers to Sufism, is the hidden, secret or unseen. The mystery or hidden knowledge is that unity exists yet is not accessible or perceived through the physical senses. This knowledge must be understood through inner experience. (Pryor, 2000, p. 21)

The Sufi-based psychospiritual approach integrates the wisdom teachings of unity in the human being's search for inner knowledge and peace for the treatment of depression.

According to Sufi theory, the ultimate goal of life is to achieve unity. Unity is found in the most basic profession of Sufism: there is no god except God (la illaha illa allah).

The human being is but a part of this eternal Being, capable of knowing the rules and laws of this eternal Divinity, for the microcosm of the self contains within itself the capacity to understand the macrocosm of Being. Such awareness is that inner treasure hidden behind the world of change. (Angha, 1998, p. 21)

There are many types of human experiences. However, Sufi-based psychotherapy focuses specifically on profound transformative treatment and healing experiences. The profound healing experience is based on the inner witnessing of the sacred point of unity concentrated within the center of every human being. This point resides within the spiritual heart. This essential point connects the individual's heart to the eternal cosmos, to God, the Divine. Sufi wisdom teaches the unity of humanity and existence as a fundamental nexus of the psychological and spiritual in terms of human development and personality structure.

Avicenna (980-1037) was a Sufi philosopher, psychologist, and scientist who developed an integrated understanding of the personality structure of the human being. His work led to an integrative perspective that guides Sufi theory to view the circle of human evolution. This circle encompasses an existential communion, which is a universal intellect of all peoples (see Shafii, 1988).

> The heart is a catalyst between emotion, affect, and thought processes, religious values, and, above all, human beings constant drive toward and search for existential communion. The heart is the river which brings the restless soul to the vast Ocean of Reality (haqq). (Shafii, 1988, p. 44)

The depressed individual is searching to understand the vast inner darkness and emptiness. The quest to know is a longing to experience existential communion with the universal intellect of all of humanity.

Sufism reflects a mystical understanding of unity that facilitates growth, change, and healing through an integrative psychospiritual approach. Unity brings together the existential angst, isolation, and inner emptiness reflective of a loss of self suffered when depressed. The emptiness is the result of separation from divine, the sacred, or spirit which functions as if the person loses himself or herself. Sufi psychology provides a framework that facilitates a bridge between the loss of self and the witnessing of the transformative or transcendent Self.

> Western psychologies, particularly psychoanalysis and dynamic psychotherapies, have ignored the study of the psychological significance of the "loss of self" . . . Richard M. Bucke, William James, Carl G. Jung and Erich Fromm have, like voices in the wilderness, tried to bring to the attention of the healing professions and the community the significance of "loss of self." (Shafii, 1988, p. 162)

Many aspects of the cosmic consciousness of Bucke and James reflect the qualities of the loss of self through unity as described by the Sufis. The qualities of the experience of unity include the observation of light, loss of self-centered personality, ecstasy, balance, and harmony as an inner awareness grounded in self-experience.

The Sufis have developed practical techniques, including the use of breath, concentration of awareness, balance, and intention, which guide the individual human being to experience an existential unity and the self as an integrated whole person. This wisdom guides healing and treatment practices. A Sufi teacher explains,

> Thus, we ought not necessarily to consider illness our enemy; rather, we may see it as an event, a mechanism of the body, that is serving to cleanse, purify, and balance us on the physical, emotional, mental, and spiritual planes. (Chishti, 1985, p. 11)

This communion is the experience of unity. There is no separation from the divine in unity. This knowledge guides psychospiritual transformation and healing.

> When we are touched by mystic grace and allow ourselves to enter its field without fear, we see that we are all parts of a whole, elements of a universal harmony, unique, essential and sacred notes in a divine music that everyone and everything is playing together with us in God and for God. (Harvey, 1996, p. xi)

This grace is the unity experienced as relief from depressive symptoms and prevention of relapse due to an inner healing of the loss of self within the psychospiritual paradigm.

The inner witnessing experienced by mystics of all traditions reflects advancement through levels, states, and stages of development. "There must be a knowledge and consideration of the physical, mental, and spiritual planes of existence for there to be true health" (Chishti, 1985, p. 16). This is a nonlinear process of unfolding the Self essence within the heart. Mystical traditions reflect the illumination and allow the individual to grasp this knowledge that guides us toward psychospiritual integration, healing, and transformation.

> It is in the face of mysticism, the soul of religion, that the modern science of psychology may realize its strength and its limitations. In the state of such realization, psychology may move toward a longing for understanding the wisdom of the ancient, and take a fruitful step toward opening a communication between the ancient mysticism of Sufism, and the modern science of psychology. (Angha, in Pryor, 2000, preface)

The application of the psychospiritual teachings of Sufism to the treatment of depression adds valuable insights and approaches to clinical psychology.

SUFI PSYCHOSPIRITUAL THERAPY

Heartbeing Therapy for Depression (HBT)

I work with the Sufism and Psychology Forum to integrate Sufism and Western psychology. The Sufism and Psychology Forum (SPF) is a department of the International Association of Sufism (IAS). IAS is an invaluable resource that serves a vital role in opening lines of communication among Sufism and those interested in the wisdom teachings of Sufism. It was established by Sufi Masters of this century, Shah Nazar Seyed Dr. Ali Kianfar and Seyedeh Dr. Nahid Angha. SPF was created to achieve the following goals:

1. To bring together the application of principles and practices of Sufism and the study of psychology through research, translation, and discussion
2. To publish and distribute a Sufism and psychology newsletter
3. To publish books on Sufi psychology
4. To sponsor lectures and seminars presented by Sufi psychologists
5. To create a forum and line of communication between Sufi psychologists, including the online dialogue on the Internet. This is a continuing dialogue between people of the mind and soul.

In order to make psychospiritual treatment accessible, I began the Community Healing Centers (CHC) with a group of psychotherapists. CHC is an integrative psychospiritual psychotherapy practice of the body, mind, spirit, and heart providing individual and group psychotherapy within the community. CHC integrates psychospiritual treatment as the primary modality for healing. Heartbeing Therapy works by cultivating inner balance based on understanding the material and spiritual realms.

Body, mind, nafs (which includes desires and ego), and spirit are aspects of Sufi psychology. This is the realm of heart and soul, the seat of healing grounded in compassion, breath, inner balance, and concentrated energy. Healing the physical, psychological, and spiritual realms is based on several practices, including clarifying intention to increase self awareness, balancing the system, use of practices to cultivate attention to breath, meditation, Self-remembrance, and concentration of energy within the heart. All of these practices increase awareness and may lead to cleansing, presence, nonjudgment, freedom, and healing. Sufi psychology integrates awareness of body, mind, and spirit with the heart. The body is the domain for healing work since the body contains the sacred temple of heart and the breath of divine.

The body language of the depressed client is distinctive. The shoulders are usually stooped, the chin is pulled in toward the chest so the eyes are averted from direct contact with the world, the ankles are often crossed, and the client speaks with a monotone, saddened quality. Working with the body through the breath and inner attention becomes an important treatment method in order to help the client integrate body, mind, and spirit. By working with the depressed body posture, the clinician can make a concrete shift in the client's psychological system. All body postures used by a depressed client tend to share one common factor: suppressing the breath. The client's system effectively shuts down.

> Try a simple exercise: sit down, hold the depressed posture for a minute, and try to breathe. Check in with yourself and ask, how do I feel? You likely feel depressed rather than happy or relaxed.
>
> Alternatively, sit with your back straight, breathe deeply with your feet on the floor, gather your energy from everyone and concentrate it within one point within your heart, then see how you feel. You may begin to feel inner balance and peace.

Concentration practice allows the individual to shift into being present within the heart, which leads to inner cleansing and healing. Sufi psychology is an unfolding process of psychospiritual integration and transformation, based on inner balance. These practices are the source of healing and treatment for depression.

Case Example: Alice

Alice is an artist in her late fifties who presented with relationship problems, insomnia, a crisis with her aging mother, struggles with her rebellious adolescent daughter, and depression (major depressive disorder, single episode). Her depressive symptoms included isolation, insomnia, low energy, low self-esteem, difficulty making decisions, and feelings of hopelessness. The client was a student and healer with the Native American Shamanic tradition. She was very interested in integrating her spiritual work with her psychological treatment. She was very sophisticated in terms of cultivating insight and using her awareness for healing.

As she progressed in the treatment process, her awareness of her journey through the darkness of depression into the healing light of spiritual awareness became transformational. Alice was able to clarify her intention to increase self-awareness, balance her system, and use breath practices to cultivate attention and concentration of energy within the spiritual heart. She became aware of an inner journey within the inner eye of her heart. Her paintings transformed and depicted an essential quality of breath, dark, light, and heart; it was as if the sun and cascading water in her art reflected her inner strength overshadowed by a tremendous feeling of unconditional love. This love became integrated into her pain about her needs, feelings, and the meaning of her depressive symptoms. Because Alice is an artist, her meditation experiences related to her transcendent world were filled with color and beauty, while her depression was frequently depicted through darkness in her art. Her inner wisdom was depicted by a radiating sun and a jeweled flower in a mandala drawing.

Progressing through psychospiritual treatment, the client expressed an inward shift from an empty heart with no awareness of herself to a gentle, warm heart, which was open to psychospiritual experience and illumination. The client recognized within herself and in her heart the truth of her being alive.

Within four months of weekly psychospiritual treatment, which included talking, art, concentrative heart-centered breath, and meditation practice for achieving inner balance and healing, the work had advanced to a stage that the client was able to receive and absorb levels of light. Different colors of light are experienced as an aspect of the spiritual journey depending on the stage and state of the individual. Alice experienced a color of light linking her with her deepening awareness of the transcendent life. The experience of light guided the work into understanding her depression and integrating her feelings. The light relieved her painful symptoms of depression. Her awareness opened her to enter into a deepening of the psychospiritual process. Alice was no longer empty or alone. Her depressed symptoms lifted and she experienced peace, tranquility, and inner witnessing. Concurrent with this therapeutic shift, the client noticed a mirroring of compassionate positive feelings toward others in all aspects of her life experience. She increasingly submitted herself to a heart-centered awareness. This transformative process was a point of inner opening that was mirrored within the client's heart and outwardly in her relationships. She was then able to begin therapeutic work with her daughter, make decisions about the care of her mother, and begin a committed relationship with a man. Her sleep problems and depression were alleviated at this time in treatment. The client continued treatment to deepen her awareness and to cultivate greater understanding of her self-transformative process.

In psychospiritual work the level of awareness is enhanced and the ability to concentrate energy within the heart grows stronger. This creates an internal shift in the structure of the personality, changes the appearance of the individual, and leads to insight into the essence of the core self. The client experiences surrender, which is an expansion of self beyond the limitations of the presenting complaint of depression into transformation. This experience of surrender within the psychospiritual therapeutic relationship arises within the intersubjective field from the totality of empathic inner witnessing to a magnetic interconnection between client, clinician, and the spiritual realm. When the therapist and client experience a mutuality of knowing the truth, this clear epiphanic experience inspires the journey as a process of self-actualization that can open the door to attainment of unity and alleviation of depression. Self-discovery is a process of deeply understanding one's reality. Exploring the nafs (desires, suffering, ego) allows the individual to unveil the layers of multiplicity and separation. Uncovering frees the individual from the layer upon layer of information, thoughts, emotions, and aspects of constant change that obscure us from ourselves. This is a transformative process of inner witnessing (ma'arefat) embracing the goal of knowledge (erphan), which is a universal truth. This leads to inner states of peace, patience, and freedom.

Case Example: Amanda

Amanda is a thirty-three-year-old Caucasian woman who suffered from major depressive disorder. She entered therapy presenting as anxious and angry due to the humiliation and loss of her fiancé who had decided not to marry her. She suffered with the rejection, trying to understand how he could change from love to hate so quickly with no apparent warning. Anger, anxiety, and grief worked against her, gradually building into depression and suicidal ideation. Her depression was experienced as badness and anger directed at the self filled with loneliness, emptiness, and fear. The depressive symptoms included depressed mood, diminished interest or pleasure in almost all activities most of the day, loss of energy, feelings of worthlessness, and diminished ability to concentrate. Around the time of her loss she had been baptized into the Catholic religion, which she had studied with her fiancé. Initially, she consulted with a priest in conjunction with her work in psychotherapy. Amanda declined a referral for a medication evaluation with a psychiatrist.

The initial phase of treatment was focused on building a therapist-client relationship and stabilizing her depression. The therapeutic relationship developed slowly. Amanda expressed considerable anger, humiliation, and shame about her grief. We proceeded to work through her feelings. As she shared her grief and the depths of her aloneness I intervened with the use of her breath to clarify her healing intention, create inner awareness, and increase her ability to be present within herself. She was eventually able to increase her self-awareness, leading her to activate and obtain a job. At that time she became stable and began talking about the meaning of life. Her existential angst was pivotal for her shift into the psychospiritual realm. She discovered that she did not know the meaning of her life and did not value herself. She found solace in God through her conversion to Catholicism.

In our therapeutic relationship, I began by evaluating the client's psychological condition and discussed it with her. Once a therapeutic relationship had been established, I was able to suggest a treatment plan based on the psychospiritual process of transformation. This is especially useful in the treatment of depression.

The clinician cultivates balance by moderating between different aspects of the client's self that are in conflict. In this case, the aspects in conflict were the client's need for admiration to define and stabilize her sense of self while simultaneously fearing the harsh judgments of others. This clinical approach involves practices, including clarifying intention to increase self-awareness, breath control work, meditation, cultivating attention to breath, and concentration of energy in the heart. In this case, I stabilized my capacity to serve as a mirror for the client's painful abandonment. The clinician practices inner stability and purification to develop the capacity for awareness. By holding an emotionally stable inner state, giving feedback neutrally, attuning to the client's state, the clinician awakens an observer position in the client. When the clinician works as the moderator within the intersubjective dynamic, then the depressive symptoms and pain are opened up.

The clinician holds the awareness, breath, and concentration in heart also practiced by the client. This mirroring dynamic necessitates the use of internal resources in the clinician to expand or open the limited perspective the depressed client is locked within. This psychospiritual approach allows for a transfer of energy, the electromagnetic energy that connects all of life and intensifies between clinician and client, thereby facilitating transformation. This process takes great skill and concentration by the clinician. The client maintains engagement in her own internal process through breathing exercises, attunement, and meditation practice between sessions. Problems arise when clients become disinterested in healing and therapeutic change and remain attached to their pain and suffering.

The clinician stays energetically present with the client's process and thereby guides the healing from within the relational frame. Rather than detachment, matching the state, then leading and pacing, adds new reaction to the released feelings and cognitions. The practice of awareness, intention, concentration of energy, and breathing facilitate opening to release suffering and heal depression. This leads the client toward an inner experience of unity or wholeness.

Sufi-based psychospiritual treatment is similar to the process of alchemy, which is the transformative process through which the mind and heart are gradually illuminated by spiritual knowledge until the human being becomes the embodiment of this knowledge. Alchemy is an ancient Greek science of transmuting one impure substance into a pure substance, such as turning a base metal into gold. In its original pre-Socratic form it was concerned with the nature of Being itself. The Sufis apply alchemy to the transformation of self, the quest to discover a universal elixir of life. The alchemy of heart necessitates a transformative process engaging stages of the heart toward the final destination of unity. The clinician acts as the moderator just like the alchemists moderated between stable and unstable metals. When the moderator is used, all pure and impure metals are mixed together, united; each is then transformed by the others and transmuted into the purest essence of all the metals. United they no longer carry their original essence. Rather, they assume the highest quality of purity, which is gold. Similarly, unity is the essential goal for the individual engaged in the transformative psychospiritual process. Unity is the elixir of the alchemical process for therapeutic healing. In Sufi healing, the transformative process is similar to the alchemical process.

In this case, the treatment supplied the client with insight, cognitive understanding, and wisdom into her depression, symptoms, and healing process. Amanda experienced a loss of self and inner emptiness characterized by badness, negativity, evil ways, and self-weakness. She suffered from low self-esteem and lack of a cohesive sense of her self. Her abandonment by others, shame about her lack of self, and disappointments in life tortured her daily existence. She also experienced success in school, her work, and some relationships. Gradually, Amanda was able to embody those painful qualities of herself and to heal them emotionally, cognitively, and spiritually as she developed an understanding of her pain.

The initial signs of healing include peacefulness, self-awareness, the development of rapport, truth with oneself, and honesty about one's pain. Healing becomes a process that shifts into a gentle opening of defense mechanisms and the painful affect of nafs (Arabic word translated as ego, desires) that hide within the psyche and traumatize the client. In this case, many signs of healing were present, such as when the client became increasingly able to tolerate friendships and improve communication in social relationships. She became accepting of her limitation and developed a greater capacity to empathize with herself and others. A major shift was evinced in terms of her sense of entitlement and expectations of being healed. The client began to accept responsibility for her treatment and became actively engaged in the transformation of herself. This is good, as it provided a beginning reliance on interactive social engagement and modeling an empathic witnessing of self.

The recovery process involved focusing on polishing the mirror of heart through concentration on the meaning of darkness and light as vital complementary aspects of unity in the treatment of depression. The client practiced self-remembering, which is a system for holding the positive qualities of love, peace, and compassion. In Sufism, remembrance can be through recitation of a word or phrase or experienced in silence. Remembrance is the concentration on creating inner awareness of the beautiful qualities of divine through the use of the breath and heart-based concentration to increase awareness and confidence during the healing process. The treatment lasted for four years and had a positive outcome. She experienced how depression can be alleviated and controlled by practices that immerse the individual in a state of inner balance, stability, and concentration in the heart. At this advanced level of treatment, her practice cultivated psychospiritual awareness and integration of the darkness of depression within the light of inner knowledge.

The client continues to delve into her own psychospiritual work and practices integrated during her treatment. She was able to move progressively through transformative stages: from the stage of nafs, through the process of alchemical transformation, which reveals the significance of heart, and embark on the journey toward understanding that leads to unity within the psychospiritual healing of Sufi psychology. These techniques aid her in preventing relapse, maintaining inner balance, and cultivating self-awareness.

CONCLUSION

Psychospiritual healing guides the individual to profound experiences that transcend ordinary consciousness. Such experiences inspire and guide the individual to a deep inner peace and awareness of a connection among human beings. This connection is a universal oneness or unity. Unity within the human being heals depression. Understanding the search for and meaning of psychospiritual healing as profound and mystical experiences is a vital aspect of the process of self-realization for human beings.

Psychospiritual wisdom forms the nexus that bridges the scientific, medical, and psychological paradigms, guiding our understanding for the effective treatment of depression. A psychospiritual approach necessitates the cultivation of the practice of the human being moving through stages of nafs, opening within alchemy into the awareness of heart and the significance of love, creating inner awareness of understanding that radiates toward unity. Heartbeing meditation and practices provide clear intention, self-awareness, remembrance, and balance. Breath and concentration techniques facilitate Self-discovery.

The essence of Sufi psychology is the twelve principles of *tasawouf*, which include abandonment, repentance, virtue, patience, honesty, purity, love, remembrance, faithfulness, solitude, poverty, and annihilation. These principles guide the individual to his or her psychospiritual change, healing, and growth. A psychospiritual approach links body, mind, spirit, and heart within the whole existence. Principles and practices of Self-knowledge facilitate the coordination of body, mind, spirit, and heart beyond the limitations of current psychological theories and Western thinking. The healing of Sufi psychology begins with the longing to attain Self-knowledge, freedom from the emptiness of depression to which we become attached, a magnetism of love that creates inner purification, and ultimately ends with the awakened heart of divine grace, wisdom, and peace in unity.

BIBLIOGRAPHY

Ali-Shah, O. (1995). *Sufism As Therapy.* Reno, NV: Tractus Books.

American Psychiatric Association (2000). *Diagnostic and Statistical Manual of Mental Disorders* (Fourth Edition, Text Revision). Washington, DC: American Psychiatric Association.

Angha, M.G. (1984). *Destination: Eternity.* San Rafael, CA: PWP.

Angha, N. N. (1991a). *The Journey: Seyr va Soluk.* San Rafael, CA: Phoenix Word and Press.

Angha, N.N. (1991b). *Principles of Sufism.* San Rafael, CA: PWP.

Angha, N. N. (1993). *The Nature of Miracle.* San Rafael, CA: Phoenix Word and Press.

Angha, N.N. (1998). *The Journey of the Lovers.* San Rafael, CA: IAS.

Arvidson, P. and Davis-Floyd, R. (Eds.) (1997). *Intuition: The Inside Story.* New York: Routledge.

Atwater, P. (1997). Illusions of Perception. *The Quest,* June, pp. 30-54.

Benjamin, J. (1988). *The Bonds of Love.* New York: Pantheon Books.

Bucke, R. M. (1969). *Cosmic Consciousness.* New York: E.P. Dutton.

Capra, F. (1981). *The Tao of Physics.* Bungay, Suffolk, England: Fontana.

Capra, F. (1982). *The Turning Point.* New York: Bantam Books.

Capra, F. (1996). *The Web of Life.* New York: Anchor Books.

Chishti, S.H. (1985). *The Book of Healing.* New York: Inner Traditions International, Ltd.

Cortright, B. (1997). *Psychotherapy and Spirit.* Albany: State University of New York Press.

Crick, F. (1994). *The Astonishing Hypothesis.* New York: Simon and Schuster.

Edinger, E. (1984). *The Creation of Consciousness.* Toronto, Canada: Inner City Books.

Frager, R. (1999). *Heart, Self and Soul.* Wheaton, IL: Quest Books.

Friedman, M. (1992). *Religion and Psychology: A Dialogical Approach.* New York: Paragon House.

Gough, W. (1997) An Inquiry. Developing a Bridge Between Science and Sufism, *Sufism Journal,* 6(4), 26-37; 46.

Grof, S. (1990). *The Holotropic Mind.* San Francisco: Harper.

Grof, S. (1998). *The Cosmic Game.* Albany: State University of New York Press.

Harding, M. E. (1965). *The I and the Not I.* Princeton, NJ: Princeton University Press.

Harvey, A. (1996). *The Essential Mystics.* Edison, NJ: Castle Books.

Hayward, J. (1992). *Gentle Bridges.* Boston, MA: Shambhala.

Henderson, R. (1998). Out of the Blues. *Common Boundary,* January/February, pp. 18-26.

Hoeller, S. (1989). *Jung and the Lost Gospels.* Wheaton, IL: The Theosophical Publishing House.

Hoffman, E. (1999). *The Right to Be Human.* New York: McGraw-Hill.

James, W. (1980). *The Principles of Psychology,* Volume 1. New York: Dover Publications, Inc.

Jani, A. (1995). An Integral View of Body, Health and Disease. *The Inner Directions Journal,* Winter, pp. 22-23.

Khan, Inayat. (1963). *Sufi Teachings: The Art of Being.* Rockport, MA: Element.

Kihlstrom, J. (1987). The Cognitive Unconscious. *Science,* 237(4821), 1445-1452.

Kohut, H. (1977). *The Restoration of the Self.* New York: International Universities Press.

Larson, V. (1986). An Exploration of the Nature of Resonance in Psychotherapy. *Dissertation Abstracts International* (UMI Accession number 8612428).

Lawlis, G. (1996). *Transpersonal Medicine.* Boston, MA: Shambhala.

Leonard, G. (1997). Living Energy. *Ionics,* Fall, pp. 8-15.

Lycan, W. (1996). *Consciousness and Experience.* Cambridge, MA: The MIT Press.

Maghsoud, M. (1991). *A Meditation: Payam-e-del.* San Rafael, CA: Phoenix Word and Press.

Maghsoud, S.A. (1975). *The Hidden Angles of Life.* Pomona, CA: Multidisciplinary Publications.

Maslow, A. (1964). *Religions, Values and Peak-Experiences.* New York: Penguin Books.

Maslow, A. (1968). *Toward a Psychology of Being.* New York: John Wiley and Sons, Inc.

Maslow, A. (1971). *The Farther Reaches of Human Nature.* New York: Viking Press.

May, R. (1958). *Symbolism in Religion and Literature.* New York: George Braziller.

McGrath, E., Keita, G., Stickland, B., and Russo, N. (1990). *Women and Depression: Risk Factors and Treatment Issues.* Washington, DC: American Psychological Association.

Meador, B. (1992). *Uncursing the Dark: Treasures from the Underworld.* Wilmettek, IL: Chiron Publications.

Metzner, R. (1998). *The Unfolding Self.* Novato, CA: Origin Press.

Monroe, R. (1982). *Far Journeys.* New York: Doubleday.

Murphy, M. and Donovan, S. (1996). The Physical and Psychological Effects of Meditation: A Review of Contemporary Research with a Comprehensive Bibliography. *Institute of Noetic Sciences Bulletin,* pp. 73-86, 120-129.

Naranjo, C. and Ornstein, R. (1971). *On the Psychology of Meditation.* New York: The Viking Press, Inc.

Nasr, H. (1991). *Sufi Essays.* Albany: State University of New York Press.

Perera, S. (1981). *Descent to the Goddess. A Way of Initiation for Women.* Canada: Inner City Books.

Pryor, A. (2000). *Psychology in Sufism.* San Rafael, CA: International Association of Sufism.

Radin, D. (1997). *The Conscious Universe: The Scientific Truth of Psychic Phenomena.* San Francisco: Harper Edge.

Raymo, C. (1998). *Skeptics and True Believers.* New York: Walker and Company.

Rogers, C. (1961). *On Becoming a Person.* Boston, MA: Houghton Mifflin Company.

Schafer, R. (1959). Generative empathy in the treatment situation. *Psychoanalytic Quarterly,* 28, 342-373.

Searle, J. (1998). *The Rediscovery of the Mind.* Cambridge, MA: The MIT Press.

Segal, R. (1992). *The Gnostic Jung.* Princeton, NJ: Princeton University Press.

Segal, Z., Williams, J., and Teasdale, J. (2002). *Mindfulness-Based Cognitive Therapy for Depression.* New York: The Guilford Press.

Shafii, M. (1988). *Freedom from the Self.* New York: Human Sciences Press, Inc.

Siegel, B. (1997). A Way of Healing. *Parabola,* Winter, pp. 59-64

Smith, H. (1958). *The Illustrated World's Religions.* New York: HarperCollins Publisher.

Steere, D. (1997). *Spiritual Presence in Psychotherapy.* New York: Brunner/Mazel.

Suzuki, D.T., Fromm, E., and DeMartino, R. (1960). *Zen Buddhism and Psychoanalysis.* New York: Grove Press.

Swimme, B. (1996). *The Hidden Heart of the Cosmos.* Maryknoll, NY: Orbis Books.

Swimme, B. and Berry, T. (1992). *The Universe Story.* San Francisco: Harper San Francisco.

Tart, C. (1969). *Altered States of Consciousness.* San Francisco: Harper.

Templeton, Sir John (2000). *The Nature of Spiritual Transformation.* A Review of the Literature. West Conshohocken, PA: Templeton Foundation Press.

Thompson, W.I. (1996). *The Time Falling Bodies Take to Light.* New York: St. Martin.

Thuan, T. (1992). *The Birth of the Universe.* New York: Abrams.

Wade, J. (1996). *Changes of Mind: An Holonomic Theory of the Evolution of Consciousness.* Albany: State University of New York Press.

Wallis, C. (1996). Healing. *Time Magazine,* June, pp. 58-68.

Wilber, K. (1977). *The Spectrum of Consciousness.* Wheaton, IL: The Theosophical Publishing House.

Wilber, K. (1980). *The Atman Project.* London, England: The Theosophical Publishing House.

Wilber, K. (1998). *The Marriage of Sense and Soul.* New York: Random House, Inc.

Wilson, R. (1995). The Art of Psychic Healing. *Gnosis,* Winter, pp. 14-21.

Women and Depression (n.d.). APA online. <http://www.apa.org/ppo/issues/pwomenand depress.html>.

Chapter 13

Mindful Awareness and Self-Directed Neuroplasticity: Integrating Psychospiritual and Biological Approaches to Mental Health with a Focus on Obsessive-Compulsive Disorder

Jeffrey M. Schwartz
Elizabeth Z. Gulliford
Jessica Stier
Margo Thienemann

INTRODUCTION: FOCUSED TRAINING AND EFFORT CAN CHANGE BRAIN FUNCTION

The ancient insight of Gotama Buddha has surfaced in modern Western medicine and psychology as an effective tool for the treatment of a variety of mental and physical conditions (Schwartz and Begley, 2002). A number of scientific studies have confirmed that the practice of mindful awareness (mindfulness) can calm and balance the mind, as well as alleviate imbalances in the brain (Schwartz, 1999; Segal, Williams, and Teasdale, 2002). The use of mindfulness has potentially profound implications for the clinical application of therapies that acknowledge the importance of spirituality in the practice of modern scientific medicine.

Studies using state-of-the-art brain imaging demonstrate that mindfulness-based treatments are associated with significant changes in brain abnormalities (Schwartz et al., 1996; Schwartz, 1998; Paquette et al., 2003). Of particular interest, research shows that people are capable of rewiring brain circuitry associated with obsessive-compulsive disorder (OCD) (Schwartz, 1998). Brain metabolism changes when patients apply basic principles of mental training developed in the course of work at UCLA over the past decade (Schwartz and Begley, 2002).

Fundamental to this OCD treatment is the principle of developing specific self-treatment skills that utilize mindful awareness practice (Schwartz and Beyette, 1997). The treatment focuses on the patient developing the ability to practice the "Four Steps," a method designed to enable sufferers to enhance mindfulness while becoming active participants in their own treatment. The basic approach discussed in this chapter is designed to lead patients through an active learning process in order to develop the skill and ongoing practice of self-therapy. The authors of a recent book, *The Mind and the Brain,* coined the term *self-directed neuroplasticity* to describe the principle that focused training and effort can change brain function in ways that permit people to become active agents in the treatment of their own medical and psychological conditions (Schwartz and Begley, 2002).

OCD: A Natural Candidate for the Practice of Mindful Awareness

Obsessive-compulsive disorder, a neuropsychiatric condition (Jenike, Baer, and Minichiello, 1998), affects about 2 percent of the population worldwide. The symptoms involve intrusive thoughts, urges, and feelings that something is amiss. The most common symptoms are obsessions that something is dirty or contaminated (for example, the sufferer's own hands) or that something is left undone, or is potentially hazardous (such as a door left unlocked or an appliance left on). These obsessive thoughts, in turn, lead to repetitive washing and checking behaviors. Also common is an intrusive, worrisome feeling that some familiar behavior, such as straightening a rug, must be done repeatedly until one achieves "just the right feeling" of completion.

A critical aspect of these bothersome thoughts and feelings, and the very thing that makes them particularly conducive to treatment with mindfulness-based approaches, is the fact that they are generally accompanied by insight: people experiencing these obsessions fundamentally know that they do not make sense. They recognize the bad feeling and associated worry are excessive and inappropriate to the actual situation. This makes obsessive symptoms natural candidates for being more clearly and mindfully observed.

Clear-Minded Contemplation

The consistent and disciplined development of the ability to practice dispassionate self-observation is the key to the practice of mindful awareness (Nyanaponika, 1973). This type of self-observation requires willful mental effort, and this effort is a critical element in the effective practice of self-directed therapy. The practice of mindful awareness *always* involves an act of will. In Sanskrit the terms *will*, or *willful action*, are translated by the word "Karma." Gotama Buddha said, "It is will, monks, that I call Karma" (Nyanaponika Thera and Bhikkhu Bodhi, 1999, p. 173).

The mental act of clear-minded contemplation has a long and distinguished history. The canonical texts of classical Buddhism describe mindful awareness most systematically and extensively (Nyanaponika Thera, 2000). Although some of its most refined descriptions in English are in texts concerned with meditative practice, acquiring the mindful mental state does not require any specific meditation practice and is *certainly not* in any sense a "trancelike" state. One particularly well-established description, using the name "bare attention," is as follows:

> Bare Attention is the clear and single-minded awareness of what actually happens *to* us and *in* us at the successive moments of perception. It is called "bare" because it attends just to the bare facts of a perception as presented either through the five physical senses or through the mind . . . without reacting to them. (Nyanaponika, 1973, p. 30)

In mindful observation you are simply watching, observing all facts, both inner and outer, very calmly, clearly, and closely. This mental action is the base from and means by which all self-regulating strategies are performed. It is also the essential component of what the ancient Stoics called "self-command," the core element of controlling one's own responses to life's ups and downs (Smith, 1976). Mindful awareness is the mental activity whereby one monitors whether the act of regulating one's responses is actually being effectively performed. Put simply, bare attention is the key to putting self-regulating strategies into practice. In order to help patients with OCD apply these principles of mindfulness and self-command during the difficult and distressing periods of symptom exacerbation, we developed a simple treatment strategy called the Four Steps, which are described in detail in the book *Brain Lock* (Schwartz and Beyette, 1997), and are illustrated in Exhibit 13.1 and in the following case example.

Case Example: Susan

Susan was diagnosed with OCD at age twenty, having spent many years not knowing that what she was suffering from was not simply a personal flaw or emotional weakness. For as long as she could remember, her life had been plagued with incessant "worries," which she now realizes were obsessions. At seven she would lie in bed, unable to sleep because of a feeling she had done something wrong. For the next thirteen years Susan would fight sleep with compulsions of reviewing the day's events, repeating them over

---

EXHIBIT 13.1. The Four Steps

1. *Relabel:* Recognize that the intrusive thoughts and urges are the result of OCD.
2. *Reattribute:* Realize that the intensity and intrusiveness of the thought or urge is caused by OCD; it is probably related to a biochemical imbalance in the brain.
3. *Refocus:* Work around the OCD thoughts by focusing your attention on something else, at least for a few minutes. Do another behavior.
4. *Revalue:* Do not take the OCD thought at face value. It is not significant in itself.

(*Source:* Schwartz and Beyette, 1997, p. 219. Copyright J. M. Schwartz.)

and over to examine what she had done wrong and what she should have done instead. Consequently, evenings became imbued with anxiety and dread.

Other obsessions took root and Susan began to perform checking and repeating rituals. Ashamed of what she assumed was her personal weakness, she carefully hid her compulsive behaviors from family and friends, who regarded it as nothing more than "type A" perfectionism. Because Susan was a successful student, friends and family saw nothing wrong, and the obsessions and compulsions continued to torment her. The symptoms exacerbated when she left home to attend college. At nineteen, Susan spent hours trapped in her dorm room. She could not leave without feeling she had forgotten something important for class, neglected to turn off an iron, hang up the phone, or lock the door. Her bedtime worrying continued while the lack of sleep made everything worse. Her anxiety was overwhelming.

Finally she confided in a friend who, coincidentally and fortunately, understood her suffering. He had been diagnosed with OCD in his early teens and had used *Brain Lock* and the guidance of a therapist with great success. Immediately Susan acquired a copy of the book and, after reading the first two chapters, felt incredible and "completely free." It seemed simple, and her symptoms dissolved to almost nothing. Just knowing it was not her fault, that what she had assumed were her own weaknesses and deep character flaws were actually the obsessions and compulsions of a clinical disorder, afforded her a different perspective. With this new frame of reference she could dismiss intrusive thoughts with ease. She stopped checking altogether, other compulsive behaviors were reduced by 90 percent, and for the first time in more than a decade, Susan could sleep soundly. Simply by being conscious of her condition her whole life seemed different.

The relief lasted three days before OCD began to infiltrate Susan's thoughts. Most of the time she identified the thoughts as obsessions, but that was no longer enough to keep her anxiety at bay, and it became difficult to dismiss them. At the most basic level, she could recognize the OC thoughts and urges but was plagued by doubt and became fearful when she could not distinguish between valid concerns and obsessions. Certain preoccupations seemed necessary (finances, for example) and she did not want to bounce a check, so it was important to ensure the numbers were right. She began to check repeatedly and make lists, feeling she had forgotten something or written a check incorrectly. She was desperate to know for sure which thoughts were obsessions and dismiss them. Again, seeking relief, she resorted to compulsions. Although release from OCD had been brief and temporary, she had tasted real freedom and the experience inspired her onward.

Unfortunately, this desperation for relief prevents the essentials of true mindful awareness from taking root. In this early stage, many patients, similar to Susan, are incapable of observing their suffering impartially. The natural response is to attempt to extinguish pain or discomfort as quickly as possible: the reaction to an itch is to scratch. With OCD, however, as with a mosquito bite, seeking immediate relief only makes things worse.

Encouragingly, Susan did not give up and persevered with the Four Steps. She negotiated Steps 1 and 2 (Relabel, Reattribute) and applied Step 3: Refocus. Again, she felt unburdened: refocusing seemed to achieve the impossible. When she felt the pull of an obsession and the urge to perform a compulsion, Susan immersed herself in activity—it was amazing how much she could accomplish. When she could not sleep, she knitted while on the phone or listening to music. When she wanted to check her finances she pushed them aside and painted or walked. She learned to stay busy and avoid OCD. Her symptoms reduced by 90 percent, this time lasting weeks.

Unfortunately, OCD would again return. Susan became complacent and depended on activities to avoid the OCD. The operative word here is "avoid." Without mindfulness, Susan did not develop the mental muscle to deal with OCD. She was only avoiding it, and its return was inevitable. When the OCD rallied again, Susan sought help and began participating in a weekly OCD support group at UCLA. Over six months, she learned the deeper and true application of the Four Steps and mindful awareness practice. She gradually incorporated mindfulness into her approach to life. She learned to apply Step 4 (Revalue) and view the intrusive thoughts and urges as merely passing events in the mind—admittedly unpleasant but intrinsically empty and unsubstantial. Meditation, mindful breathing, and yoga became part of her daily practice.

THE RELATIONSHIP BETWEEN
THE MIND AND THE BRAIN

When observing and modulating one's own mental states the mind plays a willful role in which it actively *affects* the brain and is not merely *affected by* it. Highlighting the active role of the mind in self-regulation is critical for a proper understanding of what actually happens when a person directs his or her inner resources to the challenging task of modifying emotional responses. It takes *effort* for people to do this because it requires a redirection of the brain's resources away from responses controlled largely by lower brain centers toward higher level functions, which are associated with parts of the brain unique to human beings. This cannot happen automatically. Rather, it requires willful training and directed effort. This is precisely why Adam Smith, one of the leading philosophers of the eighteenth-century Scottish Enlightenment, following the Stoics, so extolled the development of self-command as the source of all human greatness.

As he put it, "Self-command is not only itself a great virtue, but from it all other virtues seem to derive their principal luster" (Smith, 1976, p. 241). The use of mindful awareness is the practical key that opens up the human capacity for self-regulation. The application of bare attention to one's own mental processes is the activity that leads to the development of the human mind's full potential. As advances in scientific understanding have demonstrated, an act of the mind is capable of rewiring the brain (Schwartz and Begley, 2002).

Much neuroscientific research carries the implicit assumption that what the brain does in a given situation can be fully understood mechanistically. For instance, while participating in a neuroimaging study, Susan observes slides depicting emotionally arousing scenes while scans are taken of her brain. Certain brain areas are activated, and the scientist commonly concludes that the observed brain activity is the *cause* of the emotional and physiological responses Susan is observed to have.

However, this "explanation"goes only so far and implies that Susan is passive in the encounter with the arousing stimuli; all she had to do was remain reasonably awake and alert while the pictures were shown. What was being studied was how her brain machinery operates in that situation. Although this may be of some scientific interest, it fails to tell us very much about Susan as a person and tells us close to nothing at all about her as a spiritual being. However, if, as in a growing number of studies, Susan were encouraged to make an active response aimed at systematically *altering* the nature of her emotional response to what she was being shown, for example by actively performing a new therapy skill she had been taught, understanding the experiment merely as a study of her brain's machinery would actually miss the point. In such a situation the point would be to show that Susan was able to *change how her brain works* by applying her new knowledge. In such a case we would be working together *with* Susan, a human person who was applying her new knowledge to help discover better ways to treat brain-related emotional problems. In doing that, she would also be demonstrating that she could use her mind to change how her brain works—and this is an action that, beyond doubt, has true spiritual content. When examining the entire process, the spiritual aspect is obviously not separate but an integral and essential element to be acknowledged and considered.

In studying psychological treatments and their physical effects the distinction between mind and brain becomes absolutely critical. If one simply assumes the most common belief of this era of medical research, namely, that all aspects of emotional response are passively determined by biological (and especially brain) mechanisms, then developing genuinely effective, self-directed psychological strategies that cause real changes in how the brain works becomes, in principle, impossible. The treating clinician thus becomes locked into the view, often without even realizing it, that the psychological treatment of ailments caused by physical brain-based problems is not a viable goal.

THE PRACTICE OF MINDFULNESS IN DAILY LIFE

According to the Venerable Nyanaponika, bare attention should be "applied, as far as practicable, to the normal events of the day, together with a general attitude of mindfulness and clear comprehension" (2000, p. 73). As Nyanaponika's own meditation teacher, Venerable Mahasi Sayadaw, expressed it:

> A yogi should begin his contemplation from the moment of awakening. To be fully occupied with intense contemplation throughout his waking hours is the routine of a yogi who works hard with true aspiration. . . .
>
> [T]he mind is used to wandering without any restraint whatsoever. However, a yogi should not lose heart on this account. This difficulty is usually encountered in the beginning of practice. After some time, the mind can no longer play truant because it is always found out every time it wanders. It therefore remains fixed on the object to which it is directed. (Mahasi Sayadaw, 1990, pp. 45, 51)

For people who have OCD (or, as we shall see in a moment, a susceptibility to depression) this "general attitude of mindfulness and clear comprehension" (Nyanaponika, 2000, p. 73) becomes a primary mode of doing therapy.

Considering the details of how this is done can be quite illustrative of the general principle, which anyone can apply. The key is for the person with OCD to take note, mindfully and with clear awareness, when a bothersome obsessive thought or compulsive urge intrudes into the mind. This will significantly enhance one's power to respond to these unpleasant intrusive thoughts with reason and foresight. One particularly useful way of doing this is to make use of what are called "mental notes" as an aid to developing and sustaining mindfulness. As Venerable Mahasi Sayadaw put it, "the exercise is simply to note or observe the existing elements in every [mental, verbal, or bodily] act . . . keeping the mind fixedly on the object with a view to knowing it clearly" (Mahasi Sayadaw, 1990, p. 12).

The mindful recognition of OCD symptoms for what they really are, namely false and bothersome thoughts and urges associated with feelings of anxiety and dread, can help patients avoid taking feelings "at face value," which leads to repetitive compulsive responses. If a person is inundated with obsessive thoughts, mindfulness will allow awareness of these symptoms to occur with clear-minded equanimity, enabling one to make mental notes that "these are obsessive thoughts" and realize the unpleasant feeling of contamination is no indication of real danger and should not be heeded. Although great effort is required to implement a mindful response to painful unpleasant thoughts and feelings caused by OCD, over several weeks sustained mindful practice yields significant clinical benefits. The first two of the Four Steps (Relabel and Reattribute) facilitate making mental notes to perceive accurately when obsessive thoughts are present and label them as the result of faulty brain circuitry: the disease process of OCD.

Brain imaging studies of patients who have coupled this use of mindfulness with other well-studied psychological treatments using cognitive-behavioral approaches have documented significant changes in the brain circuitry underlying OCD problems (Schwartz and Begley, 2002). Although we do not have the opportunity to cover details of the treatment and subsequent brain investigations here, the crucial point is that even for medically caused neuropsychiatric symptoms the insight gained through the proactive use of mindfulness has significant effects both psychologically and biologically.

Disengaging from Depressogenic Thinking: The Role of Mindfulness in Alleviating Depression

Another important and interesting advance made using mindfulness in a mental health setting involves work with depressed patients, directed by John Teasdale at Cambridge University, United Kingdom. Teasdale and colleagues (2000) developed a technique called "mindfulness-based cognitive therapy" that helps "depressed patients to disengage from depressogenic thinking" that can cause depressive symptoms to flare up (p. 615). The description he gives of how mindfulness is used to achieve this offers an overview of how to develop "a general attitude of mindfulness and clear comprehension," as Nyanaponika put it (2000, p. 73). Practitioners of mindfulness-based cognitive therapy

> focus on awareness of experience in the moment. Participants are helped to cultivate an open and acceptant mode of response, in which they intentionally face and move in to difficulties and discomfort, and to develop a decentered perspective on thoughts and feelings, in which these are viewed as passing events in the mind. (Teasdale et al., 2000, p. 618)

The distinction between mindful awareness and what one might call mundane, "default" awareness is often illustrated by reference to the experience, when driving a familiar route, of realizing one has been driving on autopilot, unaware of the road or other vehicles, preoccupied with planning activities or ruminating on a current concern. By contrast, mindful driving is associated with being fully present in each moment, consciously aware of sights, sounds, thoughts, and bodily sensations as they arise. When one is mindful, the mind responds afresh to the unique pattern of experience in each moment instead of reacting mindlessly to fragments of a total experience with old, relatively stereotyped, habitual patterns of mind. In this way, people who have a tendency to suffer from repetitive negative thoughts such as inappropriate self-blame and self-denigration can learn to enter "a mindful mode of processing [that] allows disengagement from the relatively automatic ruminative thought patterns that would otherwise fuel the relapse process" (Teasdale et al., 2000, p. 618), often resulting in depressive symptoms spiraling out of control.

Rigorous scientific investigation of this mindfulness-based treatment approach has demonstrated that it can almost halve relapse rates for people at serious risk of depression (Teasdale et al., 2000), and that the reduced relapse is related to a changing of the relationships between conscious awareness and negative thoughts, rather than by a changing belief in thought content. Thus mindful awareness is a therapeutic modality that operates by means of a change in the mind's observational perspective rather than by a change in belief or thought content per se (Teasdale et al., 2002). The great importance of this will be elaborated on later.

These scientifically verified effects of mindful awareness in treating well-established mental health problems within mainstream Western cultural settings have potentially profound implications for the use of bare attention-based practice as part of daily living in Western societies. However, this in no way should detract attention from the use of mindfulness meditation as a means of spiritual development, and especially as a vehicle for attaining and deepening insight *(vipassana)* for the goal of final liberation from suffering. Much can be gained along the path to this ultimate realization. As the results of modern medical research attest, many benefits remain to be accrued by those practicing mindfulness and insight for more immediately pragmatic purposes.

Mindfulness in Western Philosophy

Through the centuries the idea of mindfulness has appeared, under different guises, in branches of Western philosophy. Adam Smith, whom we encountered earlier, developed the idea of "the impartial and well-informed spectator." This is "the man within," Smith wrote in 1759 in *The Theory of Moral Sentiments,* an observing power to which we all have access and that has intimate access to our internal feelings, yet is able to observe them as if from without. This distancing allows us to witness our actions, thoughts, and emotions not as an involved participant but as a disinterested observer. In Smith's words:

> When I endeavor to examine my own conduct . . . I divide myself as it were into two persons; and that I, the examiner and judge, represent a different character from the other I, the person

whose conduct is examined into and judged of. The first is the spectator. . . . The second is the agent, the person whom I properly call myself, and of whose conduct, under the character of a spectator, I was endeavoring to form some opinion.

In this way, Smith concluded, "we suppose ourselves the spectators of our own behavior" (Smith, 1976, pp. 112-113).

Smith's purpose for developing the concept of the "impartial spectator" was to present a practical method to enable people to engage in clear-minded moral judgment. Although its use may not yield the kind of direct observational experience that meditation does, it undeniably shares family resemblances with Buddhist teachings, long before they were introduced in the West. In the technical Theravada Buddhist psychology, as canonically presented in the Abhidhamma (Bhikkhu Bodhi, 2000), any moment of consciousness containing the mental factor of mindfulness is assured of being a wholesome state of consciousness. Clearly, Smith's use of the "impartial spectator" as a practical application of moral philosophy was insight indeed—and this is just one of many examples in the history of Western philosophy and psychology. Perhaps a general conclusion is that whether one is seeking cutting edge approaches to treating neuropsychiatric conditions, applied uses of moral reasoning, or full and final Enlightenment, as the Buddha said, "Mindfulness, monks, I declare to be always beneficial" (Nyanaponika, 2000, p. 72).

A TRIPARTITE APPROACH TO THE TREATMENT OF OCD

The most broad-ranging view of the psychological treatment for OCD would perhaps encompass a tripartite classification of different treatment modalities. At the level of treatment in which the patient has minimal insight and/or mindfulness capacity, the classical behavioral approach is required. If a person does not have the capacity to take the perspective of the impartial spectator to a clinically significant degree, treatment must utilize techniques that would, in effect, operate primarily on animal brain mechanisms. This is precisely what behaviorist approaches do, insofar as they are designed and validated largely within a scientific framework that uses animal behavior as the primary model. The use of treatment modalities validated by animals, however, systematically neglects the unique human capacity for mindful awareness. To use strict behaviorist approaches for individuals capable of the "impartial spectator" perspective is, therefore, inherently reductionistic and not compatible in principle with a psychospiritual approach.

Cognitive approaches, on the other hand, accentuate people's capacity to mobilize rational capabilities, enhancing their ability to adopt a mindful perspective. The cognitive approaches, extremely well validated for the treatment of depression (Beck et al., 1979) and, as discussed previously, recently conjoined in a profoundly creative way with mindful approaches in the work of Teasdale and colleagues (2000, 2002), have recently also been systematically applied to the treatment of OCD (Frost and Steketee, 2002).

However, when cognitive approaches are used as the primary treatment modality, the use of language-based self-statements and linear thinking become the sine qua non of, and an absolute prerequisite for, treatment. Although this is not, in and of itself, problematic, the spiritually oriented clinician would naturally prefer treatment approaches that utilize directly experiential phenomena as core aspects of the treatment approach. This is where mindful awareness and the impartial spectator perspective make their most profound contribution to creative developments in the advancement of psychological treatments.

Mindful awareness enables the practitioner to directly observe his or her own experience and utilize that impartial perspective as the essential dynamic that moves therapeutic progress forward (Schwartz and Beyette, 1997). It is clearly most difficult and spiritually challenging to maintain the mindful perspective when one's conscious awareness is assaulted by bitterly painful and emotionally distressing experiences generated by pathological brain circuitry. This is precisely why the cognitive-based approaches are so helpful as a means of transition from a strictly linear language-based therapeutic approach to the direct observation of experience that mindfulness requires for therapeutic advancement. In this way, the development of skill in performing cognitive interventions can pave the way toward enhancing one's ability to maintain the "impartial spectator" perspective so critical for mindfulness-based therapeutic approaches.

Behavioral interventions may be a starting place for patients with low insight, who are currently unable to process the cognitive distortions in their symptoms. They target animal brain mechanisms and do not require significant cognitive awareness for successful application. Exposure and response prevention (ERP) is a technique that utilizes therapist-assisted exposure to the patient's feared stimuli while systematically preventing the patient from responding until anxiety dissipates. This process often lasts over an hour, causing the patient significant distress. When successful this can generate improvements in anxiety. As the primarily behavioral techniques such as ERP lead to improvements in anxiety, the opportunity arises to use the lessened anxiety as a means of engaging in a more cognitive approach, with the goal of systematically strengthening the sufferer's ability to apply mindful awareness. This is a hallmark of what might be called the psychospiritual approach to therapy: we are not merely seeking symptom improvement, but rather are actively using behaviorist techniques, such as exposure, as mindfulness exercises. Analogous reasoning applies to the use of medication in treating OCD symptoms. The key is utilizing decreases in anxiety as a means to increasing insight.

Thus the shift we are making now in our approach to treating OCD is that we are not using medication and classical behavior therapy simply to make bothersome feelings less acute, and we are not calling a decrease in anxiety, fear, and even compulsions, per se, the complete treatment. In fact we want to *use* that decrease in fear and anxiety to allow us to understand what is going on more clearly. With a reduction in fear and anxiety, more mindfulness power can be mobilized. When one is less distracted and uncomfortable, one can think more clearly, and when one thinks more clearly, one can really begin to understand, in a deeper way, "this is just my OCD bothering me and this is something I don't have to listen to." Thus the use of mindful awareness and the impartial spectator perspective becomes a direct means to strengthen insight and understanding: symptom decrease is no longer considered the sole, or even the primary, goal of treatment.

The use of ERP as a mindfulness exercise, not merely as a symptom improvement vehicle, is achieved by training sufferers to actively use mindfulness during exposure as a primary means of accomplish-